Fragments
of Grace

Also by PAMELA CONSTABLE

A Nation of Enemies: Chile Under Pinochet
(with Arturo Valenzuela)

Fragments of Grace

My Search for Meaning in the Strife of South Asia

PAMELA CONSTABLE

Brassey's, Inc.
Washington, D.C.

All photos by Pamela Constable

Library of Congress Cataloging-in-Publication Data

Constable, Pamela.
    Fragments of grace : my search for meaning in the strife of South Asia / Pamela Constable.
        p.   cm.
    Includes index.
    ISBN 1-57488-618-5 (cloth : alk. paper)
    1. India—Description and travel.   2. Pakistan—Description and travel.   3. Afghanistan—Description and travel.   4. Constable, Pamela—Travel—South Asia.   I. Title.
    DS414.2 .C66   2004
    915.404'53—dc22   2003025519

Printed in the United States of America on acid-free paper that meets the American National Standards Institute Z39-48 Standard.

Brassey's, Inc.
22841 Quicksilver Drive
Dulles, Virginia 20166

First Edition

10   9   8   7   6   5   4   3   2   1

*For my parents
and in memory of William E. Merriss,
who taught me to love words*

Contents

beginning to fail, while our relations have remained in a state of frozen formality, cordial rather than close. I am a professional communicator, but I have never figured out what to say to them, and there is not much time left.

I have also never done the one thing I was built to do. I have cheated biology year after year, taking one more trip and one more assignment, terrified that having a child would tie me down and sap my energy and change me into someone else. Now, at fifty, the choice is no longer mine. Instead, I have adopted: cats, dogs, men, homes, surrogate families. I have taken in neglected or stray animals, fattened them up—and then had to stash them with friends when I rushed off to the next crisis. I have turned empty rooms into cozy nests, and back again. I have become aunt and daughter, sister and godmother to successive families—in Santiago and Port-au-Prince and Kabul and New Delhi—some of whom I lost track of years ago. I have fallen in love a dozen times, in a dozen countries, a condition that always intensified and ennobled the struggle of the moment— "mejor con guitarra," as the Spanish saying goes—but inevitably I moved on and lost touch.

So what, then, have I accumulated in this peripatetic pilgrimage? What have I learned of lasting value, what do I have to say that is more meaningful than the sum of perhaps 2,000 newspaper stories and a handful of longer writing projects published over the last twenty-seven years? Much of what I have thought and felt and experienced on my travels has remained in my private journals, too subjective or emotional to be called journalism. Some of it is more personal than I wish to reveal.

But there is also a strong, single thread that runs through my journeys, a search for human dignity and hope in the stories of anonymous people, struggling to survive in places that seem godforsaken. That search began when I read "Let Us Now Praise Famous Men," James Agee's haunting, Depression-era word-portrait of Alabama sharecroppers, in a college sociology class. It has sustained and inspired me through nearly three decades as a journalist, and it has gathered recent focus and momentum as I explored the deeply spiritual and conflicted worlds of Hinduism and Islam. It is a search in the ruins for fragments of grace.

When I set out to write this book, several publishers were uncomfortable with my proposal because it had no clear ending, offered no final answers to the questions it raised about the choices I have made and whether they were right. But just as no parent can predict how a child will develop, I do not yet know where this book will lead; I only know I must write it. If I had to guess, I'd like to think it will end like *Stuart Little*—a bit wistful, a bit wiser, and setting out on a glorious spring day in search of a new adventure.

Washington, D.C.
January 2003

Acknowledgments

I WOULD like to thank the following people for their companionship, moral support, hospitality, and insights during my travels in South Asia, my visits home, and my preparations for this book.

In India: Amit Agarwal, the late Agha Shahid Ali, Ashok Bahn, Scott and Kashmira Baldauf, Robert Boggs, Beth Duff Brown, Isabel Callejas, Pran Chopra, Ambassador Benjamin Concha, Gordon Diugud, Jonathan Harley, Parvez Imroz, Muzamil Jaleel and his family, Massood Khalili, Rama Lakshmi, the late Abdul Ghani Lone, Robert Marquand, the late Qaiser Mirza, Pankaj Mishra, Tahir Mohideen, Ravi Nair, Venkat Narayan, Smita Narula, Ashok Pandey and his family, S. Prasannarajan, Michael and Martha Ann Sullivan, Jim Teeple, Lea Terhune, and Ajay Upadhay.

In Pakistan: Salman Abassy, Senator Aitzaz Ahsan, Haroon Akbar and the staff of the Chez Soi, Ayaz Amir, Scott Anger, Baker Atiani, Hannah Bloch, Shahnaz Bokhari, Tasgola Bruner, Stephanie Bunker, Azim Chaudhary and his family, Fawzia and her family, Stewart and Marlene Georgia, Ejaz Haider, Yusuf Hassan, Professor Riffaat Hussain, Shabbir Imam Hussain, Tahir and Samra Ikram, Anwar Iqbal, Cindy Irwin, Jalil Abbas Jilani, Behroz Khan, Kamran Khan, Sahibzada Yaqub Ali Khan, Afrasiab Khattak, Khalid Mansour, General Talat Masood, Ambassador William Milam, Hamid Mir, Suzy Price, Dr. Akmal Rana, Ahmed Rashid, Salim Shaheed, Rahimullah Yusufzai, the late Asif Zahir and his family, and Kashif Zaman.

In Afghanistan: Nisar Ahmed, Kurt Amend, Qudratullah Ander and his family, Paul Barker, Mohammed Bashir, Mohammed Amin Farhang, Alberto Fernandez, Wojtek Jagielski, Alina Labrada, Zia Mojaddedi, Sayed Amin and Jamila Mujahid, Wakil Ahmed

Muttawakil, Shirzai Najibullah, Humaira Nematy, the late Elizabeth Neuffer, Nasrullah Noori, Colonel Wayland Parker, Thomas Ruttij, Sayed Salahuddin, Noor Ahmed Sarboz and his family, Michael Semple, Najeeb Sharifi, Nasrullah Stanakzai, Noel Spencer, Jake Sutton, Rone Tempest, Gary Thomas, Chris Tomlinson, General Abdul Rahim Wardak, Ivan Watson, Tim Wiener, and Omar Zakhilwol.

In Nepal: Kanak and Kunda Dixit, Steve Farrell, Durga Ghimire, Yubaraj Ghimire, Daniel Lak, Gunaraj Luitel, Ambassador Ronald Nash, and Kapil Shrestha.

In Sri Lanka: Dikshika Jahamaya, Drew Mann, Savanamuttu Pakiasothy, Joseph Pararajasingham, Ravinatha, Trini Rayan, Kingsley Rodrigo, and Maheswary Velautham.

In the United States: Dr. Nasim Ashraf, Ambassador Harry G. Barnes Jr., Christina Davidson, Jane Dystel, Mark Kukis, Erick Calixto Lopez and his family, Rashid and Bano Makhdoom, Alan and Jackie Mayers, and Connie Wilkinson. Thanks also go to John Schidlovsky and the Pew International Journalism Program, which provided me with the time and privacy I needed to think, and to Phil Bennett and David Hoffman at the *Washington Post*, who encouraged me to pursue my solitary project when all hell was breaking loose in the world.

Introduction

OFTEN I dream that I am struggling uphill, alone, through a mountain of rubble or ruins, searching frantically for someone or something through derelict buildings or abandoned caves. But sometimes I dream that I am skimming over the earth from a great height, observing the terrain as it whooshes by, recognizing entire continents and oceans and marveling at God's creation.

I had such a dream one night in the summer of 1998. As I soared past one curve of the planet below, a brilliant purple jewel winked up at me as if in invitation to swoop down and grasp it. As I awoke, I instantly identified the source. It was India.

A few weeks later, I was unexpectedly summoned to the office of the foreign editor. My heart leaped to my throat. I had been working at the *Washington Post* for four years, writing about the metropolitan region's burgeoning Hispanic and immigrant communities. It was a fascinating beat, but I yearned for a chance to return to Latin America, where I had spent much of the 1980s and 1990s as a foreign correspondent for the *Boston Globe*.

Perhaps there was a new crisis in Haiti or Peru or Cuba, and someone had finally thought of me. The foreign editor's face was inscrutable as he motioned me to sit. "Is Castro dead?" I blurted out. He shook his head and smiled. "No, actually we were wondering if you'd like to go to India."

Suddenly, in mid-career, a new world had been opened up to me. I would be immersed in unfamiliar cultures and unrecognizable languages. My new beat would cover a billion and a half people, three major religions, two of the planet's most enduring guerrilla conflicts (Kashmir and Sri Lanka) and one of history's most hermetic and draconian religious experiments (the Taliban of Afghanistan.) It was totally new territory, and yet my entire career as a journalist—every reflex and instinct, every sleepless night and sweltering journey, every revolution and recalcitrant regime—had prepared me for whatever lay ahead.

At first, I planned to ease into South Asia through India, its most freewheeling, democratic portal. I studied the pantheon of Hindu gods, the structure of the Indian parliament, the 1971 war between India and Pakistan and the 1998 nuclear tests by both countries. It was summer, and news was slow. I would take my time, establish my credentials, make a round of teatime calls on the Delhi intelligentsia and a few forays into the heartland, cover a bride-burning here or a caste riot there. Nothing too taxing at first.

My leisurely plan lasted less than a week. I was still unpacking when the United States launched a missile strike on eastern Afghanistan in retaliation for a pair of deadly, simultaneous terrorist attacks on two American embassies in East Africa. That night I found myself on a flight to Pakistan—the only country through which foreigners could enter Afghanistan—armed with a couple of journalists' phone numbers and a sheaf of semi-legible faxes about a man I had barely heard of—a Saudi fugitive and Islamic fanatic named Osama bin Laden.

I never did finish unpacking. For the next four years, I hopped from one crisis and conflict to the next, chasing a relentless barrage of news that took me from Kashmir to Colombo, from Karachi to Kandahar. I covered a military coup in Pakistan and a royal family massacre in Nepal, a massive earthquake in northern India and a passenger plane hijacking in southern Afghanistan. I followed Afghan refugee treks and Hindu pilgrimages; I saw the cruelties of guerrilla war in the lush tropics of Sri Lanka and the alpine heights of Srinagar.

Even though I was officially based in New Delhi, I spent so little time there that it never came to feel like a home, and so much time on the road that my friendships with other India-based correspondents were forged in plane or jeep rides to far-flung crises. Soon I was keeping clothes, files and stray pets at four houses in four countries.

In the late summer of 2001, the news in South Asia seemed to slow again, and I was sent to South Africa to cover a United Nations conference on racism. I was there on September 11 when the World

Trade Center was attacked. Staring numbly at my hotel TV screen, I did not fully comprehend what had happened—let alone imagine it would lead to another American assault on Afghanistan and the collapse of the Taliban regime—but I was certain that it would lead back to my beat.

My next three months passed in a single adrenaline rush of round-the-clock reporting and writing, first working in Pakistan as American bombs pounded Afghanistan next door, then entering Afghanistan just after the Taliban fell. By the beginning of 2002 I was living in Kabul full-time, and I would spend that entire year chronicling the messy, exhilarating rebirth of a nation.

I never did find the time to become an expert on South Asia or nuclear doctrine, or Islam or Hinduism. I was moving too fast, taking in too many layers of sensation, tearing off too many chunks of history in the making. But along the way, I learned lessons that transcended time and place, I found unexpected parallels with my past experiences in Latin America, I recognized universal patterns of human need and response in places that seemed to have nothing in common.

I saw the generosity and moral ideals of several new religions, and the cruel behavior and twisted theories they excused. I experienced both the benefits and constraints of clannish societies where individuals had no voice and every decision was made by committee. I discarded oceans of official propaganda and clung to small rafts of personal insight, and I discovered a dozen ways to look at polarized conflicts.

I saw how even well-intentioned people—Muslim and Hindu, Eastern and Western—could view the same world, the same events, through irreconcilable prisms of myth and history and emotion. I hope my stories, even those that provoked defensive denials, helped to bridge some of those gaps. I hope this book, a work of intuition and reflection rather than scholarship, does the same.

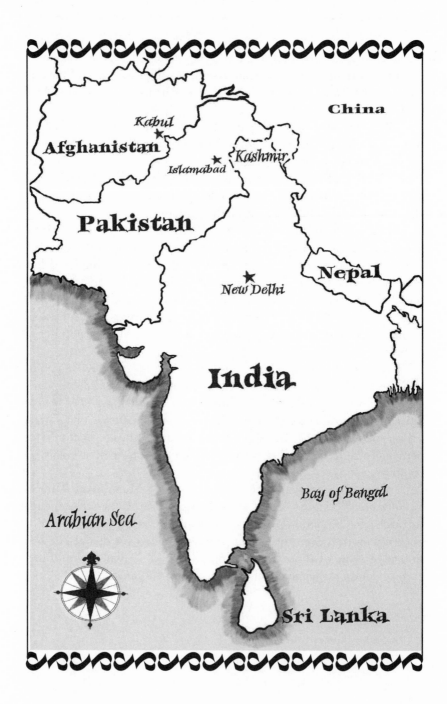

CHAPTER ONE

Into the Fog

A thousand words lie under the dust
Unsaid within my heart
I am not the only one in the world
To be awestruck and speechless
The whole of creation had its lips sealed,
And lost its face.

—Mir Taqi Mir (1722–1810)

 BEHIND me rose the barren brown foothills of the Hindu Kush; below me a narrow footpath led between two massive metal gates with squat stone turrets at each end. An extraordinary parade of human and animal traffic poured through the opening. Tiny donkeys staggered under huge loads of bricks, carpet-laden camels plodded in file. Filthy urchins lugged sacks of scrap metal, refugee families trundled all their worldly goods on hand carts.

This was the Khyber Pass: the dateline of my dreams, the ancient gateway from Central Asia to the subcontinent. Alexander the Great crossed here with his armies, I thought to myself, and Genghis Khan, and probably Marco Polo. Now I, too, was about to cross into new territory, an isolated and forbidding land ruled by men with turbans, assault rifles, and a draconian vision of Islamic utopia.

On the Pakistani side, uniformed border guards rifled through refugees' pockets and chased after darting children with sticks. I saw one officer pick up a screaming, ragged girl of perhaps seven, shake her like a dustmop and drop her in the dirt with a laugh. She never let go of the bundle she was desperately clutching, and I realized she would face a worse beating at home if she did.

On the Afghan side, the scene was even more disturbing. From

1

the elevated border checkpost where I was waiting for my exit visa, I could make out men in white robes and black turbans squatting behind rooftop machine guns. Below, more robed guards held back a mewling, pressing crowd with shouts and whips.

I shuddered and turned away, ducking back inside the little office where a Pakistani border agent was laboriously copying my passport details in a huge ledger. He rolled a piece of paper in an ancient typewriter and began typing out my exit visa with one desultory finger. Then he paused, glancing up at me with a dark grin. "Sure you want to take the risk?" he asked.

It was a good question. Even two weeks before, I had never dreamed I would be frantically trying to enter a country most foreigners and professionals had fled long ago; a country ruled by an army of semiliterate Islamic extremists who stoned adulterers, flogged drunks, and seemed to revile everything that defined me: a woman, a journalist, a Christian, a Westerner.

But the U.S. missile attack changed everything. Suddenly, Afghanistan was the focus of urgent international attention, the purported launching pad for Osama bin Laden and his Islamic "holy war" against the West. Once the wealthy Saudi construction heir had been an American ally, bankrolling Afghan guerrilla groups against Soviet military occupation. Now he had become an enemy, building camps in the sere Afghan hills where young Muslims were imbued with an ardent anti-Western vision, and given the military training and tools to carry it out.

My first foray into Taliban land was a journey made in stages, leading backward through time. From Islamabad, the leafy, modern capital built only decades before, I drove west toward Peshawar, an ancient, labyrinthine border city that was crammed with Afghan refugees. With each passing mile there were fewer offices and signs in English, more donkey carts and mosques. I saw my first camel caravan, and my first burqa, briefly wondering why any woman would willingly cover herself with a stifling, head-to-toe veil.

In Peshawar, I also received my first whiff of Taliban fire: pure, fierce, and frightening. In an Islamic religious academy, the turbaned director informed me solemnly that every one of his adolescent students would be happy to die for Islam.

In an Afghan exile office, a beautiful, green-eyed actress from Kabul described stepping out of her house and being seized by Taliban police, who lashed her ankles with whips because they were not covered with dark socks. In a hospital, I stood beside the beds of young Islamic militia recruits who had been injured in the American bombing. Swathed in bandages and ashen with pain, they remained adamant that the Taliban's religious crusade was righteous and invincible.

Now, after a week of pleading with inscrutable Taliban consular officials in Islamabad and navigating the friendlier but frustrating Pakistani bureaucracy, I was finally poised to cross the border. I was scared, but I was even more excited. It was the first of perhaps a dozen moments over the next five years when I would stop and say to myself: Yes, this is it, this is why I do what I do, this is why I don't have children, this is history.

I took a deep breath, fighting off a powerful impulse to snatch back my passport and run after my taxi driver, who was still sipping tea in the bazaar before heading back to Peshawar. I smiled at the border agent and nodded. He shrugged, stamped my exit visa and tossed my passport across the table.

∾

Thus began my first sojourn in one of the most bizarre, closed societies on earth, the first of ten nerve-wracking but fascinating visits I would make to Afghanistan under Taliban rule. I did not fully realize what lay ahead, but my instincts told me that merely to set foot in this forbidden world was newsworthy. I had a two-week visa to the "Islamic Emirate of Afghanistan" pasted in my passport, but I felt like a trespasser in a perverse Wonderland, where every sight was novel, every scrap of conversation was precious, and every opportunity might suddenly be snatched away.

Emboldened by urgency, I began talking to anyone I could find as soon as the border was behind me. I was traveling with a photographer from Peshawar who spoke one of the two major Afghan dialects, which helped enormously. As we made our way west toward Kabul in a battered Corolla taxi, we polled every passenger who got in, every teashop owner and mechanic at rest stops, asking as neutrally and as casually as possible what they thought of the Taliban.

The responses were not always what we expected. Some drivers complained bitterly that they had been thrown into prison for wearing too-short beards; others said they had been yanked out of their cars and beaten by Taliban police for playing forbidden tapes of commercial pop tunes from India and Pakistan. In the city of Jalalabad, a doctor confided in whispers that his daughters were being secretly tutored because the Taliban had banned girls from school.

In a roadside café, the proprietor showed us an official notice tacked on the wall banning all music and television, then slyly drew his hidden transistor radio from under the counter. At police checkposts, we saw bouquets of confiscated black cassette tape fluttering from poles, but once we were safely past, the driver would dig under the upholstery once more and shove the tape of Hindi music back in the player. The excessive purism of the country's new rulers, it seemed, was creating a society of deceit and double lives.

But along the way we met other Afghans who praised the Taliban for saving their country from the mayhem of civil war among armed Islamic groups. Even those who grumbled about the strict new rules often expressed relief that law and order had returned. For most of the 1980s, Afghan militias had waged a "freedom struggle" against occupying Soviet troops. But once victorious, they had degenerated into bands of brigands, their crusade into a vicious dogfight for power and turf. Civilians were robbed and raped, houses were destroyed in crossfire. With the Taliban takeover, all that ended. One woman, huddled under a burqa in our taxi, kept murmuring how thankful she was that it was finally safe to travel without fear of highway bandits. Who was I, a visitor from a highly policed and law-abiding society, to argue or to judge?

It was not until we reached Kabul that we understood both the appalling amount of destruction wrought by the war and the crushing grip of Taliban rule on the stunned and weakened populace. The capital, once bustling and cosmopolitan, was a shell-shocked ruin, abandoned by half the original populace of one million and reoccupied by tens of thousands of destitute refugees. Block after block lay in a frozen state of collapse, so untouched and monochromatic that driving past was like viewing a grainy newsreel of Dresden or Warsaw after World War II. Factories and embassies, slums and mansions—all had been reduced to rubble by militia rockets.

Majestic Darulaman Palace, built by a king in the 1920s on a hill overlooking the city, was a gaping, graffiti-marred jumble of cracked marble, surrounded by statues that had been beheaded by Taliban troops as idolatrous. What war had not destroyed, the new rulers had: music was banned, the state television station was shut down, banks and ministries were empty, and commerce was little more than sidewalk haggling over piles of secondhand shoes and sweaters.

There was so little traffic that I could stand on a major boulevard, close my eyes, and hear only the quiet creak of horse-carts and the sad jingle of bicycles. At such moments, I felt as if I were in a city of the dead, like Hiroshima or Pompei, surrounded by thousands of silent, invisible ghosts. After dark, the only sounds were the barking of dogs.

Our first official destination, and our principal point of contact with the Taliban, was the foreign ministry, a moldy formal building with a forlorn rose garden outside. To my pleasant surprise, I was greeted with tea and a plate of raisins and almonds. Some of the officials were solemn religious men, clearly uncomfortable with women, who looked down when they spoke and declined to take my offered hand; others, I learned much later, were well-traveled career diplomats who had donned beards and turbans as a professional survival mechanism.

After a short formal speech welcoming us to the country and requesting that I write about the "ground realities" of Afghanistan, the senior official then handed us a list of the rules governing foreign visitors and journalists in particular. We were forbidden to take photographs of any "living creatures," visit private homes, or speak with any Afghan woman. We were instructed not to "wear immoral clothes and walk naked," play loud music, or use drugs or alcohol in public. We were not to disseminate "non-Islamic" materials such as books and cassettes, or to "invite Afghans to any religion other than Islam." Anyone caught flouting the rules was subject to arrest and immediate expulsion from the country.

For journalists, there was more: We must stay in a government-run hotel, travel in an official "tourist" van, and remain in the company of an assigned official translator at all times. I was familiar with such restrictions from visits to communist countries like Cuba— the guided tours of busy farms and clinics; the always apologetic translator-spies. The lifestyle regulations didn't bother me much either; after all, I was a guest in a conservative Muslim country. I wanted to fit in as much as possible, and I always cringed with shame when younger Western colleagues dressed like rock stars or ramp models on location in the desert.

But the Taliban had gone much further than any regime in my experience, taking away the most basic tools of journalism and declaring half the population totally off limits. The Islamic authorities had invited us here in hopes of achieving some minimal credibility abroad. They said they wanted us to understand the historical and social context that had given rise to their rule, rather than viewing it through a prism of secular Western disapproval. But how did they expect us to learn what their people really thought, if we never had the chance to ask?

Torn between prudence and professional self-respect, we began looking for ways to skirt the rules. It proved physically impossible to escape our hotel, a haunted, 500-room palace in which we were the only guests. Built in the early 1960s, the InterContinental had been the hub of Kabul's social scene during the modernizing cultural thaw of the monarchy's final days and the hard-drinking, highly politicized atmosphere of the communist-ruled 1980s. Now the wine cellar was smashed, the grand piano locked in the cellar, the handicraft boutiques and travel agencies shut and darkened. In a vast, empty dining room, ancient waiters in frayed uniforms served us from tattered menus.

At night, vigilant Taliban "clerks" dozed outside our doors with Kalashnikov rifles beside them. Once I experimentally poked my head outside at 3 A.M., and the guard snapped awake, politely asking what I needed. Another evening after we had been dropped off by the guide, my Pakistani traveling companion and I tried to slip out of the hotel in a waiting taxi, but we were stopped halfway down the driveway and sent back. Our unfortunate Afghan driver was hauled down to the cellar and questioned in detail about our little plot. Every night before I fell asleep, I dragged a heavy bureau against my door. Every morning I awoke with a fearful start, remembering where I was and counting the days left on my visa.

During the day, it was possible to find ways to speak with Afghans, though always briefly and nervously, and almost always hampered by language, since most of the educated elite had fled and most other people were illiterate and ill at ease with foreigners. The best opportunities were inside United Nations charity offices, where some English-speaking Afghans were allowed to work. Our guides, a series of young medical students, were helpful and hinted at their own frustrations with the Taliban system, but I always suspected this was a ruse to elicit rash criticisms on our part, and I always worried whether there would be repercussions against anyone who spoke to us frankly.

I was equally determined to evade the ban on photographs. Afghanistan was a visual smorgasbord of burqas, beggars, and scenes out of the Bible; no written story alone could capture Kabul's texture. My friend from Peshawar often slipped a camera in his jacket pocket and shot from waist level. After observing him for a while, I started wearing mine on a neck strap underneath my scarf. If I saw a picturesque scene, I quickly looked around for the Taliban police, whipped the camera out for a few seconds and hoped for the best. Usually, to their credit, our official guides would grimace but pretend not to notice.

Often the result of my panicky attempts was a blurry, unusable snapshot of a child or a horse-cart, but occasionally something clicked. One frozen morning, I was interviewing people waiting outside a UN bakery for free rations of *nan*, the flatbread that is a staple of the Afghan diet. A small door opened and, on impulse, I darted inside the dark, cave-like room. Focusing my camera out toward the street, I caught a poignant scene of ragged men, eagerly reaching through the tiny window for their nan. The photograph could not be developed or published until I had left the country, but when I finally saw it, months later, filling half a page in the *Washington Post*, I felt a strong, secret glow of triumph.

∾

During all my visits to Kabul during the Taliban era, I virtually never saw another Westerner on the streets. The handful of foreigners I did meet were aid workers, doctors and nurses and managers who commuted hurriedly in utility vehicles between their guarded offices and sleeping compounds. They too operated under severe restrictions and were loath to defy them for fear of jeopardizing programs that provided food and medicine to tens of thousands of desperate people.

It was impossible to relax, and I always felt lonely and isolated. There was no foreign press corps to swap stories with, and the few local journalists were cordial but nervous if we lingered in their offices for more than a few minutes. There was no place to unwind after curfew, no newspapers or magazines to read, no local telephones or e-mail connections. In the hotel rooms, there was no television and the light was too dim to read. Often I was in bed by 9 P.M., staring at the ceiling.

The one place foreigners could mingle socially was the United Nations staff complex, where we could buy a drink and watch BBC World News, the only conduit of information in English from the outside world. The Taliban forbade journalists from staying there, but on certain nights we were allowed access to the bar until the 8 P.M. curfew. It was a dark, smoke-filled room where the bartender usually had only whiskey on hand and rang a little bell when curfew was approaching. Within minutes, the room would be empty as we all raced to our vehicles, praying we would reach our lodgings without encountering a suspicious Taliban patrol.

There were also very few public bathrooms, and only two for women in the entire capital. Fortunately there was no lack of bombed-out ruins, and I soon became shameless about ducking inside them for a moment. Crossing the open desert was trickier, but after half a dozen trips I had memorized the locations of suitable boulders and culverts near the highways. Once I ran out of tampons and combed Kabul frantically for a new supply, only to meet with bewildered headshakes from pharmacists across the city. Finally I ripped up several T-shirts from a street stall, cursing a country where women's needs simply did not exist.

As a foreign non-Muslim woman, I was not required to don a full *burqa*, and as a journalist, I was treated as an honorary man; I was allowed to speak and eat with any official in the all-male government, and I was even permitted to conduct "man-on-the-street" interviews. But I took the ban on "immoral clothes" seriously and did my best to resemble a sack of potatoes whenever I left the hotel. In Peshawar I had purchased several shapeless, long-sleeved tunics with pajamas, an ensemble known as a *salwar kameez*. Over this costume I wore both an extra-large man's shirt and an oversized scarf that covered my shoulders and chest as well as my hair.

Despite my best efforts, however, I still drew startled stares and lewd, disapproving comments from passing men, especially the turbaned village gunmen who had entered Kabul as part of the Taliban forces. To them I was an exotic and unclean creature, possibly a prostitute, and therefore fair game. There was only one restaurant in Kabul that served foreigners, and women were required to sit in a separate back room. To reach it I sometimes had to pass by tables full of Taliban officials or Arab gunmen devouring huge platters of rice and beef. Usually they pretended not to see me, but one group gestured angrily and shouted at my translator.

"They say you must cover your face or leave," he murmured. I was furious, but also curious. Were these thugs afraid of me? Did they think I would give them the evil eye or infect their food? I started to ask a question, but my translator firmly dragged me out the door, apologizing as we retreated.

The Taliban leaders were no different from these militiamen: the products of ultra-conservative Islamic schools, deeply traditional tribal upbringings, and war. They were inscrutable men, polite but unsmiling and uncomfortable in my presence. Some refused to look me in the eye; others withdrew from my proferred hand as if it were a toad. It was easy to offend their sense of propriety, especially their notions about how women should behave.

My guides often warned me to be solemn and soft-voiced when I met with officials, but occasionally I forgot myself—and paid the price. Once, I was interviewing a Foreign Ministry official in Kandahar with another American woman journalist. The two of us started giggling over the translator's mistakes, then finally burst out laughing. The official was so discomfited that he rose without a word and walked out of the room, ending the interview. We learned later he had recommended we be expelled from the country.

On another trip, my official escort was a handsome young Taliban official whose piercing blue eyes were enhanced by black mascara, a popular adornment among men from the Pashtun ethnic group. He had been a fulltime Islamic fighter for a decade, but he clearly had never been exposed to women. One of my traveling companions, a waggish Afghan-American businessman, urged me to flirt with him, but the young warrior was so painfully shy that it seemed cruel to try. I caught him staring at me a few times during long formal dinners, but we virtually never spoke. When I shook his hand good-bye at the airport, it was as limp as a rag.

I never really figured out what the Taliban thought of me, or whether they had even read my newspaper stories about them.

Sometimes they dropped hints that suggested they had scrutinized every line of an article, but other times they seemed barely to have heard of the *Washington Post*. Our conversations always went in circles, and it was never clear where their orders came from. Whenever I made a request, I would be told "no problem" over several cups of tea. But invariably, when I tried to follow up, the promised interview or permission simply never materialized.

Obtaining a visa to visit Afghanistan, available only at the Taliban embassy in Islamabad, was often an exercise in diplomatically cloaked futility. Sometimes the visa was denied with no explanation, and I would be secretly relieved. Sometimes the consul would shrug and tell me to come back the next day, every day for three weeks in a row. Sometimes the visa would unexpectedly materialize, and I would steel myself for another nerve-wracking stint under Taliban scrutiny, knowing the trip would also produce another round of unique insights and adventures—and that despite the hostility and hardships, I was enormously privileged to be there.

After each foray into Taliban territory, my nerves were shot, my hair felt like straw and my skin like leather. Every time I spotted the green-and-white Pakistani flag at the border, I felt as relieved as if I were passing through the Berlin Wall. Once I reached Islamabad, I would take a long, scalding shower, get drunk at the United Nations Club, and sleep for ten straight hours. But within a few days, I would invariably be back at the Taliban embassy, filling out another visa application and fuming as I waited behind a curtain in the women's section.

The Taliban believed women had no place in public life, and they were obsessed with preventing improper mingling of the sexes, a taboo that took priority over women's health, hygiene, literacy, and economic survival. Mothers, wives, and daughters were to be protected at all costs, but women who stepped outside traditional roles or adopted Western fashions were to be suspected and punished as potential seductresses. All women were Eve and all men were Adam: one beckoned with a tempting apple, the other was too weak to resist, and the remedy was to ensure they never met. Kabul was Sodom and Gomorrah, a place where sin and wickedness flourished as an inevitable result of men and women sharing buses or offices or class-rooms, and the authorities were determined to cleanse the capital as an example to the world.

Within weeks of taking power in September 1996, the Taliban decreed that women could not attend school, work outside the home except in gender-segregated hospital wards, travel without a male chaperone who was related by blood, or even wash in segregated public bathhouses. They also ordered that all women of childbearing age (roughly fifteen to fifty-five) be fully covered with a burqa when appearing in public. Later edicts added new prohibitions—clearly the result of close, prurient scrutiny—against wearing white stockings or high heels that clicked provocatively and risked inspiring "impure thoughts" in men.

One of the most onerous restrictions was the ban on unescorted travel, especially for women in rural areas. In 1999, I visited one village an hour's drive south of Kabul, where the elders told me the community's most acute health problem was the high number of women who died in childbirth. The nearest hospital was in the capital, and men were scarce since many had fled abroad or died in fighting. If a woman in labor began to hemorrhage, and her husband or brothers were off working in the fields, she simply lay there and bled to death.

The principal enforcer of the Taliban's draconian moral creed was the Ministry for the Propagation of Islamic Virtue and the Prevention of Vice. Its special goon squads, who commanded far more power than ordinary police, were feared by every resident of Kabul. Soon after the Taliban takeover, they became notorious for careening through the streets in powerful pickup trucks, crouching in the back and then leaping out to surprise religious scofflaws. Wielding whips and wire cables, they slashed at women who revealed a pert ankle or uncovered their eyes to examine a piece of merchandise.

By the time I reached Kabul in 1998, virtue-and-vice squads were less rapacious in their public attacks on women, partly because of international criticism but mostly because women had learned their lesson. Even an innocent oversight, though, could still provoke a vicious whipping. Years later, a dignified woman of fifty-four recounted to me, her voice still trembling with rage and humiliation, how she had been lashed by a Taliban policeman who saw she had pulled back her veil while she was washing dishes in her own front yard.

Although I never witnessed such a beating, I did see Taliban police leap out of their trucks into busy bazaars, shouting at shoppers
to head toward the nearest mosque at prayer time and flailing away
with their cables like SS police in the ghettoes of 1940s Europe. I
would shrink back into an alley, hoping they hadn't spotted me but
trying to see as much as I could. Around me, grown men grimaced
in fear and scurried to obey illiterate thugs half their age. I imagined
how humiliated they must feel, and I wondered how prayer could
possibly retain any meaning when a person was lashed into the house
of God.

Yet the Taliban rulers clearly believed in their mission, and the
officials of the virtue and vice ministry saw themselves as guardians
of the nation's purity. During my first trip to Kabul, I spent an astonishing half-hour in the office of the deputy minister, a huge, scowling
mullah named Qalamuddin. He seemed perfectly cast for the part,
with a fat black turban, thick black eyebrows and enormous feet
straining his sandal straps. I wondered if he enjoyed beating his prisoners, and I immediately remembered not to shake his hand.

The mullah was polite enough, offering me tea and raisins and
almonds as soon as I was ushered in. But after a few sips, he launched
into a stern lecture on the dangers of "foreign contamination" that
turned Western women (presumably myself included) into sex
slaves. In Afghanistan that could never happen, he reassured me, because both law and culture made men responsible for the chastity
and comfort of their daughters and wives, from cradle to grave. "We
shelter women for life," he said, with evident pride. I smiled wanly,
shivering at the thought.

The most frustrating aspect of my visits to Kabul was being shut off
from other women. I was dying to know how urbanized Afghan
women felt about the Taliban, and about wearing the burqa. I had
many theories but no opportunity to test them. In numerous visits to
the capital between 1998 and 2001, I never saw a woman outdoors
who was not covered in a full veil. If I was invited to a meal, the
host's mother and sisters cooked and served it but were never introduced. If I chanced to encounter an unveiled woman in a shop or
office, my guide quickly pulled me away.

At first I was obsessed with the burqa, or rather what I could not see behind it. I watched fascinated as Afghan women navigated the streets, encased in the pleated nylon capes that billowed like breezy spinnakers but masked their eyes behind small mesh squares of crocheted cloth. I watched for clues: bracelets, stocking mesh, anything that would hint at the personality or social background of the woman behind the veil. I wondered if they felt hot and angry behind the heavy cloth, or simply safe from leering eyes and police whips.

Burqas were hardly a Taliban invention; in conservative rural areas of the country, they had been worn by Muslim women for generations as a form of protection from prying male eyes. By making them mandatory, the Taliban in part were trying to restore decorum and safety to a traumatized, vulnerable society. But mostly, burqas were a punitive, blame-the-victim method of enforcing strict Islamic norms. The Taliban sought to create a primitive, puritanical utopia, isolated from the lures of the modern, decadent world. The burqa, a blue cocoon of silence and invisibility, was its starkest symbol.

Feminist groups in the West, seeking to raise funds and awareness over the plight of women under Taliban rule, circulated protest cards with tiny squares of blue eye-mesh pinned to them, but I wondered if the truth was more complicated. As a journalist in Afghanistan, I could have benefited enormously from wearing a burqa: it might be harder to see, but it would be a lot easier to observe. Even men had been known to use the all-encompassing veils as a form of emergency disguise to escape death or capture at enemy hands.

In spite of my natural curiosity and empathy, though, the ubiquitous burqa was having the exact effect on me that the Taliban authorities had intended. The streets of Kabul swarmed with women beggars, mostly war widows with no skills, social status or means of supporting their families. They haunted bazaars and traffic circles, they waited outside mosques on prayer days, they camped around the gates of U.N. charities. As soon as I emerged from a taxi or government van, I was instantly surrounded by a dozen women in patched blue- or mustard-colored burqas — pleading for money, waving crumpled, unfilled medical prescriptions and clutching at my clothes with scarred, leathery hands.

I could see they had endured enormous hardship; I had watched them fight their way past whip-wielding Taliban police to reach trucks piled with sacks of donated wheat. And yet it was hard to feel pity for people whose faces I could not see. Their eyes couldn't haunt me, so it became easy to spurn them. The window between our souls was shut. Every time a mob of masked beggarwomen crowded around me, clawing and pleading, I recoiled in nervous distaste, imagining them to be hideous, toothless crones. In an appallingly short time, I came to think of Afghan women as annoying, anonymous blue blobs.

Only two or three times during my early visits did I manage to exchange a few furtive, hurried words with unveiled Afghan women. The conversations were frustrating for both of us, and invariably we stumbled over language, since most spoke only the Afghan dialects of Dari or Pashto. Yet I sensed an enormous, pent-up urgency to communicate, especially with foreigners.

During one tour of an international hospital for land-mine victims, an English-speaking nurse drew me aside and whispered that she and her colleagues were frustrated and unhappy, barred even from working in the same wards with male doctors. Another day, a housewife beckoned shyly from her doorway, pulling me inside as she flung off her burqa to reveal a flushed and perspiring face. Mutely, she took my hand, pointed to the heavy cape, and sighed.

Finally, I decided the only way to pierce the veil separating me from half the Afghan population was to try wearing a burqa myself. The chance came one day in a crowded bazaar in the city of Kandahar, a decrepit but bustling desert city that was a stronghold of both the Taliban and Afghanistan's deeply traditional ethnic Pashtun tribes. There was no need for the religious police; young men sporting fashionable Taliban turbans and rifles swaggered through the streets. The day before we arrived, two murderers had been shot by a firing squad in the city's sports stadium before a hushed audience of several thousand.

There were many burqa shops in the bazaars lining the muddy streets, and I stopped in one where a young man named Abdullah sat surrounded by bundles of blue nylon cloth. Offering me green tea, he confided shyly that he had been married the year before, and was now the father of a son. No, he and his wife had never met before the wedding, which had been arranged by their parents. Yes, she always wore a burqa outdoors, and so did his sisters and mother. His family shop had been selling them for seventy years.

"Our traditions are even more strict than Islam," Abdullah explained earnestly, referring to the Pashtun tribes that comprise 60 percent of all Afghans. "The Taliban are the system we want. If you have a tradition of so-called freedom in your country, that's fine, but we have our own. Our women like to wear the burqa," he declared, "because every glance has a cost."

When I asked to try on a burqa, Abdullah laughed delightedly and helped me into a brand-new, bright blue cape. It weighed far more than I expected, and the face mesh squeezed tightly against my eye-glasses. Almost immediately, I tripped on the shop steps. Feeling foolish but determined, I hiked up the dragging skirts and set out along the sidewalk.

A thick mist surrounded me, making me feel claustrophobic and off-balance. The heat was stifling and I could barely breathe. I stumbled again, cursing in anger and fighting off panic. I could barely see three feet ahead, and yet I had the acute feeling that every eye in the bazaar was watching me. Suddenly I realized I had nothing to worry about, and I laughed ruefully to myself. Like every other woman in Afghanistan, I was now invisible.

Kabul under the Taliban was not only a place of religious oppression, but also of crushing poverty and hardship; anyone with a few dollars had long since fled. By 1998 there were more than 4 million Afghan refugees living in Pakistan and Iran, the two large neighboring countries, and tens of thousands more in Europe and North America. The economy was in ruins, and the government apparatus was in the hands of religious zealots with no money, no experience in governance, and far more interest in promoting piety than public service.

Thousands of teachers, police, engineers, and other government workers were fired in massive ideological purges, turning entire ministries into empty shells. Middle-class professionals took menial jobs to feed their families, while their skills atrophied and their self-respect sank. I met an English teacher selling vegetables from a pushcart, a policeman who sold used sweaters in the bazaar, a constitutional lawyer who had worked clearing landmines by hand. I stood in food lines with worried-looking men who wore shabby jackets of good-quality wool over the dirty cotton robes required by the Taliban. Sometimes they looked at me ruefully, ran their fingers over their scraggly beards and shook their heads in mute resignation.

Chicken Street, the block of antique and gourmet stores that had been a haven for Western tourists and counterculture drifters in the 1960s and 1970s, was now a deserted row of darkened shops whose proprietors spent their days sipping tea. I befriended one curio shop owner who spoke passable English and often visited him at teatime, finding a quiet haven in his carpeted cave. Not once did a customer enter. The glass shelves, crammed with china cups and lapis lazuli boxes and silver swords and intricate earrings, were thick with dust. Like everyone else in Kabul, the owner was simply waiting for the day that change would come.

The capital was also overrun with thousands of destitute refugees who had fled from fighting in the north, where Taliban forces waged a see-sawing battle with opposition militias for the entire five years they were in power. A few hundred of the displaced families were housed in an old Soviet embassy compound, but most took up far more precarious residence in the blocks of abandoned ruins that reached several miles west and south of Kabul. There they lived like cave-dwellers, without water or light or fuel, cooking on wood fires and surviving by their wits.

Many of these refugees were from the Shomali Plain, a once-verdant region of vineyards and orchards north of Kabul, where whole villages had been attacked and razed by Taliban troops. Shomali was behind the front lines now, heavily mined and inaccessible to journalists. But the portrait painted by the refugees was of a vengeful pogrom. Old men in tears told me how their fields had been torched, their trees chopped down, their irrigation wells dynamited. One refugee family described how an elderly uncle and a newborn had died in the forced march to Kabul; then the mother carefully unlocked a metal trunk and brought out the only gift she had to offer me: a handful of almonds from their lost farm. I was so touched that I kept them in my purse for months.

While their mothers begged, the children of the displaced roamed the streets of the capital, forming gangs of sharp-eyed urchins. Fatherless and uprooted by war, without skills or formal education, they survived on a combination of elfin charm and calculating combativeness. They shined shoes, sold cigarettes, scavenged in the garbage, and followed people around with little tin cans of smoking incense, asking for alms. Their fingernails were filthy and their cheeks pitted by sand-fly infections. Their stature was stunted by poor nutrition, but their expressions were hardened far beyond their years.

Some of them broke my heart. I especially remember Ziamuddin, a scavenger of eleven or twelve whom I encountered brushing his teeth at a charity workshop for street children. I wanted to talk but he was in a hurry to gulp down his bowl of soup and be gone; his younger brothers and sisters were still out begging, and he had to look after them. Every night they pooled their resources for dinner, and a beating would follow if they did not bring home enough. As the boy hoisted his scavenger's sack to set off, I snapped his picture. He grinned and stuck out his hip, but there was something else in his eyes: the infinite weariness of a burden he was much too young to shoulder.

The Kabul street boys were expert at spotting targets blocks away, and they would chase after me with practiced smiles and pleas for "baksheesh, mister." But in larger groups they could become instantly menacing. One shove would lead to another, then someone would throw a rock, and suddenly I realized they could easily tear me apart. This happened a dozen times: the crowd pressing in, the taunts growing louder, until someone—usually my translator or a policeman—picked up a stone and screamed a stream of expletives, scattering the mob long enough for me to escape.

Afghan culture had a brutal, primitive element, and animals were often the victims. Organized fights between dogs, roosters, and partridges were major weekly attractions in Kabul until the Taliban banned them—not because they were cruel, but because they encouraged gambling. The national sport was *buzkashi*, a violent form of polo in which there were no rules of conduct, the ball was a goat carcass, and a chaotic field of horses and riders lunged after it in a muddy, bloody blur of whips, teeth, spurs, and hooves. To me, it seemed the perfect metaphor for a feral society.

An especially popular pastime for Kabul's roving adolescent gangs was to harass the animals at the Kabul Zoo, a bedraggled cluster of shell-pocked buildings whose rusted cages contained a few monkeys, wolves, and eagles, along with an aged, one-eyed lion who had been famously maimed by a grenade. One day I came upon a group of boys clustered around the monkey cages, and I watched with growing horror and rage as they threw rocks and jabbed long sticks into the cages, lit cigarettes and poked them through the bars for the monkeys to eat, snickering and egging each other on.

Periodically an old guard wandered by, shouting threats and swinging half-heartedly with a stick. But as soon as he moved on to another cage, the boys were back, taunting and tormenting the creatures within. I made several attempts to lecture them, asking my translator to explain that monkeys had feelings like human beings, and asking them to imagine what it was like to be in a cage with people trying to hurt you. They stared at me in astonished, shrugging disbelief. "This is our fun," one boy told me.

They had grown up in a society without pity, a place where the most common phrase in Islam, "in the name of Allah, the merciful and benevolent," had become a perverse joke. They were beaten by the police, by older relatives, by bigger boys—so they turned on caged animals to victimize. The monkeys, normally playful and polite under more civilized circumstances, had also become half-mad. They cowered and grimaced in the corners of their cages, then lunged forward in a frenzy, baring their teeth and attacking the wire mesh. Trusting no one and permanently prepared to defend themselves, they had become a different species altogether.

∾

When I arrived in Afghanistan, I had never spent time in a Muslim country, and I had no means of comparing the Taliban to any other Islamic government. I knew that the Saudis also meted out harsh and primitive punishments, stoning adulterers and amputating thieves' hands, and yet faced relatively little international outcry. Moreover, the Taliban leaders I met presented themselves as moralists and their repression of women as an effort to protect them from the depredations of a war-savaged society and the temptations of the modern world.

But the more Afghans I managed to meet out of official earshot, the more I realized how extreme the Taliban's religious vision was, how much it was based on exaggerated fears of Western life—and how little it had to do with Islam. Unlike the Saudis, who embraced the technology and comforts of the West, the Taliban sought to keep out both the benefits and the dangers of modern world, and to cast a veil of stultifying conformity over the entire society. Afghanistan, conservative and rural by tradition, wounded and weakened by war, was a vulnerable vessel for one of the most draconian religious experiments in history.

The Taliban repressed men as well as women, forcing them to grow long beards and wear flowing robes instead of suits, firing thousands of trained professionals from the government and replacing them with semiliterate Islamic clerics. They stymied the physical and intellectual energy of youth, banning chess, kite-flying, pigeon-raising, and other forms of recreation as distractions from religious devotion. They required sports teams to wear long pants on the playing field and spectators to watch games in silence.

The Taliban rejected modern knowledge, substituting school classes in Koranic studies and Afghan Pashto—an obscure dialect spoken in no other country—for courses in English and science. They shut down libraries and banned Western reading material. They shunned foreign investment and technology, asserting with tragic conviction that "God will provide" while the populace of 20 million struggled in desperate poverty and drought.

Yet sometimes I could sense that these men—mostly rural Islamic clerics who had been exposed to little in life except Koranic verses and combat—were gamely struggling to come to terms with the alien, modern world I represented, weighing its evils and advantages. They were puritans trying to re-create the seventh-century world of the Prophet Mohammed, but the barren, battered country they governed was in desperate need of technology, education, and foreign investment.

Once I traveled to Afghanistan with a group of foreign businessmen who hoped to rebuild the defunct telephone system and modernize several ministries. We were taken to meet the deputy communications minister, a turbaned mullah who was curled up barefoot next to an empty, ornately carved desk. One visitor opened his briefcase, bringing out a laptop computer and a cellular phone that played "Can-Can" when he pressed the hold button.

The official's eyes lit up as he marveled at the strange gadgetry, but then narrowed in thought. I could see he was wrestling with his conscience. Finally he spoke. "When we go to religious school, they don't just tell us to pray," he said, "they tell us to work for the people and the society." His office, like other Taliban ministries, was in a deserted building where no telephone rang, no typewriter hummed.

He fingered the cell phone, then handed it back politely. "This is all in the hands of Allah," he concluded. "If it is his will, we will do the job as he wishes."

At the same time, these Afghans seemed bent on wiping out much of their country's own heritage. They banned not only Hindi pop music but also traditional Afghan story-poems and songs, in a country that was 80 percent illiterate. They slashed museum paintings and smashed priceless artifacts from a dozen historic periods and cultures, condemning them as un-Islamic.

The greatest irony—and the gravest error—of Taliban rule was that it soured many of its own people on Islam. For conservative rural Pashtuns, the ideas of the Taliban were not unwelcome, but their methods of enforcement were insulting and redundant. Some people enjoyed watching public punishments, but more were disgusted by them. Afghanistan was virtually 100 percent Muslim when the Taliban seized power. But by dragging devout citizens into mosques and prisons, the Taliban gave their religion a bitter new taste.

Although most of Afghanistan was rural and conservative, it was much easier to gauge people's true opinions once I could escape the intense official scrutiny of Kabul. Whenever I did secure permission to leave the capital, I grabbed a cab and departed immediately, lest the authorities change their mind, and tried to make each drive last as long as possible without arousing suspicion. Even with a government guide at my side, I could hear stories and jokes and forbidden music on long, slow rides across the countryside. I could talk to shepherds worried about the drought and shop owners whose wives had lost their teaching jobs. I could glean my own impressions of the country's "ground realities."

On one trip to the north, I toured a Soviet-built cement factory, half-ruined by war and looting, that the Taliban were trying to revive. The manager, a young Taliban fighter, was dead serious about his task but totally dependent on the ancient workers who had tended its roaring open furnaces for decades. I also toured the ruins of a surreal, Disneyesque palace where a former warlord had built himself a monument to childlike megalomania, with his own waterfall, exotic aviary, imported rose garden, gold coin factory, and a miniature train that chugged up his personal mountain to a cloud-painted eyrie topped with a huge metal eagle.

I also made numerous trips to the south, traveling the three-hundred-mile desert highway between Kabul and Kandahar and becoming intimately familiar with every bomb crater and collapsed bridge along the way. The road had been built with American aid and engineering in the 1960s, a smoothly paved product of Cold War competition. But twenty-five years of war, neglect, and truck traffic had pounded it into a spine-jolting slalom course. By day the heat was searing, and the gritty dust worked its way into our hair and teeth.

Afghan drivers and passengers stopped frequently to wash and drink in desert streams, as well as to recite their prayers. I resisted fresh water as long as the supply of warm sodas lasted, knowing how devastating the medical consequences could be. But on one trip I grew too thirsty to care about germs any more and scooped a handful of cool water from a stream running through a culvert, practically inviting the attack of dysentery that knocked me off my office chair in New Delhi, like a dagger in the stomach, one week later.

Every so often on the desert road, a caravan of camels would materialize on the horizon like a mirage, heaped with carpets and tents. The convoys plodded silently along the sand, following invisible grazing and trading routes Afghan nomads had used for centuries. Often they were led by young girls in swirling, filthy skirts of emerald and purple and scarlet, and always they were followed by a single, shaggy-headed dog. There was never any sound but the occasional bleat of a baby camel and the tinkling of tiny bells around the placid beasts' necks.

Sometimes, to avoid the relentless heat, we made the journey at night, driving under stars that glowed intensely in the pitch black sky. To keep awake, taxi drivers raced each other across wide, trackless stretches of sand, past the ghostly shapes of abandoned mud villages. Or they unearthed hidden music cassettes from under their seats, and we would listen to the piercing, melancholy chanting of Afghan boys, accompanied by an ancient stringed instrument called a *rabab*, until the repetitive rhythm merged with our dreams.

Late one night, a traveling companion pulled out his notebook and read a poem he had written in Afghan Dari. It was about a man living through a long night under a starless sky, with no mother's or lover's arms to console him, always seeking an elusive patch of light. There was no need to say that the poem was also about Afghanistan, an entire nation that had become dark and bereft. I held my breath, and my fingers crept across the seat, silently intertwining with another passenger's in the dark. I remember thinking, very clearly, that this was another moment I must never forget. It had nothing to do with the news, but it was what I had come to Afghanistan to feel, and I wished it would never end.

∽

Interlude

Dubai——I am exhausted, disgusted, and guiltily grateful. My flight from Kabul has landed in this glittering oasis of oil wealth on the Persian Gulf, a replica of Beverly Hills dropped in the desert. The first thing I see when I enter the airport terminal is a brand-new Lamborghini, mounted on a display pedestal. Outside, the wide, palmy boulevards are lined with surreally familiar logos: Baskin-Robbins, Nieman Marcus, The Gap. In the distance, I can see the silhouettes of high-rise hotels lining the white Gulf beach; out in the desert, imported race horses are stabled at an exclusive track.

After my first hot shower in weeks, I sit down in my comfortable, well-lit hotel room to write my final story from Kabul. It is a piece about winter and poverty under the Taliban, the one that will run with the photograph of frozen people lining up for bread at dawn. I smelled that baking bread, saw those desperate faces, took that picture less than a week ago, but already the experience seems oddly remote. After the ragged misery and the muted atmosphere of Kabul, I feel as if I have landed on another planet.

A few more weeks, another swoop through the skies, and I am back in America, trying to come to grips with more startling contradictions. On the airport lobby TV screen is a red-faced President Clinton, describing in legalistic but prurient detail his office antics with a girl of twenty. My first thought surprises me: Thank God the Afghan people can't see this. I know many Americans must share my squeamish embarrassment, but after several weeks of immersion in such a modest Muslim society, taking pains to keep my head covered and listening to sermons about the decadence of the West, I also feel ashamed to be an American. The Taliban were right, I scribble angrily in my journal.

It is the shock of reimmersion in so much ease and affluence, though, that really jolts. It has never gotten easier, this transition between affliction and security, between hunger and excess. Even after twenty years of reporting from countries as desperate as Haiti and Peru, even after witnessing so much petty cruelty and greed abroad that I long ago stopped romanticizing the plight of the world's poor, I still have trouble adjusting to the abundance of consumption and choice that engulf me each time I return to the United States.

Life here is too easy, too insular. It chokes me, it makes me feel dead, like furniture showrooms and television gossip shows. I am afraid of being lured into somnolence and status symbols and debt. I dread going to work in a building full of padded cubicles and insincere smiles, where the atmosphere feels more like a bank or an insurance company than a force for truth. I would rather do without hot running water for a week than forget what a rare luxury it is.

When I finally reach my parents' home in rural Connecticut, I am exhausted. It is Christmastime, the village lights are blazing, the shops are selling cashmere sweaters and gift-packaged Scotch. The people who live here are affluent retirees with spacious, landscaped homes, people whose greatest personal worries revolve around tax law reform and creeping arthritis and their son's latest divorce.

Once, when I was much younger, I would have immediately begun railing about the unfairness of it all, would have made a pointed contrast between the bread lines of Kabul and the bon-bon boutiques of Connecticut. I would have goaded my parents into a useless political argument because they were the handiest target for my rage at the inequities of the world. Like Mencken, I wanted to "comfort the afflicted and afflict the comfortable," but I didn't yet understand they could be one and the same.

Now, I am finally beginning to appreciate the values that truly make Connecticut different from Kabul: the dignity and graciousness, the kindness and refinement that are the real luxuries of wealth. My parents are part of a dying breed of genteel Easterners for whom honor and propriety are the highest values, frugality and self-reliance a matter of pride. They believe in modesty rather than ostentation. They never lie or cheat on their taxes. They live in an exclusive, insular world, and they are uncomfortable with people from other racial and ethnic backgrounds, but they are unfailingly polite and fair to everyone.

I know more about the world now than I once did. I know that poverty breeds cruelty, and that people in places like Afghanistan would always rather work for Americans because they are kinder and don't try to take advantage. I know that affluence is no guarantee of happiness, that people with privileged lives can be haunted by childhood slights or hardships, that mansions can become prisons just as prisons can become churches. I know that haranguing always backfires, and that true generosity is always repaid. I know that despair is relative, and that when my mother bursts into tears because the soufflé has fallen just as the guests arrive, her anguish is no less real than the old men shivering in line outside the bakery in Kabul.

When I think of the corruption and cruelty I have encountered in my travels, the hideous unfairness of people's fates, the contempt for law and the irrelevance of moral merit, I thank God for the WASPy roots that once embarrassed me, for a family who educated me to strive for success without stepping on others. I see my parents only once or twice a year now, and I often think sadly that when they and their generation are gone, the qualities they represent will fade away from American life. I know I am a lot more like my parents than I ever imagined, even though I can never admit it and they would never believe it.

But in other ways, even when we are in the same room, we remain worlds apart. Style and appearance matter enormously to them, and they have spent years surrounding themselves with objects that define their history and identity: an antique silver tea service, a French brocade chair. I, on the other hand, have acquired almost no possessions and lived out of a suitcase for years. They love to give parties; I am so afraid of being a clumsy hostess that I have never bought a house with a dining room. They believe in "breeding," and in associating with people of one's social and ethnic background. I have fled their homogenous world, imagining myself as a bridge to other cultures and races and languages, seeking out friends and mates they were never able to accept.

Although I know my parents are proud of my professional success and public achievements, faithfully following my byline on stories from one trouble spot to the next, I think they are still bewildered and disappointed by the choices I have made; still worried that I have never settled down or decorated a house; still trying to "improve" the way I look and dress. My mother was a fashion designer before she married, and for twenty years she made me exquisite party dresses, bending over her sewing machine in the basement. Now those dresses hang under plastic bags in my attic, while I have spent the past twenty years happily slogging through the mud in sneakers.

Tonight is Christmas Eve. The tree is twinkling in the corner, symmetrically hung with the same hand-blown glass ornaments that are carefully wrapped and unwrapped every year. The house is perfect, the silver candelabra are polished and the fireplace logs blazing, the turkey and eggnog and hors d'oeuvres displayed on pink damask cloth. This is the highlight of my family's year, the annual holiday party they plan for months in advance. They no longer attend church regularly, but this party comes close to being a religious ritual.

My father looks jaunty in his Santa tie; my mother looks elegant in her green satin dress. The doorbell rings, the ice clinks, the laughter rises. My mind is already far away, restlessly steeling myself for the transition ahead. In a few days I will be back in a shapeless tunic, my hair and teeth full of sand as I jolt along the road to some troubled village. But tonight I am wearing a velvet skirt and pearls and lipstick. My role is to look pretty and make polite conversation about my exotic travels. Somehow, once a year, it seems the least I can do.

CHAPTER TWO

The River

My life is nourished by the river,
And through its veins
The gifts of many mountain peaks run down;
The fields grow richer from many rivers' silt . . .

The river, messenger of the universe,
That brings near the Far
And brings, even to one's door,
The welcome of the Unknown,
That river has wound all my births into one.

My nest, moving in its stream,
Freed of fetters,
Floats from shore to shore . . .

— Rabindranath Tagore (1861–1941)

I LOVE the monsoon. I love the word itself, long and low like a distant moan, evoking visions of cool, refreshing rains that sweep across the parched earth, bringing everything back to life. I never want it to stop, this drenching miracle from God. Driving along the flooded boulevards of New Delhi under the downpour, I see people crouched beneath fruit carts, crammed into telephone stalls, shrinking under trees, or simply standing and dripping. But for once, no one shoves or complains. People are smiling with gratitude and relief, as if the shower were washing away the sour, surly habit of urban living, along with months of dense, asphyxiating heat. The city can breathe again.

I too need the rain. I need it to wash away my exasperation with traffic jams and tea-sipping bureaucrats and sidewalks that are human obstacle courses and office machines that never work and airports where well-dressed passengers insinuate themselves ahead of you in line and pretend you do not exist. I need it to refresh my compassion for the people sleeping on cardboard scraps at noon and the children begging beside stoplights at midnight and the gaunt, scarred teenager with filthy nails who snatched my purse on the Rajasthan Express.

It has always been my nature to plunge into every new assignment heart-first, to immerse myself in new cultures and languages and experiences, however grim or discomfiting. When I arrived in New Delhi, I saw how easy it would be to shut myself off and circulate in a pleasant, air-conditioned, neocolonial microcosm of leafy, high-walled neighborhoods, embassy pools and receptions, five-star hotels and guarded children's schools. But that was not what I had come for, and I was determined to resist the temptation.

For months I sought out slums and shantytowns, visited lepers' colonies and prisons, interviewed butchers and beggars as well as cabinet ministers and diplomats. I was fascinated by the sheer human density of India and its cities, and by the idea that one billion people, at least two-thirds of them desperately poor, could coexist in a cauldron of caste, ethnicity, and faith without violent upheaval or state repression. Having spent years covering brutal regimes and bloody revolutions in much smaller, more manageable countries of the West, I couldn't believe democratic India existed and endured, and I wanted to explore every corner of it.

What I found was a society of perplexing contradictions, a massive subcontinent overwhelmingly united by democracy, a dominant religion, and a militaristic national pride—and yet psychologically an archipelago of a million tiny islands, divided by invisible barriers of caste and language and religion and family. People identified with the state; even the humblest villager knew he had the right to choose his leaders. Yet Indians lived in such dense proximity, with such glaring economic disparities, that they created impenetrable walls around themselves, their property, their relationships, and their capacity to empathize.

In cities like New Delhi, the rich protected their islands with high walls, alarm systems, and guards who shooed away a stream of peddlers with knapsacks full of socks and keychains, rural migrants looking for work as gardeners, and snake charmers who tootled mournfully on little horns, coaxing a pair of weary cobras out of straw baskets. Even government census takers were turned away by guards under orders from their employers. No one bothered to clean or beautify one meter of ground beyond his property line, and no one dared do so either, because the space would be instantly occupied by armies of sharp-eyed squatters.

The floating urban poor created flimsy but equally inviolate islands of their own: makeshift tents erected at construction sites for as long as the project lasted; narrow sidewalk sleeping spaces around which thousands of pedestrians stepped while the occupants dozed in exhausted oblivion. For months, while a highway overpass was being built near my house, several hundred laborers lived in a camp of plywood huts around the site, hanging their clothes on pegs and erecting tiny religious shrines on shelves inside their temporary homes. Then one day they were simply gone, replaced by a green park with shrubs.

Privacy, in a place this poor and densely populated, existed only as a pure act of will. Tinny music blared all night from neighborhood temple festivals, and everyone slept through it but me. People bathed at public taps, stripping to their undergarments while they soaped their bodies and clothes, rinsed, and then dressed again. I once saw a shoeshine boy leap from a train during a brief stop, perform this entire ritual, and leap back on before it left the station.

Many people had neither bathrooms nor latrines, so they simply squatted in open spaces, creating invisible curtains. Often, leaving Delhi on a train or highway in the early morning, I would see a dozen solitary figures, perhaps fifty yards apart, hunkered half-naked in a field or weedy back lot, gazing unhurriedly into the distance and studiedly oblivious to the human activity around them. I remembered how embarrassed I was every time I had to relieve myself in the Afghan desert, and I marveled at people who had, though sheer necessity, acquired the art of making themselves invisible.

Traffic operated on the same principle. On any urban boulevard, vehicular traffic was a perfect replica of India's human hierarchy and its corresponding velocities. Dangerously overburdened buses and cargo trucks groaned along, three-wheeled rickshaws zipped casually among lanes, families of five balanced precariously on motorbikes. Powerful new Mercedes and Maruti sedans honked their way past old bicycles stacked high with merchandise, and the occasional elephant serenely plodded along with a mahout on its back.

The veteran Delhi driver, entering one of the capital's landscaped roundabouts, never paused to gauge the relative speed and distance of the diverse conveyances surrounding him. He gripped the wheel, stared ahead, and sailed across five lanes of traffic, ignoring the chain reaction of swerving and braking he caused. An elephant trainer once told me that one of his favorite animals, a large, middle-aged female, had been killed in Delhi traffic by a car that ran straight into her backside. In court, the driver swore he hadn't seen her.

The streets of Delhi were also haunted by beggars—not the product of war or emergency, but of chronic poverty and crowding. Barefoot urchins hawked newspapers, men on crutches held up truncated limbs, women clutched infants so tiny they seemed like dolls. Tapping on car windows, they scratched at the consciences of the affluent, always with the same wheedling whine and the same unmistakable, hand-to-mouth gesture they must have practiced a thousand times. They stood on the same corner day after day, year after year, and passed on the turf to their children.

Many affluent commuters simply rolled up their windows when the light turned yellow. Sometimes I did too, especially once I recognized the same beggar, proffering the same deformity, for the tenth time. I knew some were professionals employed by gangs, with borrowed babies and deliberately malformed limbs. I knew the lepers waving their shiny stumps of knuckles were long since cured and housed in government shelters. I knew the cripple at the Bhikaji Flyover was a fake, because I caught him one day as the signal changed, stomping off in disgust with his crutches under his arm.

Sometimes, though, a brief encounter with a beggar stayed with me for months. One night, as I was returning from a party, my taxi pulled up at a stoplight. It was almost midnight, and a light rain was falling. A girl of about ten was waiting on the curb. When she saw me, she rose shakily on a single crutch and held out her hand. Her eyelids were half closed, and I realized she was exhausted. In my country, most children her age would have been fast asleep. This one was clearly under orders to remain at her post until the last bar had closed for the night. I fumbled in my purse, overcome by pity and guilt, but the light had already turned green. As we pulled away, I saw tears rolling down her face.

Then there was the elephant boy who plied the train station at Agra, where thousands of tourists alighted each day to visit the Taj Mahal. I was waiting to return to Delhi after a weekend visit, sitting on a railside platform that swarmed with humanity: beggars and shoeshine boys and pickpockets, peddlers with trays of peanuts and greasy newsprint cones full of chips, soldiers napping on duffel bags, Hindu pilgrims half-wrapped in dirty orange cloths, and entire families camped on pieces of cardboard.

Amid this splendid panorama a single, grotesque figure caught my eye. He was not yet 12, and one leg had swollen from elephantiasis into a gargantuan rubber sausage. The foot was a gigantic clown shoe on which the boy flapped efficiently about the platform, matter-of-factly marketing his deformity to waiting passengers. When a train pulled out, he drew his balloon-limb under himself like a hideous ottoman, squatted on it and begun gulping from a metal bowl of rice and lentils. Then he hopped toward the public water tap near my bench, poured himself a cupful, and offered one to me.

This boy had by far the best scam of any beggar in the station, and he knew it. He seemed inured to the startled stares he evoked, as brisk and businesslike as if he were peddling candy. Yet I shuddered to think of his approaching adolescence, the moment hormonal awareness dawned and he would suddenly, desperately, long to be normal. I wondered if he had any idea what awaited him, and whether his parents had deliberately allowed his lucrative disease to progress.

As I handed the boy a crumpled bill and watched him flap toward a scrum of newly arriving passengers, I thought again about the extreme contradictions of Indian society. This was a country with a world-class elite of doctors, engineers, and nuclear scientists, and a vast rural underclass that weeded rice paddies by hand and patted cow dung into fuel cakes. It was a country where imaginary families on TV ads relaxed in sparkling white rooms full of modern appliances—but where real families in miserable shacks maimed their children and sent them into the streets to beg.

Inevitably, every few months, the moment would come when I felt overwhelmed by the oppressive poverty and heat and traffic, when I could no longer squeeze another drop of compassion from my pen. There were too many beggars whining at my window, too many repairmen demanding bribes, too many bureaucrats out to tea when I desperately needed their signature. I felt used and manipulated by an entire society, a foreigner who existed only to be flattered and fleeced. I wanted to go home, but that was ten thousand miles away.

Finally, I learned to accept defeat and retreat for an afternoon to the only sanctuary I had found in Delhi: the cool, arching marble atrium of a five-star hotel. It was an island of polished marble and stone, rising abruptly from a wasteland of garbage that no one ever collected, fetid puddles that never dried, and piles of moldering construction material that would never build anything. Beggars and peddlers swarmed the nearest intersection and migrant laborers dozed on pieces of cardboard, their barefoot children scampering in the dirt.

Inside, only foreigners and well-dressed Indians dared enter. The waiters were discreet and efficient, and there was soothing jazz in the air. The guards checked every license plate at the gate, and the doormen, wearing slightly ridiculous uniforms designed to recall maharajahs' guardsmen of yore, summoned taxis by murmuring into microphones hidden in their lapels. I could sip chablis with my friends in a bar decorated with British equestrian prints, or nibble salad in a café overlooking a landscaped pool. For a few rejuvenating hours, I could do what thousands of affluent Indians did every day: pretend that India did not exist.

My first impression of Hinduism, the religion shared by more than 90 percent of Indians, was of a perfect opiate for the suffering and illiterate masses. It was childish and circuslike, a form of mass entertainment and escapism that seemed too messy and commercial to allow for spiritual contemplation. Its chief gods included an elephant, a monkey, a bright blue baby, a woman astride a tiger, and a man with snakes coming out of his head. Its festivals were like a Rose Bowl parade or Brazilian samba competition, with enormous floats and marching bands and devotees in fantastic stage costumes.

Its temples, rising above every neighborhood and village, were often noisy, crowded, smoke-filled pagodas with a carnival atmosphere. Inside, worshippers scattered flowers and coconut shreds while bald frowning priests lit incense and droned chants. Live elephants with flowers painted on their heads blessed children with their trunks, monkeys scampered over the gables, vendors hawked marigold wreaths and other trinkets, and new taxis pulled right up to the door, their drivers waiting for the priests to sprinkle them with holy flowers for good luck.

Yet somehow, the faithful seemed to find solitude and solace amid the cacophony and claustrophobia, emerging from the gloomy din of a village temple to start their day with renewed vigor and a smear of scarlet dust on their foreheads. Somehow, in the pageant of noise and color and dirt that left my senses reeling and my nerves jangled, ordinary Hindus conjured up a zone of privacy as contemplative as the silence of a Quaker meeting hall.

Because most of the people working in my house and office were Hindus, their religion gradually became an intimate part of my daily life, in ways that ranged from amusing to startling to profound. During more than four years, the family that lived and worked in my house—Ashok Pandey, the shy, gangling night watchman and office clerk; Asha, his plump, determined wife; and Ravi, their little boy— became the prism through which I came, gradually and reluctantly, to appreciate the abiding power of an alien, multitudinous faith.

The initial episode was not a promising one. I decided to move to a new house and office, and on the first day there, I was horrified to find a dripping red swastika freshly painted on one door. It turned out to be Hindu blessing from the staff—not a Nazi curse from unseen enemies—but the incident unsettled me for several days. Then Ashok approached me and asked if we could have a *puja*: a spiritual housewarming ceremony conducted by a Hindu priest. It seemed a harmless gesture, perhaps even an encouragement to domestic harmony.

I had no idea what was to come. On the appointed day, a plump priest with a sour face arrived, wrapped in a saffron skirt and carrying a bulging satchel. After pocketing a large fee, he plopped down on the parlor floor and proceeded to build a campfire. First he laid down a row of bricks, then arranged a pile of twigs on top and lit them. As the flames rose, he fed them with sprinklings of leaves, flower petals, rupee notes, dirt, and cooking oil. The entire time, he rocked and chanted in a nasal monotone.

Soon the room was filled with nauseating smoke, and embers spilled off the bricks. I had visions of the carpets and curtains going up in flames, but the staff, chanting dreamily along, did not seem to notice. Finally the priest declared the blessing complete, stuffed his fee inside his robes with a grunt, and departed. As I feared, the stone floor was crisscrossed with indelible char marks. Dragging a rug over the spot, I prayed the landlord would not discover it until I was long gone—and vowed never again to succumb to such foolishness.

It took another, far more serious domestic incident to break down my exasperated resistance and replace it with awed respect for the power of the Hindu faith. Ashok, dignified but diffident, was a lifelong devotee of Hanuman, the monkey god. One of the most beloved figures in the Hindu pantheon, Hanuman represents strength and valor and is depicted as an armored warrior, striding forward and clutching a mace. In the "Ramayana," the legendary Hindu epic-poem of godly exploits, Hanuman hoisted an entire mountain in his hand so his master, Lord Ram, could find a sacred medicinal herb to save his brother's life.

Many Hindus call upon Hanuman for succor in times of stress or travail, and Delhi is full of Hanuman temples, decorated with carvings of enormous, leering monkey figures that reminded me of amusement parks. There was one in our neighborhood, and Ashok visited it faithfully twice a week. In the spring of 1999, I noticed he was looking pale and thin, and he confided he was having stomach problems. A doctor had prescribed some medicine but it had not helped, so he had stopped taking the pills and begun taking extra offerings of flowers and coconuts to the Hanuman temple instead.

Over the next several weeks, Ashok grew more gaunt and demoralized, and one day he collapsed in the driveway. We rushed him to a private clinic, and for the next four days he was treated by a team of specialists, but his condition worsened. He lay on the bed, drifting in and out of consciousness, too weak to move and too sick to eat. With each day, his will to live visibly slipped. Each time he awoke, he begged to be sent back to his village. Asha, slumped in tears by the bed, beseeched me to let him go, so he could pay respects to his ancestors before he died.

It was a startling request. As an educated Westerner, I had no doubt that Ashok was getting the best medical care available and needed to remain where he was; to send him on a bumpy, seventeen-hour train ride across India would surely be a death sentence. But it disconcerted me even more to realize that I wielded such enormous power over his fate. It was I who paid the clinic bills, I who appeared each day to make sure Ashok was being treated properly.

I had not been in India long, but I already knew that my stature as an affluent foreigner was a useful cudgel to wield in an emergency, even if it made me uncomfortable. I was an American, independent and egalitarian, and yet here I was suddenly surrounded by servants who insisted on performing chores I was perfectly capable of executing myself, and in return called upon to take an almost feudal responsibility for their welfare.

Now, the family that depended on me for its survival, that obeyed by requests and indulged my whims without question, was asking me to relinquish that power, to accept tradition and superstition over modern medicine, to give up on my gods and bow to the will of theirs.

I took a deep breath and said no. Ashok had to remain in the clinic and he would improve very soon, I explained as authoritatively as possible. The problem, the gastroenterologist with the cellphone on his belt confided to me, was that he might not recover. He had waited too long, consulted too many Hindu priests and neglected to take too many pills, while bleeding ulcers ate away at his insides. If he died in the clinic, his family would never forgive me, and never believe that Western medical mumbo-jumbo hadn't been to blame.

What I needed was insurance, some familiar source of healing power that would convince Ashok and his distraught family to trust my judgment. Hanuman. Feeling both foolish and inspired, I headed for a curio shop and spotted a small metal figurine of the monkey god, posed in his fierce, legendary stance. It cost me the equivalent of $1.25.

When I returned to the clinic that afternoon, Ashok's face was sunken in shadow, and his eyes were too weak to open. Asha was there, weeping disconsolately. His two brothers patted his head and conferred in worried murmurs. One of them bent down and told him I was here, and his eyes opened briefly. I put the little Hanuman figure in his hand, and he pressed it to his forehead with a brief smile. Then his eyes shut again and his head fell limply on the pillow.

I dreaded the next day, dreaded seeing Ashok's skeletal frame in the bed and the look in his family's eyes—resigned, faintly accusing, not quite daring to meet mine. But when I entered the ward, I heard laughter. There was Ashok, sitting up against a pillow, grinning at his family. His eyes were bright and his color was back. He asked for a radio, so he could hear what was happening in Parliament. He asked Asha to bring some porridge. He asked me how soon he could go back to work.

On the nightstand, amid a litter of plastic pill bottles, was the little metal figurine, striding forward, eyes fierce, mace held high. All night Ashok had clutched it in his hands. In the morning, his fever had suddenly broken. Intellectually, I had little doubt that modern medicine had turned his illness around. But I also knew, with absolute certainty, that Ashok's faith in Hanuman had given him back the will to live. Who was to say which force was the more powerful?

∾

When I first came to India, I was advised to avoid certain journalistic clichés, known as snake charmer or sacred cow stories. A democracy and nuclear power of one billion people needed to be taken seriously, not reduced to a Kiplingesque zoo tale. But animals were the great passion of my life, and I was fascinated by the extraordinary roles they had played in the history of India—revered as spirits, ridden to war, hunted as trophies, worked to death, paraded as spectacles, and spoiled as pets.

In Delhi, I was immediately drawn to the creatures that haunted the fringes of urban civilization, clinging to niches in a vast metropolis that inexorably ate away the surrounding equatorial plain. Every day at 4 p.m., I noticed that a pack of wild monkeys appeared outside the Ministry of Defense, where there were several banana vendors, and then vanished at a silent signal into the trees. They lived in the ruins of an old pre-Mughal fort, built by Ghiasuddin Tughluk, and on weekends I sometimes drove out and climbed into the ruins to watch them.

I loved feeding them bananas, which they accepted with grave politeness before dancing away. I loved watching the teenagers cavort on the rocks, the mothers suckle babies that clung to them like burrs, the males establish simian seniority with brief, shrieking fights. They were so sociable and clever that I kept thinking they would make companionable pets, and eventually I arranged with a man to bring me a pair of adolescent monkeys from Rajahstan. I hired a carpenter to cover the back porch with wire mesh and arranged some branches inside.

When the monkeys arrived, I instantly fell in love. They were perhaps six months old, with sad eyes and chirping cries. They nuzzled my hand when I fed them grapes, they huddled together in their traveling cage at night. But the next day, disaster struck. I took them to a vet for rabies shots, and as soon as he opened the cage, they shot straight to the ceiling—leaping among the light fixtures, raining down shattered bulbs, and trying to squeeze out through an exhaust vent. It took several hours to catch them, and when I released them into my porch, the same thing happened. Over and over, they tried to rip holes in the mesh, desperate to escape.

I knew then that I had made a selfish, almost criminal mistake. These little creatures were terrified, and they no more belonged in my home than in a zoo. That night I stayed up with them, feeding them grapes in their cage, listening to their melancholy chirps. If I kept them another day I would not be able to bear parting with them. If I kept them another week they might begin to lose their wildness, to become resigned to captivity. I had to act now.

The next morning I drove out to Tughlukabad Fort, climbed onto the rocks and opened the cage. In a flash, they had scampered over the boulders and vanished. I was weeping uncontrollably. That night I prayed that they had found a friendly monkey pack to join, that they had not starved. Several times I went back, hoping to recognize them in the roving simian bands. I never found them, but for many months, when I was alone in my room late at night, I could still hear them, calling out plaintively in the darkness.

The other creatures that fascinated me were the elephants I glimpsed from time to time, plodding serenely along the boulevards of Delhi like majestic, solitary visitors from another planet. They towered over the traffic, oblivious to the careening din. Their ancestors had been the pride of India's maharajas and the might of its emperors, riding into armored battle and bearing royalty through the streets.

By now, the era of elephant glory was long past, and there were only twenty-three of them left in the capital, all working animals who were hired out for upper-class children's parties, religious processions, and military parades. At night, they retired to a dilapidated camp under a highway bridge that crossed the Yamuna River, where my assistant Rama Lakshmi and I spent several evenings, learning their names and listening to the tales of their keepers. One was Ghayar Ali, a fourth-generation *hathi-wallah*, or elephant keeper. "It was my forefathers who were really fond of elephants. They worked with them on royal estates, they went to war on them, they loved them.

For me, it's a business," he explained. Ali said his children liked play-ing with the animals, but that he hoped to prepare them for a more modern trade. "By the time they're grown, there may be no elephants left at all," he said.

One night, Rama and I accompanied the Ali family elephants to a festival in another city. We watched as five of them were loaded into open cargo trucks. The youngest, Ranjili, panicked and tried to back out, dragging six men with her, and had to be forced back in chains while the mahouts jabbed and shoved and cajoled her. We drove until dawn, when the patient beasts were unloaded, painted with fluorescent designs and draped in velvet. Groups of costumed officials mounted wooden platforms on their backs, and off they marched.

All morning, they paraded through the streets while brass bands thumped and tootled alongside. Adults showered them with rose pet-als and children stared in awe, many seeing an elephant for the first time. By noon it was 100 degrees, and still the animals trudged on. When the procession finally ended, they were fed water and molas-ses, then loaded on the trucks for another long, jolting trip back to their riverside camp in Delhi.

That night we finally left them at rest, munching hay to the soothing strains of a transistor radio, their huge shapes silhouetted against the evening sky. I knew that one day in the not-too-distant future, when someone else drove across the highway overpass and glanced down by the river, the last of the Delhi elephants would be gone forever.

ༀ

India's public life is one of the great success stories of the developing world, with a modern, secularized legal system and an open, free-wheeling political system. But Indians' private and social behavior are often a very different story. Over the years, Indian parliaments have passed laws against every traditional form of social evil, from child marriages to widow suicides. They have banned discrimination on the basis of caste and religion, and established an elaborate hierar-chy of set-asides for jobs, education and social benefits for hundreds of different caste groups.

Yet to a great extent, the unwritten codes of class, caste, and reli-gion still determine how people treat each other within families and communities, whom they marry and how many children they have, how far they rise in politics, what kind of work they do and how much they earn. Where India's political life is open to scrutiny by an aggressive press establishment and marked by free debate on every controversial issue, its private life is cloaked in a thousand veils, governed by a tangle of taboos, prejudices and traditional boundaries that are both subtler and more enduring than the law.

In some ways, these practices help preserve order in a huge, complicated, heterogeneous society where four-fifths of the population lives in poverty, six major languages are spoken, and four major religions are followed. In other ways, though, they hold back that society from developing the values of tolerance, merit and individual freedom that it needs to truly progress. India has become "Westoxified," as one Indian essayist dubbed its insatiable yearning for modern fashion and technological know-how, but it has yet to become modern.

During the time I lived in New Delhi, I traveled widely but not deeply across India, usually to cover some traumatic or transient news event—a natural disaster, a peasant massacre, a religious controversy, a health crisis, an election or a political scandal. I was always in a rush, always on deadline, always racing in a taxi or train or rented car past scenes of daily life I wished I could stop and explore—a village temple festival, a wheat-threshing brigade, a wedding procession with the groom on a white horse prancing through the town square.

Still, I was able to catch many tantalizing glimpses of the rituals and prejudices, the fervent adherence to the certainties of faith and caste, that enveloped the lives of hundreds of millions of people in both a mantle of reassuring guidance and a web of suffocating constraint. Rama, a gracious and quick-witted young woman, proved an indispensable interpreter of Indian culture and society, as well as language. Every time we waded into a crowd of angry villagers or blissful pilgrims or chanting protesters, she knew intuitively which voices to listen to in the din, and how to capture the spirit as well as the letter of what they said.

In Orissa State, where a cyclone swept in from the Bay of Bengal, drowning more than 7,000 people and 200,000 farm animals, Rama and I spent two days wandering among half-drowned coastal villages. We watched Hindu volunteer squads, wearing rubber gloves and masks, tenderly pick up victims' bloated bodies and cremate them on campfires with a brief prayer to the Hindu god Ram. But we also saw villagers nudge a baby's tiny corpse out of their yard, holding their noses, so it would not bring them bad luck.

In Bihar, a parched and poverty-stricken state where Maoist guerrillas were waging a violent campaign against wealthy landlords, we learned how a volatile mix of caste rivalries, feudal traditions, and revolutionary politics could produce an endless cycle of tragedy. One night a village of prosperous farmers from the *bhumihar* caste would be massacred by the Maoists as punishment for exploiting laborers from the untouchable class; a few nights later a village of untouchables, or *dalits*, would be massacred in revenge by the landlords' private vigilantes.

In Uttar Pradesh, where local elections were being held, we saw how a village had been divided for generations along immutable lines according to caste, with the dalits relegated to the lowest forms of labor: tanning buffalo hides and hammering metal washers in dim workshops. But dalits were also beginning to emerge as a political force, forming their own party and electing a woman from their own group as chief of the village council. Her main campaign platform was one every village woman instantly supported: how to stop men from spending their wages on liquor instead of providing for their families.

Both Rama and I were especially intrigued and disturbed by the problems of Indian women. By law, they had the right to vote and go to school, to divorce and inherit property. In practice, they still suffered from enormous pressure to conform to the traditional or arbitrary dictates of family, clan, and caste. In state after state, in village after village, we saw how illiteracy, ignorance, and tradition trapped poor Hindu women in lives over which they had almost no control.

Girls were generally unwanted at birth and sometimes allowed to starve to death. (In the cities, where prejudice against girls has combined with access to technology, women widely used sonograms and abortions to get rid of female fetuses before they were born.) They were married too young, in widespread defiance of the national minimum age of eighteen for girls, and often in exchange for onerous dowries that indebted their parents for years. They were pressured to bear as many sons as possible and sometimes sent back home in disgrace if they failed.

If their husbands died, they lost all stature in their families and could be enslaved or discarded. The traditional practice of *seti*, in which Hindu widows jumped on their husbands' flaming funeral pyres, attaining instant popular sainthood in the process, has long been illegal and now happens very rarely. But thousands of unwanted widows, their heads shaved in a stigma of sexlessness, still survive only by chanting and begging outside Hindu temples.

During the national census of 2001, Rama and I accompanied government surveyors to dozens of interviews with village women; the results were frustrating but revealing, the answers sometimes sad and often hilarious. "How old are you?" the surveyor would ask. A shrug and giggle: "I don't know, ask the neighbors." When did you marry? When I was still playing with toys. How many children do you have? That depends if you include the ones who died. What work do you do? Nothing. I only milk the cows, fetch the water, weed the fields, and take care of the children. Where is your husband? He's dead, but please write down he is the head of the household.

Sex remained a taboo topic in India, rarely mentioned in polite conversation. Mass-entertainment movies sent mixed messages of titillation and prudery. No matter what the plot, the formula never varied: every ten minutes or so, troupes of handsome men and coquettish women shimmied across a parking lot or village square in upbeat, choreographed routines à la *West Side Story* or *Grease*. Couples wiggled their hips in tandem, exchanged soulful gazes, and sang passionate, lip-synched duets—but they never actually kissed, and their imaginary, sanitized sex never had consequences.

Birth control, though widely practiced among the middle class, had earned a bad name among the poor because of a crude, quota-driven government sterilization program in the early 1980s. Hindu nationalists often boasted about India's billion-person population, equating size with stature, and even in 2001, a Delhi newspaper published a sympathetic feature about an illiterate, jobless rural family with twenty-six children.

AIDS, which rapidly spread through India in the 1990s, was associated with the double stigma of promiscuity and homosexuality. In Bombay, where prostitution and a long-distance trucking industry had concentrated the AIDS plague, Rama and I visited the red-light district and found that many brothel girls were from impoverished backgrounds and knew nothing about the disease; if a prostitute became infected and her health deteriorated, the family often refused to take her back. The same was true at truck stops we surveyed, where drivers—who often carried the virus home to their villages from liaisons on the road—shied away from the health-care vans where free condoms and AIDS prevention pamphlets were distributed.

Shame and honor, the evil twins of South Asian social relations, often led to hideous family violence against women, especially brides whose marriage dowries were considered too paltry and girls who dared to fall in love with young men from another caste. Under the law, excessive dowry demands were illegal, yet the maiming, burning, killing, and forced suicides of brides by their in-laws remained the most embarrassing stain on Indian democracy. Across the country, more than 13,000 dowry deaths were reported in 1998 and 1999 alone.

When I arrived in India, I started a folder of news clippings on cases of dowry violence that appeared at least once a week in the Delhi press; by the time I left, the folder was bulging. The stories were depressingly similar. A pregnant woman of twenty-six hung herself from a ceiling fan after her husband, a police officer, and his relatives repeatedly harassed her over demands for a $5,000 dowry. A man shot his wife dead because her parents had given them an Opel sedan and he wanted a Honda. An eighteen-year-old wife was starved, burned, and finally beaten to death by her in-laws, who demanded more money and a motor scooter.

One man I knew became embroiled in a tangled dowry case that led not to violence, but to an equally awful fate for his sister. The man, a security guard, borrowed heavily against his future wages to help pay for the sister's dowry. Shortly after the wedding, it developed that the groom was chronically ill, something his family had deliberately neglected to mention. He soon died, leaving his bride a widow at eighteen, her dowry not yet fully paid. In the West, the marriage would have been annulled. In rural India, the bride became her in-laws' household servant, probably for life.

Most marriages in India, even today, are arranged alliances between families. Love is not an expected or even desirable factor; the marriage is essentially a financial contract in which the bride is viewed as the less valuable property and the deal is sweetened by gifts and money. I was always convinced that the high incidence of dowry violence was a direct result of this system, because there was no mitigating emotional factor—no opportunity for a romantic bond to develop, no tenderness between newlywed strangers to soften the raw greed and cruelty involved.

On quiet Sundays in New Delhi, I often turned to the thick, pastel-colored newspaper sections of matrimonial advertisements. Their sales pitches, composed in identical, hyperbolic code, revealed more than a textbook about Indian culture, values, and ambitions. Girls were advertised as convent-educated, skilled homemakers with college degrees. Boys were trumpeted as high-tech educated, foreign-trained or, most desirably, American green-card holders. Dowry terms were never spelled out, but the most marketable grooms could demand many thousands of dollars, as well as late-model cars and household appliances.

Caste, in contrast, was always mentioned, and often the advertiser insisted on same-caste matches. With some enlightened urban families or harder-to-place candidates such as divorcees, the ad would say, "caste no bar." But outside of major cities, mixed-caste marriages remained relatively rare. In rural communities, where several castes often coexisted in precarious harmony, an adolescent Romeo-and-Juliet romance could lead to instant scandal and cruel retribution.

In one 2001 incident that attracted national notoriety, two teenagers from different castes were caught smooching in a village in Uttar Pradesh. A mob of outraged villagers, encouraged by both sets of parents, hung the couple dead from a roof. Police officials took no action at first, telling Indian journalists they had to respect local traditions. Even the girl's mother was quoted saying the romance was an unbearable stain on the family honor, which murder presumably was not. "My relatives were coming to visit, and I couldn't bear the shame," she said.

Yet despite the cruelties that could accompany arranged marriages, and despite the growing numbers of young Indians exposed to Western dating and lovematches, the practice remained firmly—and often happily—entrenched. Every older couple I met in New Delhi had been introduced and paired by arrangement; many seemed content with their married lives and most expected to arrange their children's matches too.

Young women also seemed largely content to follow the traditional path to marriage. Even in Delhi and Bombay, where girls attended coed college classes and danced until dawn at hotel discos, the freedom to mingle did not seem to weaken the tenacious hold of family culture. Premarital sex remained relatively rare, partly because of the strong cultural taboo and partly because most children lived with their parents until they married. An ambitious young Indian woman might become a doctor or engineer, might even seek a job in London or New York—but she still assumed she would eventually come home and settle down with someone her parents selected as "suitable."

"I want to get a taste of freedom, and the idea of going to America is very exciting, but the life I live here is safe, like a cocoon," said Namita Gupta, a college senior I met at a coed technical university in Delhi. She wore a T-shirt and jeans to class, but went straight home every night and had never been on a date alone with a boy. At first I felt sorry for her, but she seemed happy and well-adjusted, not trapped or resentful. "My career is very important, but I don't want to miss out on family life," she told me, sounding much more mature than most nineteen-year-olds I had met anywhere. "A lot of people go to America and never come back. I don't want to be one of those."

It was not yet dawn when we reached the Ganges. Ravi yawned in his mother's arms, oblivious to the ordeal ahead. Like thousands of Hindu families, Asha and Ashok had planned and saved all year for this journey to the river, which would culminate in the Hindu rite known as a *Mundan.* Like Christian baptism and many of Hinduism's most sacred rituals, the Mundan included a blessing of holy water which the Pandeys believed would shield their four-year-old son from harm for the rest of his life.

A seventeen-hour train ride from the capital carried us across a wide swath of India to the far eastern edge of Uttar Pradesh State, past endless mustard fields in full buttery bloom, through villages with water buffaloes grazing outside thatch-roofed huts, across back yards swept clean and adorned with patterns of cow-dung-fuel cakes drying on mud walls, past blurred figures threshing wheat and hoisting water and riding bicycles and squatting to relieve themselves in open fields.

Ravi arranged his stuffed monkey and plastic helicopter on a bunk, bouncing up and down with excitement. Asha unpacked metal tins of homemade rice, lentil stew, and crisp round pastries called *puris*. After dinner we dozed off to the rocking of the rails, and the next day we alighted at a rural junction where a cousin of Ashok's was waiting with an aging hired taxi.

The Pandey clan had been gathering for several days; this was the first important family ritual since a wedding last year, and everyone was expected to attend. They were upper-caste Brahmins, poor and semiliterate but proud and conscious of their dignified rank in Hindu social order. Some were subsistence farmers and shopkeepers who had remained in their ancestral villages. One was a dubious "doctor" who ran a local pharmacy. Others had gravitated to cities like Delhi or Lucknow to find a better life, becoming partly urbanized but still clinging fiercely to their religious and cultural traditions.

For nearly a week, I became part of this extended Hindu family, given the kind of intimate access that journalists rarely attain. It was an enormous privilege, a gesture of trust and respect that I had to be careful not to abuse. There were disturbing things I saw or heard that week that I knew I would never describe in print, and there were endearing things that I knew I would never forget.

The family's daily life was crowded and noisy, occupied by primitive tasks of cooking without refrigeration and bathing without plumbing. It was organized in a complex hierarchy of relationships, strictly observant of Hindu ritual, and influenced in a thousand ways—from petty to life-altering—by the taboos and prejudices of religion and caste.

Each time we entered a home or greeted a visitor, there was a flurry of gestures—some so rapid I almost missed them—as each relative acknowledged the other's position in the complicated family pecking order. Asha briefly knelt and touched the hem of her mother-in-law's sari; a younger sister-in-law did the same to Asha. In one home, a teenaged girl—recently married to Ashok's youngest brother—appeared covered by a veil, carrying a metal bowl of water. She knelt at Ashok's feet and started to wash them. Ashok, embarrassed in my presence, kicked the bowl away and asked her to stand.

But later that day, during a visit to his ancestral village, Ashok made a formal courtesy call on the most senior resident, an old man slumped on a frayed rug in the dirt farmyard. Without shame, Ashok crouched and bowed, hands folded and touching his forehead, before the illiterate elder. Asha showed me the hut where she had given birth to Ravi, surrounded by her female in-laws, who were overjoyed at her good fortune to deliver a son. Outside, a young man was holding two little girls, his young daughters. I told him they looked pretty, and he frowned. "I am such an unlucky man," he said matter-of-factly. "Now I will have to spend the next twenty years worrying about two dowries."

The extended family had so many members, and people came and went so busily, that it took me days to figure out who was who. The head of one household had a middle-aged wife, but he also seemed to be related to a pretty young woman with a newborn baby boy whom everyone kept cooing and fussing over. Finally, someone explained to me quietly that this was his second wife, a practice that was not strictly legal but was quietly condoned by everyone in the family because the first wife had not been able to bear him a son.

One night, after the clan assembled for dinner, eighteen relatives crammed into two rented trucks and drove all night to Vindiachal, a town of Hindu temples on the Ganges. I rode with Ravi and his parents, jammed next to a window. When we reached the town before dawn, it was still dark and silent, and we made our way down to the beach by flashlight. At spots along the sand, vendors had already set up displays of soap, incense, and resinous neem twigs used as toothbrushes. Other families were waiting in clusters for the Mundan to begin, other little boys fidgeting in their arms.

As the darkness began to lift, the Pandey clan members hovered around Ravi. His hair, deliberately uncut since birth, tumbled down over his shoulders. A barber, hired for the occasion, squatted on the beach and laid out his tools. Ravi spied the straight razor and began to whimper. His parents gently settled him on the sand, and his mother and aunts chanted softly.

The barber poured a cup of Ganges water over Ravi's head and began to scrape. Ravi shrieked and tried to wriggle free, but his parents held him down firmly. His tresses fell away in chunks onto the sand. His father and uncles bent low, telling him to be brave, but he could not stop screaming. Within ten minutes, the little boy was completely bald.

There was worse to come. Ravi's mother pulled off his clothes, picked him up and carried him into the river. He was weeping hysterically now. The first pink streaks of dawn silhouetted the pair of struggling, splashing figures as the mother immersed her sobbing son in the purifying, ice-cold water, murmuring a Hindu prayer.

Part of me was appalled. Ravi was hysterically frightened and far too young to understand what was happening. I wondered if the experience would traumatize him for life. And yet this was not a painful circumcision or ritual scarring; it was a baptism of faith surrounded by a loving family. I held my tongue and watched.

Back on the beach, Ravi's father was waiting with a towel, and his uncles rubbed him dry and popped a consolation sweet into his mouth. They opened a box and dressed him in a crisp, store-bought, Nehru-style suit. They fastened a gold chain around his neck, and then they proudly posed him for photographs like a bewildered little prince.

As the clan packed up to leave, other bald little boys were being carried down to the river, and their squeals of protest echoed through the chilly morning air. Someday, I thought, Ravi would bring his own son to a spot on the Ganges at dawn, perhaps shivering as he recalled his own childhood ordeal, but equally sure the ritual would shield his boy from the evils of the world.

That night, as we were driving back toward the Pandeys' hometown, I spotted a small black puppy howling in a puddle. I scooped her up and we continued on our way. I had no plan for her, but somehow the encounter seemed fateful. She slept in my arms that night, and the next. When it finally came time to board the train for Delhi, I could not bear to leave her behind. Ashok helped me find a small laundry basket in a bazaar, wrap it in a towel and smuggle her onto the train. For the next seventeen hours she sat hidden in the basket, napping with the rhythm or waking up to nibble cookies. All the way to Delhi, she never barked, never tried to escape. We named her Mundan.

∽

Baptism is a birth, a leap of faith, an act of grace that gives new meaning to life. It can transform a prison into a place of liberation, a cesspool into a sparkling fountain, a multitudinous din into hushed and solitary awe. Baptism is a fundamental part of Protestantism, the religion in which I was raised, but in my experience the act itself was always sanitized and symbolic, a few drops carefully sprinkled on the forehead of a prettily dressed baby—never the full, spluttering sub-mersion of an adult, joyfully surrendering his or her dignity to God.

I had experienced the transforming and treacherous power of water once before. In Haiti, a country poisoned by a history of slav-ery and despotism and parched by decades of poverty, people be-lieved in a forest waterfall with a magic healing spirit, and for a time they believed in a radical priest who promised to wash away all evil in a cleansing cascade. They believed that flimsy fishing boats would carry them to the promised land—and drowned by the hundreds each year only a few miles from the shores of Florida.

In India, with tens of thousands of miles of coastline, many peo-ple live at the mercy of the sea and hundreds die each year in floods and cyclones; yet water is the most sacred of Hindu elements. To believe in the purifying and protective power of the Ganges, as hun-dreds of millions of Hindus do, requires one of the world's great leaps of faith. In many places, the river is a meandering cesspool. Factory effluents empty into it, mud-caked water buffaloes are bathed in it, dirty laundry is slapped against its rocks, funeral pyres are lit and floated down it. An entire crusading movement has sprung up to save the Ganges from ecological disaster.

And yet every day of the year, thousands of devotees travel to temple cities like Varanasi and Allahabad and swarm over stone riv-erside pavilions known as *ghats*. Wading in waist-deep, they happily brush their teeth and dunk their heads under the water, oblivious to the rafts of scum floating by. So adamant is their belief—and so vulnerable to political manipulation—that in February 2000, when a controversial film was being shot at the Varanasi ghats, a radical Hindu group staged a protest that turned into a riot, and eventually the film was scrapped. Among other unacceptable criticisms of Hindu culture, the script had depicted the Ganges as polluted rather than pure.

The first time I saw Hindu pilgrims bathing in the Ganges, I felt a mixture of revulsion, pity, and contempt. The second time, at Ravi's Mundan, I was so moved and fascinated by the baptism ritual that I hardly thought about the condition of the water. The third time, in January 2001, I found myself irresistibly swept up in one of the most extraordinary religious experiences of my life.

It was the Maha Kumbh Mela, a month-long Hindu festival held on a vast campground near Allahabad, where the Ganges merges

with another sacred river, the Yamuna. For days religious pilgrims—
old men on crutches, mothers with newborns, entire villages in bus
convoys, holy men and hustlers—streamed toward the site from all
corners of India. There was even a sect of naked, forest-dwelling
mystics called *naga sadhus*, smeared in white ash and brandishing tri-
dents, who cavorted on the beach under heavy police guard. Within
a week, more than 25 million people were camped in the sandy delta.

Hundreds of enormous tents, candy-colored and strung with carnival lights, had been erected by Hindu sects in rows along the sand.
Inside, costumed gurus held court, dispensed wisdom, and served
rice and lentil stew to thousands of devotees. All night a rhythmic
cacophony of chanting and drumming emanated from the tent city.
The roads were so clogged that it soon became physically impossible
to reach our hotel in the city, so Rama and I eventually crawled into
one of the tents, surrounded by snoring pilgrims, and tried to sleep.

By day, the sloping beaches were crammed with waves of pilgrims, all inching their way toward the river delta to take a cleansing
dip. The sea of humanity was suffocating, and yet each person
seemed entranced in individual reverie. People chanted to themselves, murmured quiet prayers and lit tiny candles at the water's
edge, oblivious to the crush. Elderly women, who would never dream
of appearing unveiled in their village square, stripped off wet saris
without a trace of shame, wrapped themselves in spare cloths and
marched back up the beach. The crowd was transformed into a million tiny temples, in which each individual communed alone with his
or her gods, surrounded by an invisible curtain of belief.

At first, the sheer size of the gathering frightened me. My past
experience with large masses of people had been of a very different
nature: student protests against dictatorship in Chile that were
blasted by firehoses, pro-democracy demonstrations in South Korea
where every face was swollen and streaming with teargas, election
rallies in Haiti that had degenerated into deadly, panic-stricken stam-
pedes. I had been nearly trampled a dozen times, and my first instinct
was to look for escape routes.

But the atmosphere at the Kumbh Mela was so congenial, so suf-
fused with bliss, that I gradually relaxed and allowed myself to be
swept along with the other pilgrims. At one point, I even briefly
waded into the water with my ecstatic neighbors, who offered me
towels and posed eagerly for dripping family portraits. By the third

day, I was exhausted, full of sand, and ready to head back to a hot shower and soft mattress in New Delhi. But I also felt an awestruck, vicarious joy at the privilege of witnessing such a benign mass testament to human faith.

∾

To be a foreign correspondent is to learn, again and again, that nothing lasts: to tear one's self away from a family holiday or a long-awaited embrace and rush to a massacre site, to leap up from a long-planned dinner or fireside book when a bomb explodes, to learn months after the fact that a faraway friend has been married or killed in an accident, to begin to believe in something that is abruptly yanked away. It is a lesson that is very difficult to unlearn, one that inevitably lowered my expectations of others—and of myself.

As I was basking among the faithful millions at the Kumbh Mela, a massive earthquake ripped across the north Indian state of Gujarat, leaving thousands of people dead, a city of 150,000 in ruins and un-counted bodies, many still alive, buried in the rubble of a dozen villages and towns. It was a catastrophic reminder of the other extreme of life in a densely crowded and impoverished land, where millions lived in flimsy huts or shoddily built apartments, where collective bliss could give way to collective horror in an instant, where the gods could uplift or crush the faithful with equal force.

I reached the scene in less than twenty-four hours, pausing in an airport jammed with television crews arriving from Tokyo and Rome and Los Angeles. For the next three days I wandered, horror-struck, through the ruins of village after village. Dazed families slumped in front of flattened huts, pigs rooted through the debris. A young man poked hopefully through the remains of his mother's kitchen, carefully dusting off a tea set and ignoring a pile of charred bones nearby. Tiny hands protruded through the rubble of a block that had collapsed on a school parade. Frantic parents surrounded every arriving journalist, begging us to send for bulldozers and shovels, but we knew none would reach the tragedy in time.

At night, we all rushed back to a dark and silent city that was without power, water, or food. Some journalists camped in military tents set up for the emergency. Several of my friends and I made our base at a small hotel, scribbling stories on paper by candlelight and dictating them as fast as possible over shared satellite phones whose batteries were failing rapidly. The building had jagged cracks running along the walls, the lobby was full of broken glass, and the manager refused to let us sleep inside for fear of aftershocks.

Instead, we spent the night on the sidewalk, where the hotel staff had placed a circle of plastic chairs around a bonfire of crates. The manager kept vigil with a hockey stick, batting away dozens of long-horned cattle, anxious and lost in the streets, that kept stumbling into my chair. I dozed fitfully, dreaming of children's limbs protruding from rubble and of masses of people marching blindly toward a fathomless ocean. Death and deliverance merged in my subconscious; my horror of being crushed had returned.

As time ran out and the death toll rose—ultimately it would reach more than 13,800—the few stories of survival, the small miracles of individual rescues, became the intense focus of our attention and the nation's hopes. In the ruins of one city block, an army major proudly showed me the pit of twisted cables and cement where his squad had dug for forty-eight hours straight, finally pulling a seventeen-year-old boy alive from a space the size of an animal's burrow.

On the ninth day, after officials had said there was virtually no chance of finding anyone else alive, a rumor spread that a couple had been found in the town of Bhachau, calling faintly from the ruins of a collapsed apartment building where they had lain, immobilized in separate pockets, for almost two-hundred hours. It was already dark, and I stumbled through a maze of rubble-filled alleys toward the building, holding onto Beth Duff Brown of the Associated Press. A crowd of several hundred people had gathered, and we all watched in dead silence as a Russian rescue team gently probed for a way to reach the couple, periodically pausing to listen for their voices.

As night fell, the rescue workers inched deeper into the rubble, illuminated by portable floodlights. Finally they touched the man's hand, and a cheer went up. Then more silence, more agonizing minutes. I was back in El Salvador, in 1986, watching a baby girl pulled from a quake-flattened high-rise at dawn, and watching an old man sob uncontrollably in a hospital bed. For days he had lain trapped in the dark, surrounded by terrified, weakening screams and certain of his own death. Even after fifteen years, I had never forgotten his face.

It was nearly 10 P.M. when the Indian couple were finally pulled out and placed on stretchers. No sound came from the crowd, just a lonely clicking of cameras. I caught a glimpse of the man's face, half-starved and staring in horror, before he vanished into an ambulance. Like the Salvadoran shopkeeper, he was alive, but he did not yet believe it. I raced for my satellite phone, but I felt no thrill of drama-on-deadline, only a sick sadness at the duty of covering such a grim event. Everyone said it was a miracle that this couple had lived while thousands of others were crushed to death; I saw it as an act of divine perversity. A week before, I had bathed in a powerful tide of faith, but at this moment it seemed like so much dirty water.

Interlude

Chincoteague——The marsh grass ripples almost imperceptibly with the current. The salt air fills my lungs like a drug. Across the creek, I can see the solitary white heron standing motionless in the reeds, waiting for a minnow to dart by. I like to imagine it is the same heron who was here a year ago, the last time I sat on this porch; that his solemn and delicate ritual has continued each morning, outlasting the miles I have traveled and the turmoil I have witnessed halfway across the world. This is my marsh, my immutable corner of nature, my private proof that there are some things that do last, no matter how far and frenetically I flee from them.

I have always felt most at home by the sea: not the frivolous, warm aqua sea of spring breaks and expensive cruises, but the gray-green, melancholy northern sea that is patterned with wind and rain. I love the smell of salt air because it reminds me of my childhood summers in Nantucket, where I spent hours writing in the old cemetery and fell asleep to the quiet rhythm of the harbor waves and the foghorn off Coatue that sounded softly every twelve seconds. I have not heard that sound in many years, but when I close my eyes I can still hear it, and I want to believe that it, too, never stops echoing across the water.

This is my time to reflect, this is the only place where I feel safe and strong enough to look back without wincing, to look ahead without panicking. How have I changed in this year? My skin is more lined and leathery from too much sun and gritty, wind-blown sand. My weight is down, the felicitous effect of my recurring bout with dysentery. My energy has been sapped by the chronic loneliness and strain of waking up alone, in another hotel room, to face another day of trying to pry information from suspicious or grieving strangers, another night of battling recalcitrant high-tech equipment and falling asleep exhausted.

My tolerance has been tested a hundred times by unscrupulous drivers, maddening bureaucrats, clawing beggars. My faith has been shaken by mercurial acts of God that seem to mock the devotion of millions whose daily lives are dominated by religion. I cannot remember the last time I went to church, and I'm not sure what I would say to God anyway.

But each time I come home, it seems harder to pick up the threads, harder to revive the relationships I have put on hold for so many months. I have spent so much time compartmentalizing my life that I cannot remember how the pieces fit together. I have been absent for such long periods that people I love have ceased to rely on me, or even to send me important news. My best friend delivered a baby girl, and my only glimpse of her was an e-mailed snapshot. My father's only sister died in a nursing home, and I missed the most important family funeral in years. I have become a name above a story, a postcard with an exotic stamp, a static-filled phone call of congratulation or condolence.

Still, I keep trying: trading quantity for quality, scrambling to compress a year's worth of memories into two weeks of Scrabble games and bicycle rides and sunsets by the ocean. From the porch I can hear sounds of normal, mundane activities that have become amazingly precious to me: Alan reading a fairy tale to Jocelyn, Connie trying to coax Alejandra into eating her cereal, Erick pinning Nelson on the rug. I shut my eyes and cling to the moment, wishing it would never end.

I know that these few days by the sea are not enough; that this snapshot of intimacy is no less an illusion than a boozy college reunion portrait. I worry that I am missing what really matters and accumulating little except another year of newspaper clippings. I see other people's children, growing taller and more talkative with each visit, and I wonder if I will one day regret having cheated biology, year after year, until the choice to conceive was no longer mine. I worry that in my obsessive quest for novelty and news, my sequential immersion in the struggles of the world, I have become so adroit at flying that I am afraid of landing, so good at pushing people away that I have lost the ability to hold them close.

If I had grown up in India, I would have foregone romance but stayed married; my life would have been more rooted and less ephemeral, more circumscribed by tradition but less burdened by choice. Instead, I have hopped from one relationship to another, inevitably growing restless and moving on because there was nothing to stop me. Often, a new acquaintance in South Asia will ask me, out of bewildered and kindly concern, "Where is your husband? Where are your children?" Each time, part of me bristles with professional resentment, but part of me is asking the same question.

When I think of the Pandeys, I think of them as my family, and yet I know they are not. What they are, if I look at things honestly, is one of a series of surrogate families I have adopted over the years, in half a dozen countries, to stave off a wanderer's loneliness, to create a temporary sense of normalcy and belonging in an alien world. India can never be a home for me. In a society of a billion people, I have become close to half a dozen; for the rest I will always be a privileged white foreigner, tolerated but not trusted. My niche is temporary and floating, without anchors of caste or clan or faith.

I have flung myself into story after story, plumbed the suffering and salvation of strangers, and then moved on. One day I will pack up and leave India forever; I will put away the crayon drawings Ravi used to offer me shyly after school, and someone will whitewash over the trail of hand-prints he used to leave on my stairs. He is six now, and he always lights up when he sees me, but someday he will be an adult stranger with vague, fond memories of the "madam" who brought him puzzles and books from America, many years ago.

The truth is, I am no longer sure where home is. I am two people, restless and sentimental, driven and domestic. When I am abroad, I dream of building a permanent nest somewhere. When I am home, I listen for the wind. I am still not ready to settle down, and I have repeatedly abandoned people and places I love to search for inspiration and meaning in distant struggles. I am addicted to the uncertainty and danger that leave open the door to epiphany and ecstasy, even as they shut the door to stability and more acceptable definitions of happiness. I am still not sure which half of my life is real, and which half is the escape.

But I do know that if it were not for these brief, periodic interludes in a safe harbor, I could not summon the courage to head back into the maelstrom of unpredictable crises and hardships. And I know that these moments each summer—the first glimpse of the sea, the first glass of wine at sunset with old friends—are made more precious by the months I spend on the other side of the world, struggling with cold and germs and loneliness, searching for pathos and poetry in grubby places with unpronounceable names. It is the ability to jet between comfort and strife, to keep feeling jolted by contradictions instead of sinking into a cushion of security and sameness, that keeps me alive.

CHAPTER THREE

Ashes in the Snow

*"Don't tell my father I have died," he says,
and I follow him through blood on the road
and hundreds of pairs of shoes the mourners
left behind, as they ran from the funeral,
victims of the firing.*

*From the windows we hear
grieving mothers, and snow begins to fall
on us, like ash. Black on edges of flames,
it cannot extinguish the neighborhoods,
the homes set ablaze by midnight soldiers.
Kashmir is burning.*

—Agha Shahid Ali, from
"The Country Without a Post
Office"

 THE first thing that struck me was the silence.
Yesterday this had been a busy Kashmiri vil-
lage; today there was no sound at all. Piles of
rubble smouldered everywhere. Bits of blackened carpet lay next to
the remains of handlooms where women had spent months weaving
each intricate, floral-patterned rug. Families sat disconsolately, without speaking, among piles of melted cooking pots and charred clothing. I don't recall hearing even a baby wail. Inside several sheds lay
the bloated, still-tethered corpses of incinerated cows.

According to the Indian authorities, the decimation of Khargam
Village on June 20, 1999, was the unavoidable consequence of
"crossfire" between Indian troops and Muslim separatist guerrillas
who had been hiding in several houses. According to the villagers, it
was an act of deliberate revenge and terror by the army and police,
who shot two guerrillas, sealed off the village, poured kerosene

among the houses, and kept the inhabitants outside at gunpoint while their belongings and animals burned.

The report I filed to Washington the next day was professional and even-handed, quoting both sides and giving full credence to neither. But my instincts told me the villagers' account came closer to the truth, or illustrated a larger one. My photographs were of a dazed family, slumped amid charred boxes, and a little girl sitting alone on the window ledge of a burned house. My story concluded with a bitter observation from a teacher in the village, who told me the Indian forces were trying to intimidate the populace into submission. Instead, their mission had backfired. Now, he said, "each and every person has a new hatred in their heart."

It was impossible to confirm what had really happened in Khargam, though, because the murky incident fit so neatly into two ongoing, dramatically opposed versions of a decade-old conflict. After only a few visits to India's Kashmir Valley, a remote and haunted corner of the subcontinent where Indian security troops and Muslim insurgents had been fighting each other since 1989, I was already leery of both the official explanation of violent events and their political exploitation by opposition leaders. It was easy to feel pity and outrage—but it was also easy to feel used.

The extraordinary beauty of Kashmir made it an unusually seductive setting for covering a war. A verdant, alpine region of pines and eucalyptus, apple orchards and rice paddies, craggy vistas and lily-padded lakes, it had drawn tourists for half a century. Its cultural and political nerve center was Srinagar, a quaint city of wood-framed chalets and curlicued mosques and curio shops selling papier maché animals and goat's hair shawls. Houseboats with romantic names like Switzerland and Floating Castle swayed on the fringes of Dal Lake, and ancient gondoliers poled silently across the water.

The majority of the inhabitants were Kashmiri Muslims, traditional in custom and dress but tolerant in outlook. Most practiced a mystical strain of Islam known as Sufism, which was built around shrines and emphasized a believer's personal connection to God. Its religious leaders taught in riddles that provoked pupils to think, not just to memorize and obey. Kashmiri women wore head scarves but not full veils in the street, and they mixed easily with male relatives and guests at family gatherings. Kashmiri men were known as passive hookah-smokers and poets, not zealots or warriors.

But the Kashmir I came to know, during numerous visits between 1999 and 2001, was a tense and sullen place, an alpine resort
under military occupation. At every intersection in Srinagar, Indian
troops stared out from sandbagged bunkers; at every bus stop, soldiers frisked long lines of passengers. Bars and cinemas were permanently shut for fear of attacks by radical Islamic militias, and the
streets were empty after dark. A decade of warfare and terrorism had
frightened away all the tourists, leaving the houseboats bobbing
empty and the gondoliers dozing on the docks. Virtually the only foreign visitors were journalists like myself, drawn to Kashmir's dramatic irony.

Over time, the religious and political tolerance of Kashmiri tradition had been replaced by suspicion, fear, and creeping Islamic radicalism. Political factions spewed propaganda against each other and
the state; mosques were pulpits for a religion of revenge. Shops
clanged shut on cue for frequent protests and strikes. Armed violence
was so common that the local newspapers carried terse daily round-
ups of soldiers killed by grenades or guerrillas shot in "armed encounters." In this corner of the world's largest democracy, every
family had a tale of military repression, and every child was a potential terrorist. Kashmir looked like Switzerland, but it felt like the
Gaza Strip.

The modern political history of Kashmir has been one of suspicion, intransigence and bloodshed—a microcosm of the bitter half-
century rivalry between India and Pakistan. When the departing
British colonial rulers abruptly partitioned the subcontinent into two
countries in 1947, carving out the Muslim nation of Pakistan from a
wide swath of north India, the result was months of bloodshed and
chaotic dislocation that left one million people dead, 12 million displaced, and a litany of atrocities that still burn in the memories of
both nations.

Kashmir, a predominantly Muslim state ruled by a Hindu maha-
rajah, was literally caught in between, and it erupted in fighting that
lasted until the United Nations brokered a cease-fire in 1949. Under
the truce, the scenic Himalayan region was "temporarily" split between the two countries along a 550-mile "Line of Control," with
thousands of soldiers protecting both sides. India pledged to hold a
plebiscite at some time in the future, allowing Kashmiris to choose
their political destiny.

But for the next forty years, the referendum was never allowed to take place. Indian officials, fearing they might lose Kashmir to Pakistan, insisted it was an "integral part of India." Kashmiri political leaders exhausted their energies, and sometimes went to prison, crusading for the right to self-determination. Then in 1989, after elections many Kashmiris believed were rigged in favor of pro-government parties, a new generation turned to armed rebellion, launching a guerrilla movement that would lead to tens of thousands of deaths.

Throughout the early 1990s, the insurgents carried out spectacular crimes inside Kashmir—kidnapping politicians, blowing up army installations, occupying Muslim shrines. In turn, the Indian security forces blanketed the region with some 700,000 regular troops and launched a sustained counterinsurgency campaign, which reportedly included torturing suspects by dripping hot rubber on their skin and crushing their thighs with steel rollers.

The Kashmiri insurgency was never a serious threat to India's territorial integrity or defense, but Kashmir had enormous symbolic importance to India's idea of itself as a unified, pluralistic, multireligious state. Moreover, the role of Pakistan, which systematically fueled the conflict in an effort to politically wound and weaken India, transformed a local dispute into a permanent source of tension between two heavily armed neighbors with deep suspicions of each other.

Since Partition, India and Pakistan had fought two brief, conventional wars, and India had won both. In 1965, Pakistan launched a military offensive designed to support a popular uprising in Kashmir, but Indian forces quickly gained the upper hand and a ceasefire was signed after less than a month. In 1971, India forcefully backed a Bengali independence movement in East Pakistan against repressive military raids from West Pakistan, leading to the bloody creation of independent Bangladesh and a second bitter humiliation for India's Muslim neighbor.

Pakistan's revenge was Kashmir. From the beginning, its intelligence services covertly financed, armed, and promoted the insurgency. It became a rite of passage for young Kashmiris to slip across the Line of Control into Pakistan, receive military training, and return to the valley as combatants. Pakistan's involvement also provoked vicious internal disputes among guerrilla groups over money and political allegiances, leading to the cold-blooded assassinations of prominent Kashmiris who had been denounced as "traitors" by one group or another.

Indian authorities, while routinely decrying this "cross-border infiltration," confined their military response to conventional and counterinsurgency measures inside Indian Kashmir. They repeatedly declared that they did not want full-fledged war to break out with their neighbor; their aim was to maintain their territorial integrity, secure their political and military dominance in the region, and gradually expand their economic sphere as well.

Then, in May 1998, India stunned the world by conducting five underground nuclear tests in the Rajasthan desert, officially declaring itself a "nuclear power" after two decades of deliberate ambiguity. Two weeks later, despite repeated pleas for restraint and threatened economic sanctions from Washington, Pakistan responded by testing five of its own nuclear devices in the remote hills of Sindh, fulfilling a thirty-year quest to build the world's first "Islamic bomb."

Suddenly, the Kashmir dispute had acquired alarming new significance. The soldiers who eyed each other across the Line of Control were backed by rival nuclear powers. From that moment on, Kashmir would become known as the "nuclear flashpoint" of South Asia—an obscure conflict that could trigger atomic holocaust in a densely populated region of 1.5 billion people.

When I first arrived in Kashmir, I faced an odd dilemma. The conflict was an old, often-retold story, and only the abstract threat of nuclear conflagration had revived the interest of the world, and my editors. But to me, the enduring nature and human dimensions of the dispute were intriguing. What was the psychology of an endless guerrilla war and military occupation? How had constant exposure to violence and death changed the people on both sides? I wanted to know what made the insurgents keep going, what made the populace revere them, and why India's parliamentary democracy, so adroit at co-opting opponents across the political and regional spectrum, had failed so spectacularly in Kashmir.

In the 1980s, I had covered guerrilla wars in Central and South America, where peasant revolutionaries had risen against corrupt governments and repressive armies. I had witnessed massacres and funerals, disappearances and demonstrations. I had seen radical ideas take root among chronically abused people, turning them into disciplined soldiers in a bloody class war. I understood the appeal of these ideologies, extreme in their methods but rooted in a familiar struggle for social and economic equity.

Both Hinduism and Islam were new to me, though, and little in my experience had prepared me for the communal passion both religions could inspire. Kashmir could not be viewed as purely a political dispute, or as a pawn between regional rivals. Kashmiri Muslims saw themselves as oppressed by a Hindu army, acting on the orders of a Hindu state. Their role was to resist a superior force, by subterfuge or slingshot, by shutting down their shops or hiding grenades in their haystacks. This was intifadah, and it had become a way of life.

My first, and most important, guides to the Kashmiri conflict were several local journalists in Srinagar. Theirs was a grim and thankless job, a daily diet of visits to hospitals and cemeteries and bunkered bases. As Kashmiris, it was hard for them to remain dispassionate and objective; as witnesses to constant mayhem, it was hard for them not to go numb. Their knowledge of local language, history, and actors made them indispensable to me, and yet they faced the same frustrations I did, the same elusiveness of fact in a fog of propaganda, the same inadequacy of words to portray the grim repetition of events.

Each time I visited Srinagar, I would awake to the early-morning ring of my hotel phone. Invariably the call was from a Kashmiri journalist friend with sketchy news of another village burned, another army troop bus exploded, another politician shot, another young man missing and feared dead in custody. And off we would go, bumping along muddy winding roads in an old Ambassador taxi, past apple orchards and wheat fields, past clopping horse carts and old men smoking hookahs and stone kilometer markers painted with poetic phrases about Kashmir's serene beauty.

When we finally arrived in Kupwara or Anantnag or wherever the latest atrocity had occurred, it would always be the same: the men scowling and silent, the women wailing and shrieking over dead bodies, the squads of soldiers and police tense and stone-faced. A guerrilla attack had occurred, followed by a military raid or torching. A shopkeeper had been seized by police and a protest had broken out in the market and someone had been shot. It was a familiar, brutal ballet, and it was evident that both sides were well-prepared to play their roles.

I always returned from these forays in a state of both drained exhaustion and impatient exhilaration, churning over how I would begin my story. My visits to Kashmir were a whirlwind of constantly shifting events and emotions. I forgot to eat, woke at dawn, smoked cigarettes. My friends were people whose blood ran with the swift, mercurial, and treacherous currents of war. The whim of violence replaced the rhythm of life. We rarely finished a meal or a conversation. We rushed to scenes of mayhem others were fleeing, and we rushed back to pound out what we had seen, at the peak of our senses and skills. I was never happy there, but I was always high, and I always wanted more.

For a journalist, it was easy to meet, and sympathize with, one set of victims. Virtually everywhere I went in the Kashmir Valley, I was surrounded by people with horror stories to tell. I met illiterate farmers whose sons had been detained, tortured, and dumped dead by the roadside. I went to village funerals where bruised and charred bodies were being buried. I sat in teashops, surrounded by people who held up old identity cards of their missing sons and brothers. I visited graves, many graves, in overgrown fields and formal "martyrs' cemeteries" where poems and Koranic sayings had been engraved on headstones.

It was far more difficult to locate or identify with the other set of victims—the soldiers and policemen who died, almost every day, in insurgent attacks. Military operations were cloaked in secrecy, officials were vague about details, and the dead or wounded were often unidentified men from remote parts of India. Soldiers on patrol were nervous and reluctant to talk; their superiors were polite but harried, and always on the defensive.

The army spokesman, an articulate major with a neatly trimmed mustache, always received us cordially in a rose garden inside a heavily guarded base, but he never veered from the official explanation of events. The inspector-general of the state police was a thoughtful man who invited journalists for dinner and debate in his official bungalow. Yet when we suggested that many Kashmiri Muslims were alienated from the government, he dismissed the notion out of hand, and when we brought up cases of abuse by the security forces, he called them regrettable but isolated incidents. These men were serious professional officers, but they were wedded to a single interpretation of events, and no account of another charred village was going to budge them.

In public life, it was hard to find heroes on either side of the Kashmir dispute; there were few inspiring leaders who offered an example or hope for meaningful change. The state's longtime chief minister, Farooq Abdullah, was a charming but self-indulgent politician in his sixties. His father, a legendary Kashmiri leader, had spent years in Indian prisons for spearheading the Kashmiri independence movement, but Abdullah was more devoted to golf than governance. His party nominally championed Kashmiri autonomy, but it remained pragmatically allied with the central powers in New Delhi.

One of the more surreal moments of my years in India was watching Abdullah deliver a florid Independence Day speech to the nearly empty stands of Srinagar's heavily guarded sports stadium, while kilted bagpipers marched on the field and a captive audience of military recruits watched dutifully from their seats. No member of the public would ever have been allowed inside; the danger of an attack on Abdullah was simply too great. As I watched from the field, I kept thinking someone was going to start tittering, but every face in the audience remained carefully set and solemn.

The elected legislature of Jammu and Kashmir State, long dominated by Abdullah's National Conference party, had little relevance in the Kashmir Valley. Periodic elections were systematically boycotted by the Muslim majority populace—partly because of guerrilla threats but mostly because people saw the polls as an unacceptable, easily rigged substitute for the long-promised referendum. In Srinagar, turnout was often as low as 10 percent.

Most separatist leaders were also a disappointment—eloquent at decrying Indian oppression, articulate at explaining the history of the Kashmir dispute, but bogged down in internal disagreements, caught up in cynical and counterproductive logic, and splintered into pro-Pakistan and pro-independence factions. Every politician had a litany of old arguments and grievances ready to trot out, and each had created a version of history from which he could never retreat. No interview or speech dealt with the day's events until it had reviewed fifty years of history, slanted to suit the speaker.

A few leaders were more generous and open to compromise. Abdul Ghani Lone, a grizzled politician of seventy, often invited me to his office for thoughtful seminars on Kashmiri history, laced with dark aphorisms. Mirwais Umar Farooq, the hereditary Muslim leader of Kashmir whose father had been murdered in 1990, seemed remarkably wise and evenhanded at age twenty-seven. But everyone else was trapped in the narrow political calculus of self-interest. I secretly wondered whether their greatest fear was that an open, honest election might actually take place in Kashmir, leaving them sputtering in jobless irrelevance.

For their sheer courage, I found myself admiring the few Kashmiris who dared run for local or state office, venturing out on the campaign trail in defiance of public hostility and guerrilla threats. During the legislative campaign in October 1999, one ruling-party candidate was assassinated and a second attacked twice by gunmen; others toured villages under heavy guard, making quick speeches and getting out.

Yet Mahbooba Mufti, daughter of a prominent Kashmiri political and religious family, repeatedly ran for legislative office despite constant threats from guerrilla groups, who had once kidnapped her younger sister Rubaiya for ransom in an episode of high national drama when their father was a federal minister. I met her several times at her heavily guarded house, and she always spoke in a soft voice about human rights and the need for political moderation.

Most vulnerable of all were former insurgents who had decided to surrender, join the system and run for office—and who were trusted by neither side. "Our message is a return to normalcy, but there is none here," complained one such candidate, a thirty-two-year-old ex-guerrilla I met on the campaign trail. "People are in complete fear psychosis, and they do not have the freedom to vote. There is pressure from every side. I have chosen the nonviolent path, but I am choked between two guns."

Perhaps, as a Western visitor, I was too biased toward democracy and the rule of law to fully appreciate how both had failed the people of Kashmir, where elections were often manipulated, where anti-terrorist laws were misused to jail people indefinitely without trial and deny other rights. But when I try to think of someone I admired, my mind returns to a cluttered, closet-sized office in Srinagar, without a phone or a desk, where a local lawyer kept meticulous lists of men who were missing in custody, typed up a monthly newsletter, and filed petition after petition to the state courts. The missing never reappeared, but this man's quiet persistence touched me in a way no display of grenade-throwing bravado ever could.

∾

To many Kashmiri Muslims, the insurgents were indeed heroes — how could it be otherwise, when so many had died for their cause? In the early years of the uprising, many of its leaders were well-known former political or student activists who had given up on the system and picked up rifles as a last resort, carrying out bold crimes with that captured the public's imagination. Thousands of militants had been killed, and their names were kept alive in portraits and flyers, ceremonies at mosques and graveyard inscriptions across the region.

Kashmir was a place where death had become a profession, fatalism had replaced faith, victimization had become a way of life. Aging parents buried their sons and saved their bloodstained shirts as mementos; funerals were more common than weddings. There was a special vocabulary of violence, with competing euphemisms employed by both sides. To his friends, a dead fighter was a "militant" who had found "martyrdom"; to the security forces he was a "terrorist" killed in an "encounter." Grieving relatives spoke not of someone's personal character, but of his larger place in history.

In the village of Lar, bursting with apple and pear trees, an elderly farmer named Abdul Ahad Bhat showed me a small, carefully tended plot with eleven graves: his sons, cousins, and nephews. All had been members of the largest Kashmiri guerrilla group, Hizb-ul Mujaheddin, and all had been killed by the Indian security forces since 1989. Their blood, he said, had been "shed for a dream, and I cannot accept any peace unless that dream succeeds."

It was virtually impossible to meet Kashmiri guerrillas in the field, except by making elaborate arrangements in Pakistan for clandestine meetings that virtually always fell through. But in the jails and prisons of Kashmir, where hundreds of militants languished for years, it was sometimes possible for a journalist to slip through the gates with a relative or lawyer for a quiet, inconspicuous chat.

A few of these prisoners had been convicted of crimes, but most had been repeatedly jailed without trial under preventive anti-terrorism laws, or had been charged with terrorism but never tried. They were gaunt, sad-eyed men with violent pasts and saintly demeanors. They spent their days in dank group cells, debating politics while they drank endless cups of spiced Kashmiri tea.

It was in a Srinagar jail that I met Yasin Malik, one of the most famous surviving insurgents, who at thirty had been in and out of prison for more than a decade. He coughed from chronic illness and chain-smoked in the Kashmiri style, holding the cigarette upright between two fingers and inhaling through his fist. He had recently been released on one charge and almost immediately jailed again for leading an election boycott. His stare was that of someone who had suffered and expected to suffer indefinitely. Between coughs, he outlined a vision for Kashmiri independence he must have described a thousand times. "I will never abandon my cause," he said simply.

By the time I arrived in Kashmir, though, the nature of the uprising had changed dramatically. Much of the original movement and its Kashmiri ranks had been wiped out, and in their place a more radical insurgency had taken root. These were hardline Islamists, mostly from Pakistan, who had cut their teeth in the Afghan conflict and viewed the Kashmiri "freedom struggle" as a stepping-stone in a sweeping crusade to unite Muslims in a holy war against the West.

As the hard-liners' influence grew, young Kashmiris began abandoning their tolerant Muslim traditions and taking up the new banner of radical Islam. Grenades were thrown at a cable TV station; posters appeared on campuses warning girls to cover their faces or risk having acid thrown at them in the street. Meanwhile, the "guest" insurgents began carrying out bolder attacks. They formed suicide squads called *fidayeen*, which launched highly lethal, kamikaze grenade attacks on airports, urban ministries, and highly guarded military compounds.

To some Kashmiri Muslims, the religious radicalization was a cause for alarm and the Pakistani fighters were not to be trusted. Divisions among separatist groups, already split into pro-independence and pro-Pakistan camps, deepened further. A few leaders worried openly that foreign hard-liners were sabotaging the Kashmiri cause, but most people kept prudently quiet.

In some corners of Kashmir, the double appeal of Islam and insurgency was irresistible. When six young men from the town of Sopore vanished, the army said they had been killed in an "armed clash" near the Pakistan border. Their families told me they had been tortured and shot en route to an Islamic preaching retreat, but hinted they might have wanted to join the newly invigorated Islamic insurgency in Pakistan. They were buried by a duck pond, their tombstones inscribed with Koranic incantations to sacrifice.

"My son is dead, but the blood of innocents irrigates the movement," declared Abdul Khaliq, a forestry worker, showing me the engraved stone. His phraseology was chilling and rehearsed, a fanatic's comforting mantra. "This is a struggle between Islam and infidels. The solution is not dialogue but the gun," he continued. "We want the freedom to be with Pakistan. We want all Muslims of the world to unite under one leader, and let it begin here."

The pace and audacity of terrorist attacks escalated. Some were calculated to harm civilians as well as security forces, or to exacerbate tensions among religious groups. In March 2000, I was in New Delhi preparing to cover a state visit by President Clinton. It was to be an upbeat tour, with a full schedule of banquets and speeches intended to reinforce the thaw in relations between two once-hostile powers. At the same time, Clinton was expected to put polite pressure on his hosts to peaceably settle the Kashmir dispute, and to deliver a tougher version of the same message when he stopped off in the Pakistani capital afterward.

But on the same day the U.S. president was due to land in India, a squad of armed men slipped into a village of Kashmiri Sikhs after dark, lined up thirty-six male villagers and executed them on the spot. The village was called Chittisinghpora, and its inhabitants were members of a quiet, hardworking religious minority who stayed aloof from politics and mingled easily with their Muslim neighbors. It was the worst civilian massacre in Kashmir in a decade—unquestionably a more urgent news story than Clinton's visit, and almost as obviously timed to undermine it.

I reached Chittisinghpora, along with several other foreign journalists based in Delhi, about twenty hours after the massacre. The village was seething with grief and rage. Women rocked and wailed out the names of the dead; men gathered angrily in the local *gurdwara*, or Sikh temple, threatening to attack government officials—and journalists. I hurriedly tried to coax details out of witnesses, but people were agitated and confused. Some swore the killers had worn army uniforms and shouted extremist Hindu slogans. Others said they had recognized several local guerrillas, while village leaders insisted they were all "foreign militants."

As so often happened in Kashmir, the circumstances were so murky, the versions so contradictory, and the conspiracy theories so multilayered that it was possible to believe almost anything. Within days, the massacre would be variously blamed on Pakistani infiltrators, Indian troops disguised as guerrillas, and Kashmiri turncoats working as mercenaries. In following weeks and months, the incident would be exhaustively investigated, debated, and written about—but never solved.

Back in my hotel in Srinagar that night, I agonized over what to write. As usual, I dutifully tried to cast a little blame in all directions, but in a way it hardly mattered who had pulled the trigger. Truth had long since become a casualty in Kashmir, replaced by convenience and cynicism. Attempting to sound authoritative and sort out facts was hopeless; it was more honest to try and sketch a larger portrait of despair, deadlock, and passionately believed lies that had become more powerful, and more true, than any single death.

∽

The Other Kashmir, the portion that lay across the Line of Control in Pakistan, proved to be an even stranger place. Officially known as "Free Kashmir," it was a grim, isolated, and barren region populated by idle refugees, infiltrated by police agents, and off-limits to most foreigners. The capital, Muzaffarabad, seemed to exist on dreams of revenge. Walls were painted with murals of young men brandishing weapons, and a large replica of a missile was planted on a bridge, permanently aimed at India.

Once, before Partition, a winding highway had connected Srinagar with Muzaffarabad, and a truck carrying fresh apples or timber could make the hundred-mile trip in less than three hours. Now the two cities were in different countries, on different sides of a war, and the trip required a circuitous route through New Delhi and Islamabad. Many Kashmiri families had been physically separated for years, each nursing memories and myths about the other side.

Many inhabitants of "Free Kashmir" were refugees who had fled years ago from the Indian portion, which they called "Occupied Kashmir." They lived in permanent camps, dependent on the government and trapped in political limbo. When journalists appeared, they eagerly offered tales of Indian military abuses, and their camps were frequent settings for organized VIP visits. Children sang stirring Kashmiri anthems against a backdrop of colorful portraits, which on closer inspection proved to be bloody photographs of torture victims. On several visits, I was moved by the passion and suffering of the refugees, yet I also sensed that their speeches were as rehearsed as the songs.

In one camp, a grizzled old man told me his youngest son had just been killed in fighting on the border, and that his older son had died as a rebel for the Kashmiri cause years ago. He himself had once been imprisoned and tortured by Indian troops, he said. Now he pointed to his infant grandson, surrounded by other children. His finger shook, but his eyes blazed with zeal. "We are prepared to offer each of their lives for the glory of Islam and the liberation of Kashmir," he vowed. His speech gave me goosebumps—and yet I couldn't help but wonder if other visitors had heard it before.

To the Pakistani state and its agents, Kashmir was not a place, it was a cause: a rallying cry that kept a poor and disparate Muslim nation united against a militarily superior Hindu enemy next door. It was a domestic counterweight to both the alienation of economic despair and the centrifugal forces of ethnic and political regionalism. It was a foot in India's door, a stone slung at Goliath, a wound to be rubbed raw, a myth to be kept alive. State television and radio stated endlessly that Indian Kashmiri Muslims longed become part of Pakistan, and that Indian troops routinely raped women. Neither was true, but that was irrelevant.

With Indian and Pakistani troops patrolling both sides of the border, tensions flared periodically and nervous troops fired rockets or shells across the no-man's-land marked by wooden pickets and rolls of razor wire. Sometimes people were killed. I drove up to the border one day in 1999 with a politician and religious leader from a large Islamic party; his duty that day was to lead prayer services for seven villagers who had been killed by Indian mortar rounds.

One of the dead was a man who had just returned home from his job as a driver in Saudi Arabia to attend the double wedding of his daughter and son. When we reached the village, we heard the familiar sound of wailing. In one room, the men sat in a circle, palms raised, while the cleric murmured an Arabic prayer for the dead. In a separate room, mourning with other women, was the victim's new-lywed daughter, aged twenty-one. The extended family had gathered to celebrate the wedding several days before, she told me. "We had a wonderful time, but it was over so soon."

There was only one political issue in "Free Kashmir": the libera-tion of "Occupied Kashmir." When elections for assembly seats were held in the semiautonomous state, every candidate tried to outdo the other in praising the insurgency. It was also an open secret that Kashmiri and Pakistani guerrilla groups operated training camps in the area; this was the real reason foreign visitors were kept away and journalists had to obtain special permission to enter the state.

And yet the government in Islamabad, in a disingenuous effort to maintain international credibility, steadfastly refused to admit that fighters were trained, armed, and sent to fight inside Kashmir. India routinely denounced "cross-border terrorism" and refused to open political dialog with Kashmiri separatists unless it was stopped; Paki-stan routinely denied any links with guerrilla groups and described the Kashmiri cause as a "legitimate struggle for self-determination" which Pakistan supported only through "diplomatic and political" means. The phrases never changed, and the dialog never advanced.

Despite the enormous fig leaf of official denial and the clandes-tine nature of the training camps, it was relatively easy for foreign journalists to meet both Kashmiri and Pakistani insurgent leaders elsewhere in Pakistan. Several of these groups maintained semipub-lic offices in Islamabad, with telephone numbers and official spokes-men. I visited these offices regularly, presumably with the tacit ap-proval of the Pakistani intelligence agencies, who kept discreet but close tabs on all foreign journalists—especially those based in India.

Hizb-ul Mujaheddin, the largest Kashmiri guerrilla group, had its official headquarters in Islamabad. Its above-ground leader was Syed Salahuddin, a jovial former politician from Srinagar with a fluffy beard and a generous girth, who always called me "sister" and welcomed me with platters of grapes and apples. He was a cagey fellow, eager for publicity and given to sketching ambitious visions of a liberated and Islamic Kashmir, but evasive about his group's armed activities and careful not to reveal too much detail.

Lashkar-e-Taiba ("Army of the Pure") was a more radical, Paki-stani militia, the armed wing of a hardline Islamic movement based

in a large rural compound near the city of Lahore. Its branch office
in the capital was a rundown house with furnitureless, carpeted
rooms for sleeping. It was always full of solemn young men with
wispy beards, one of whom spoke English and was the designated
press liaison. Everyone went barefoot, and the front entrance was
strewn with plastic sandals. It was in that house that I first glimpsed
the burning faith, deep hatred, and powerful urge to self-sacrifice
that drove Islamic insurgency.

During one visit I met Hafiz Sayeed, the nearsighted, soft-voiced
Islamic cleric who had founded Lashkar's parent movement. He told
me that thirty-six of his relatives had been killed in the religious violence of Partition, and that his goal was to free Kashmir from the
"tentacles" of Indian military occupation. "Revenge is our religious
duty," he vowed. "They call us terrorists, but the real terrorists are
the Hindus who blasphemed our mosques and burned down our
houses. We fight with the help of Allah, and once we start the holy
war, no force can withstand us."

The solemn young recruits spoke in the same fervent whispers.
They were products of intensive religious indoctrination and military
training, plucked from poverty and taught to kill for God. Their
creed forbade alcohol or unmarried sex; all their energies were channeled into the cause. One young man proudly described to me how
he had detonated a mine while hiding in a tree and watched Indian
soldiers fly into the air. Another, barely sixteen, said his dearest wish
was to die in the holy war against India so he could secure a place in
heaven. As I listened to these pious adolescent warriors, I couldn't
help admiring their determination—and wondering how much
longer they had to live.

The highway from Srinagar to Kargil was breathtakingly beautiful.
Our bus wound upward past emerald rice paddies and alpine villages
and glacial streams, slowing for horsecarts and herds of goats. But
gradually the scenery grew grimmer, emptier. We began to pass net-
draped artillery nests, camouflaged troops guarding bridges, villages
that looked completely deserted. A range of jagged, barren ridges
rose to the north, and just beyond them lay Pakistan. Every so often
we could hear a strange, soft booming in the distance. The sound was
the echo of Pakistani shelling, and we were headed for war.

It was June of 1999. An invisible army of guerrilla fighters from Pakistan had secretly scaled the Kargil Mountains that spring, crossed the Line of Control, and seized a number of strategic peaks on the Indian side. For nearly a month, Indian troops in high-altitude combat gear had been fighting to dislodge them, enduring snowstorms and sunburn and frostbite, camping in crevices on sheer rock faces. There were probably no more than a few hundred enemy fighters in the mountains, but they had managed to surprise and embarrass India's mighty military establishment, and they were deeply dug into their positions.

The Kargil invasion also appeared to be a deliberate move by Pakistan to undermine any thaw in relations between the two rival nations—and a direct slap at India's Prime Minister Vajpayee, who had made a historic gesture towards reconciliation in February. Taking a bus across the long-sealed Pakistani border, Vajpayee had hugged Pakistani Prime Minister Nawaz Sharif at a colorful welcoming ceremony, calling on both nations to "put aside the bitterness of the past" and "make a new beginning" together.

After a day of meetings, the two leaders jointly announced that they would take immediate steps to reduce the risk of nuclear war and seek a solution to the Kashmir conflict, along with other long-standing disputes. The event was hailed around the world as a breakthrough for regional peace, and plans were made for a series of bilateral talks. But even as Sharif was shaking hands with Vajpayee, Indian officials often said later, his military and intelligence aides were preparing to send fighters across the border and into the Kargil mountains. The symbolism of that betrayal would rankle for years to come.

For journalists in New Delhi, the first weeks of the Kargil war were enormously frustrating. The authorities refused to allow us anywhere near the fighting or the troops. Instead they offered daily press briefings in the capital, with government spokesmen giving casualty figures we could not confirm and describing battles we could not see. They made frequent allegations of atrocities committed by enemy forces, including the mutilation of Indian soldiers' bodies. They also claimed that Pakistani army troops were directly involved, and displayed "evidence" such as confiscated soldiers' paybooks and letters home in Pakistani Urdu.

My foreign colleagues and I remained skeptical, but the Indian national press, caught up in an ultrapatriotic wartime frenzy, abandoned all pretense of objectivity. Every accusation against Pakistan was trumpeted, every Indian soldier's hometown funeral was covered in sentimental glory. Magazines and newspapers competed to raise funds for war widows, while advertisers quickly capitalized on the mood, using martial images and slogans to sell everything from insurance to insecticide.

To a lesser extent, the same phenomenon was taking place in Pakistan. Every day, the foreign ministry and defense spokesmen held a joint briefing to present their version of the war, which bore almost no resemblance to what their Indian counterparts were saying. Pakistan was also caught in a trap of its own making: it was dying to claim success on the battlefield, but that meant admitting its own troops were involved—a blatant violation of numerous bilateral agreements with India that could trigger world condemnation, UN intervention, and possibly even a full-fledged regional war. Even as contrary evidence mounted, officials had to keep insisting that the men up in the mountains were Kashmiri rebels.

Because I had long-term visas to both countries, I was able to cover both sides of the propaganda, if not the war itself. I flew several times between Delhi and Islamabad, dutifully reporting what was said at the rival briefings while trying to get a little closer to the action. Pakistan, the defensive underdog, was quicker to oblige. When an Indian jet fighter was shot down just inside Pakistan, army officials arranged within hours for a helicopter to fly several of us to the site. At 12,000 feet, we snapped photos of the wreckage with a telltale Indian flag decal. The regional army commander, a cordial officer who had escorted us in the chopper and on a long jeep ride through the mountains, posed proudly next to the plane's remains in his khaki uniform and beret.

Finally, in June, the Indians relented and organized several press trips, under military escort, to Kargil, the mountain town that was the major launching pad for Indian troops. Our bus arrived well after dark, and we woke up the owner of the first hotel we saw. It had no light, no hot water, no functioning telephone or kitchen, but we were thrilled. For the next several days the Hotel Siachen was home to thirty journalists. We washed with buckets of cold water, ate rice and lentils at sidewalk stalls, and wrote out our stories by candlelight. At night, the last calls to prayer would rise from the village mosques, sometimes interrupted by the soft, distant boom of another Pakistani shell. It was terribly haunting, and terribly romantic.

By day, we chafed and protested under heavy military restrictions, limited to vague official briefings and photo opportunities at hillside artillery posts. Several of us decided to remain behind in the town after the press bus left, hoping to meet some soldiers who had actually been in the mountains. Our defiant little gesture paid off. Wandering through villages along the Kargil highway, we found troops everywhere: shaving or cooking breakfast beside tents, cleaning artillery, waiting outside public phone stalls, sprawled exhausted in abandoned stores.

We didn't learn any military secrets, but during that week and a second visit to the war zone several weeks later, we learned a great deal about the pride, patriotism, and unity of India's armed forces. We met Hindus from every state, Sikhs from Punjab, and even a few Muslims. All expressed a strong desire to defeat their common enemy, but many of the Hindus also harbored deep suspicion of a "foreign Islamic conspiracy" against them. Several confided they wished they could break the rules, storm across the border, and "fight a real war" with Pakistan.

The men were reluctant to talk about their experiences in the mountains, but they hinted at appalling combat conditions. In one abandoned village, we came upon an infantry squad dozing in an empty shop. One soldier, bloodshot and sunburned after two weeks on an icy ridge, said it had snowed the entire time and that no one could walk more than a few feet without stopping to breathe. In another village early one morning, a squad of signal corpsmen offered us tea and fresh hot vegetable puris. One of them said he had trekked 14 hours into the hills, carrying radio equipment, and had lost his way in the snow. "I prayed I would survive, and I did," he said.

After a while, we stopped paying attention to the boom of shelling and ventured further into the war zone. The Mushkoh Valley had been evacuated by the army and was off-limits to the press, but four of us decided to explore it anyway. We drove through several silent, abandoned villages and finally came upon three men walking across a broad, green field. They said they were heading home despite the evacuation order, hoping to find the sheep and cows they had been forced to leave behind.

Suddenly, there was a puff of smoke across the field, then a distant boom, then another puff, this one much closer. Pakistani shells were exploding everywhere, probably aimed at our jeep. Panicking, we jumped in and raced back to the highway, glancing back guiltily. The farmers were trudging slowly across the field again, heading toward a cluster of grazing cows.

∞

The Kargil conflict abruptly ended after ten weeks, when Pakistani Prime Minister Sharif, who was on a visit to Washington, promised President Clinton he would make sure the fighters withdrew. A wider war had been averted, but the incident would remain a source of anger and embarrassment to both India and Pakistan for years to come, undermining repeated efforts at bilateral negotiations and stymieing progress toward political compromise in Kashmir.

Then, in October 1999, Pakistan's army chief of staff, Gen. Pervez Musharraf, seized power from Sharif in a bloodless coup. Musharraf did not appear to be a ruthless dictator, much less a radical Islamist, but he had been in charge of the army during the Kargil war, and thus a key architect of India's humiliation in the mountains. For Vajpayee, already fending off the hawks in his Hindu nationalist coalition, the idea of negotiating with a Pakistani general seemed suicidal. There would be no talks on Kashmir, or anything else, for a while.

Over the next two years, I returned to Srinagar again and again, filing more reports about ambushes and massacres, army torchings and insurgent attacks. I tried hard to find creative, compelling ways to describe the endless cycle of violence, new adverbs and adjectives that would add horror or humanity to nouns and verbs that never changed. I wrote about deaths in every season of the year, and when I think of each one now, I instantly remember what the weather was like that day. I remember the swirling snow mixing with black ash as an old man poked through the charred rubble of his shop, burned down by army troops. I remember the thick white blanket covering traces of blood in the market where a guerrilla bomb had killed several vegetable cart drivers and their horses.

I particularly remember one summer day when Kashmir was at its prettiest, the pink lotuses were floating thickly on Dal Lake, and the air had an intoxicating piney tang. In the morning I interviewed gondoliers who had watched while a terrorist bomb, hidden in a fruit cart, shattered hotel windows along the lakefront. In the afternoon I interviewed a family whose twenty-one-year-old son Aijaz had been picked up by an anti-terrorist squad as he drove to a wedding. His body had later appeared at a police station, its back burned and its fingernails gone.

The young man's family said he was an engineering student; the police claimed he was a "senior operative" for an insurgent group who had been killed in another "armed clash." His mother was too distraught to say much, but she took me to see his grave in the main Martyrs' Cemetery. The headstone had been inscribed with these words: "Their blood is more precious than the holiest mosque." His older cousin, a computer technician, went with us, still sputtering with rage.

"If this is a democracy, with jails and courts and laws, why do there have to be custodial killings?" he demanded. "If Aijaz was killed in an encounter, why was his back burned? Why were his hands broken? This does not make the security forces a success," he added. "It makes every small boy want to pick up a stone, and maybe later a gun."

After a week of reporting in Srinagar, I always felt as if I was in prison. The conditions were far less confining than Kabul, but all arriving foreigners were required to register at the airport, and visiting journalists were watched carefully by the intelligence police. There was no relief from the grim diet of violence and lies, nowhere to relax and unwind, nothing on TV except news from New Delhi and old Russian movies. An after-dark curfew was always in effect, and anyone walking or driving home at night could be stopped literally dozens of times at military checkpoints.

Once I spent an evening at the home of a Kashmiri poet, memorable because of its rare spirit and camaraderie in a gloomy place and time. Several times I dined with the jovial police inspector, whose armed guards drove me home. But usually I was confined to the Broadway Hotel, where there was nothing to do but eat spicy lamb kebabs and rice in the empty dining room. I finally persuaded the manager to bring in some wine from his personal cellar, and from then on I spent my evenings in the poolside bar, sipping chardonnay and chatting with Siddiq, the bored bartender.

During the day, when I was desperate for some peace of mind, I often retreated for an hour to one of the venerable wooden shrines and mosques in the old part of the city. They were truly beautiful places, quiet and cavernous sanctuaries where everyone, including women, could come to pray aloud, meditate or chat quietly. One mosque was full of majestic wooden pillars and cooing pigeons; another had been carved with ornate green and blue curlicues, and the outdoor terrace was an informal barber shop where old men shaved each other and gossiped.

It was in these shrines that I first felt a twinge of spiritual identification with Islam. The atmosphere was not unlike a country church, serene and unpretentious. The people I met there were friendly, interested to learn of my mission and often happy to be interviewed. After my harrowing introduction to the forbidding, misogynistic version of Islam imposed by the Taliban—and a first glimpse of the radical vision that inspired Pakistan's Islamic militias—it was a pleasant surprise to discover other Muslims, and other mosques, that welcomed me.

∞

Despite the intense hostility that dominated relations between India and Pakistan after the Kargil war, and the hawkish domestic constituencies that fueled the antagonism in both countries, intermittent glimmers of hope broke through the relentless gloom of Kashmir. The first came in July 2000, when Hizb-ul Mujaheddin declared a unilateral cease-fire. After eleven years of fighting and thousands of deaths, the Kashmiri militants could sense the popular longing for peace, and they were unhappy with the growing Islamic flavor their movement was acquiring via Pakistan.

For a few days that summer, the fatalistic pall lifted from village life, people stayed out after dark, army troops relaxed their patrols and a few guerrilla fighters even slipped home to see their families. The psychosis of war was replaced by a semblance of normalcy, and everyone in Kashmir breathed a sigh of relief. Within two weeks, though, the truce collapsed, largely sabotaged by Islamic hardliners in Islamabad who claimed India had made impossible demands for negotiating.

To drive home the lesson, terrorists exploded a powerful car bomb that week in busy downtown Srinagar, leaving twelve people dead and dozens injured, including journalists who had rushed to the scene after a smaller bomb exploded first. I was in New Delhi at the time, but one of my closest friends in Kashmir, a reporter from the *Indian Express* newspaper, reached the scene to find wounded and dying colleagues crawling in pools of blood and writhing in pain, with scattered bits of flesh hanging from branches and telephone wires overhead. "I was a minute late, so I survived," he wrote in the *Express* the next day.

Three months later, Prime Minister Vajpayee decided to try again, announcing a government truce in Kashmir despite opposition from Hindu hardliners in Parliament and within his own administration. This time, most guerrilla groups rejected the truce as a ploy, and the pace of hit-and-run attacks against army barracks and patrols escalated. Vajpayee repeatedly extended the ceasefire, hoping for a breakthrough, but finally gave into domestic pressure and cancelled it.

Vajpayee's Pakistani counterpart, Gen. Musharraf, was equally eager to prove himself a statesman and peacemaker in uniform. While continuing public moral support and covert military aid to the guerrillas, he repeatedly offered to discuss the Kashmir problem with Vajpayee "anywhere, anytime." In the summer of 2001, the Indian premier accepted his offer and invited Musharraf to meet him in Agra, site of the Taj Mahal.

During several days of intense private meetings between the two personable heads of state, hopes soared for a breakthrough on Kashmir, only to be abruptly dashed when a draft agreement was scuttled by powerful hardliners in Vajpayee's party. On the last night of the summit, many of us gathered outside the gates of Vajpayee's hotel while Musharraf was inside, saying goodbye. We were all hoping for an eleventh-hour miracle, but when the gates opened and the general's departing motorcade emerged, his face looked ashen and grim.

I never went back to Kashmir after that; events in the United States and Afghanistan swept me into a frantic new phase of reporting from a much hotter battlefield. But I often think about its haunting beauty, its poplar-lined roads and snow-covered rooftops and emerald fields of new wheat. I think of the friendships I forged with other journalists there—intensified by the violence we witnessed together, strained by the tension of constantly expecting the worst, interrupted by curfews and deadlines, but permanently enduring in our memories of a certain time and place in history.

I also think about the people who died on my watch in Kashmir's endless war. Some were strangers whose faces I glimpsed once, soldiers whose names I never knew, village boys whose snapshots their mothers pressed into my hand. Some were acquaintances I met briefly, sources I interviewed repeatedly, colleagues with whom I had worked and traveled. Some were friends I still miss. Not all their deaths were violent war casualties, but in my mind they have all become part of the same bleak picture, a frozen image of snow mixing with ash as it falls on a smouldering Kashmiri village.

The jaunty Pakistani brigadier who escorted us to the wreckage of the Indian fighter jet—killed the next week when the same helicopter, with the same crew, crashed in the same Kashmiri mountains.

The unfailingly polite Indian army colonel who briefed us in his rose garden in Srinagar—shot dead when a guerrilla commando squad burst into his office at army headquarters.

An Indian newspaper photographer who had been on those bus trips to Kargil—blown to bits by the car bomb that exploded in downtown Srinagar.

The Kashmiri journalist who guided me to Khargam village—killed in a car accident.

The cultured, provocative poet with whom I had spent such a rejuvenating evening—dead of a brain tumor at barely forty.

The death that hit me hardest, though, was the assassination of Abdul Ghani Lone, the veteran Kashmiri separatist politician. He was a former legislator and lifelong resident of Srinagar, from whom I had learned a great deal about the region's tragic history. In three years, I had visited his small, spare office many times, eaten with his family, traveled with him in Pakistan. He invited me to his son's wedding, he taught me Kashmiri proverbs. I called him "Lone-Sahib," a term of respect. He called me "daughter," which I suppose I should have minded, but I did not.

In a highly polarized conflict where everyone exaggerated, everyone blamed, everyone put personal and political power first, Lone was a rare exception. He was not without ambition, having formed his own separatist party after giving up on Indian legislative politics. He did not oppose guerrilla violence, though he openly condemned the rising influence of pan-Islamic extremists from Pakistan whose agenda had little to do with Kashmir. He was a wily old fox and a political survivor who trusted neither India nor Pakistan. But his tone was moderate, his observations honest, and his motives genuine. He spoke slowly and softly, but people listened.

In May 2002, I was in northern Afghanistan, interviewing a police official. A small TV set flickered in the corner. Something caught my eye, and I turned. There was a frozen picture of Lone-Sahib, and the single word, "Assassinated," in large letters across the screen. I rushed to the set and sank to the floor, sick with shock. Lone had been speaking on an outdoor stage in Srinagar when a gunman in a police uniform strode up, shot him and escaped. I was livid. I didn't know who had shot him, but I knew why. His calm call for moderation—for stopping the bloodshed and giving Indian elections another chance—was too much of a threat to the forces that fed on polarization and violence and blind zeal. He had to be silenced.

Lone's killing evoked a barrage of official hand-wringing about lost chances for peace, as well as a predictable rash of accusations that Indian security forces or Pakistani intelligence agencies had been involved. The killing, like so many in Kashmir, was never solved. Whoever they were, the assassins did something even more unforgivable than murdering a respected politician, a voice of reason, an unarmed elderly man. They murdered my friend, and even now I cannot type this sentence without tears coming to my eyes.

ᔕᔕ

Interlude

Florence———Is there ever a proper time, a proper place, to die? Does life ever become long and full and examined enough to expire gracefully, without regret, without fear? I have just reached Europe after a brief visit to Washington, where I attended the funeral of a grande dame, the former publisher of my newspaper, in a cavernous cathedral. I didn't know her, and I was a bit abashed by the celebrity-packed congregation. But I knew the liturgy and the hymns and the architecture. *Time, like an ever-rolling stream, bears all its sons away.* Everything in its place, life brought to a meaningful end. I always wondered, every time I heard those words, whether they would comfort me when the time came for my parents to die.

This morning I awoke to bells chiming outside my window in the early morning chill. It was a reassuring sound, not unlike the muezzin's call, beckoning believers through the mist. I have grown to love the hushed spaces of mosques and shrines, but it is the echoing iron and bronze bells of the West that are mine, that call me back to my roots, my childhood. I recognize the hymn that is chiming across the stone square, something solid about soldiers and saints. I know I am in Europe because I feel closer to home.

After years of fleeing as far and as fast as I can from the West, searching for forgotten causes and new religions, mastering strange dialects and pursuing international romances, I feel suddenly grateful to understand what passersby are saying, to blend into a crowd of people who pay no attention to me, to be back in the Christian world. I have spent hours staring at paintings I love, drinking in the luminous glow of Michaelangelo's holy family, and marveling that a human hand could have painted such softly shadowed, falling folds of cloth.

I needed this vacation more than I knew. The past year has taken its toll; seeing and writing about so much violent death has played morbid tricks with my subconscious. The other night I dreamed my father had died, twice. In the first dream he was lying in a hearse, impeccably dressed but gasping for air, and I was desperately trying to open the door. In the second dream he was sealed away in a cave, silent and invisible, and I never found out what he had been thinking or feeling.

That has always been one of my worst fears, that he would die while I was far away on some foreign assignment, cut off and unaware of what had happened until much later, much too late to say goodbye. I do not know him very well (though I have glimpsed terrible solitude and yearning and anger in him), and perhaps I never will. He has always been too proud and private to reveal much, and I have always been too shy to ask.

Mostly, I have simply been away. Instead of settling down, I have kept bouncing around the planet; instead of giving him grandchildren to enjoy in his old age, I have given him countless nights of worry, not so different than those that kept him up when I was fifteen. Most of the time, he doesn't know where I am, but the chances are it is dirty, dangerous, and difficult to find on a map. Maybe that's the reason he has never told me when he was sick or unhappy; I was too far away and moving too fast to listen.

Now, unexpectedly, the news has reached me in Italy that he needs heart surgery. His voice on the phone was as casual and controlled as usual, a little embarrassed, but he must feel shaken and afraid. He is in his eighties now, still debonair but growing frailer. The operation may weaken him, or even snatch him away, and I am determined to get there first. I am already due back at work, but I pray the next week will not bring another earthquake or massacre on my beat. I have something more important to do.

When I reach my parents' home in Connecticut, twenty-four hours later, I know immediately it was the right decision. My father is reading in the garden. He looks very tired, and his hair is whiter. Events in India and Afghanistan seem petty and irrelevant and very far away. Time has slowed to this one moment, space has shrunk to this single patch of lawn. We chat about doctors' exorbitant bills, about neighbors' noisy lawnmowers, about nothing in particular. As usual we avoid certain awkward topics: my divorces and romantic life, his views on immigrants and foreign aid. But for the first time I can remember, we are simply spending time together.

It feels good to slow down. It feels good to be raking the leaves and weeding the garden. I had forgotten how beautiful it is here in warm weather, with the dogwoods and cherries in bloom, the river serene and silvery as it flows past the point. Most of my visits here are frantic and formal, with holiday guests and gifts; this time there is nothing to do but breathe. Usually I am watching the clock and dashing madly to the airport; this time I want the week to last forever.

Every morning I rise early and tiptoe outside, settling on the dewy grass, watching the mist rise on the water, listening to the loons and doves and starlings warming up for their morning concert, drinking in the glory of creation. A poetic refrain comes into my mind: "If there is paradise on earth, this is it, this is it, this is it." The poem was written about ancient Kashmir, and it has often been invoked in irony since the outbreak of political violence. But here, in this peaceful garden spot, it seems blessedly free of double meaning.

What a fool I've been, to run away from all this. My parents have lived in this house for twenty-eight years, but if I added up all the time I've spent here it wouldn't amount to more than six months.

Where was I all those other dawns? Was I doing something more urgent than listening to the loons and watching the river? Why did I have to court so much horror and death to appreciate the simple gift of life? One day they will be gone, and the house will be someone else's. But the morning light and the water and the birdsong are no one's, are everyone's, are mine now forever. It is the memory of them that matters, and the renewal of spirit God brings with every sunrise, even on days that bring loss and grief and fear.

I think my father wants me to remember him in this garden by the river, not in a hospital room full of machines. A few days from now, when I am somewhere high over the North Atlantic or the Arabian Peninsula, men I have never met will cut open his chest and take out his heart and replace most of it and sew him back together. Anonymous strangers will hold his life, literally, in their hands. For once, I will be the one trying to suppress my worst fears. But this time, I will have the memory of a perfect dawn to hold onto, and the knowledge of the time we shared, and of the unspoken words that filled it.

CHAPTER FOUR

The Hidden Heart

Stay with me,
My assassin, my sweetheart, stay on.
When the night moves on
After drinking the sky's blood . . .
Wailing, laughing, singing, it moves on,
Jangling the purple anklets of pain.
When hearts sunk in bosoms
Wait hopefully for hands cloaked in sleeves . . .
When desire once aroused
No consoling will appease . . .
Stay with me,
My assassin, my sweetheart, stay on.

—Faiz Ahmed Faiz (1911–1984)

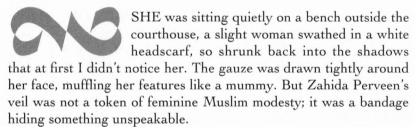 SHE was sitting quietly on a bench outside the courthouse, a slight woman swathed in a white headscarf, so shrunk back into the shadows that at first I didn't notice her. The gauze was drawn tightly around her face, muffling her features like a mummy. But Zahida Perveen's veil was not a token of feminine Muslim modesty; it was a bandage hiding something unspeakable.

Underneath the folds of cloth, her eyes were gouged-out hollows, her nose was a raw red stump of cartilage, and her ears were jagged, lobeless holes. The disfigurement was the handiwork of an insanely jealous and defiantly unrepentant husband. The face was that of Pakistan's grimmest social shame: honor crimes.

Zahida was an illiterate woman from a poor village in Punjab. In December 1998, when she was six months pregnant with her third child, her husband, a burly man of forty and a barber by trade, came home from praying at the local mosque and accused her of having improper relations with a brother-in-law.

"I told him it wasn't true, but he didn't believe me." Zahida,

83

thirty, spoke in a whisper, huddling next to her lawyer and cradling her year-old child in her lap. "He caught me and tied me up, and then he started cutting my face. The children were locked in another room, crying. He never said a word except, 'this is your last night.'"

While Zahida's injuries were unusually grotesque, the circumstances of her case were far from unusual. Every year, thousands of women in Pakistan have their faces disfigured—usually burned with battery acid or kitchen kerosene—and hundreds more are murdered by vengeful husbands or fathers or brothers who believe the women have insulted their "honor."

The offense can be as audacious as committing adultery or as innocent as chatting with a neighbor. In a society still largely ruled by male-dominated tribal codes, a woman can "dishonor" her family by seeking a divorce, eloping with a lover, or refusing to marry a man of her parents' choosing, even an abusive drunkard twice her age. And in the eyes of many Pakistanis, avenging family honor by violent means is still considered acceptable, if not strictly legal.

What was indeed unusual about Zahida Perveen's case was that her attacker was actually brought to trial. More often, such crimes have been swept under the rug; police collude with embarrassed or locally influential families, charges are never filed or judges dismiss them. The victims—usually uneducated wives and daughters with no independent resources—have nowhere to turn.

When I first met Zahida, sitting silently on the bench next to her lawyer, it was difficult for me to imagine what she was thinking or feeling. She answered most questions in shy monosyllables. After several meetings, though, she allowed me to look at her face and even posed for photographs. The first time she unwound the shroud, a dozen horrified thoughts raced through my head. I wondered if she had ever been pretty or flirtatious. I wondered how she had felt, bearing the child of a monster just months after he had maimed and blinded her for life.

On the other side of the courthouse, a prison bus pulled up and a burly bearded man was brought out. His wrists and ankles were manacled, and he was shackled to a guard with chains. It was Zahida's husband, Mahmoud Iqbal, who had been charged with aggravated assault. I approached him hesitantly, dreading the encounter but knowing it might be my only chance to hear his story.

Had he cut up his wife's face with a razor, as they said? "Yes, I did these things, but I was going out of my senses," he replied readily. The lawyer at his side explained that his defense was based on *ghairat*, the Islamic legal concept of extreme provocation that excuses violent actions from punishment.

Why was he so upset? "She was provoking me and ruining my life." He stared at me steadily, and I thought I detected a smirk. I pictured him in a blind rage, slicing away, and I shuddered. Did he regret his actions? "What I did was wrong, but I am satisfied," he answered. "I did it for my honor and prestige." The guard tugged at the chains, and Iqbal shuffled away. His words had sounded coached and confident, and a terrible thought dawned on me: He's going to get away with it.

When I wrote the story of Zahida Perveen, my editors decided not to publish the pictures of her uncovered face; it was simply too ghoulish. But the photograph that did appear—a woman's face swathed in white, with narrow slits through the bandages where the eyes should have been—was haunting enough.

The story generated enormous attention and controversy. When I visited Washington that summer, I was invited to speak about honor crimes at several conferences, and to a reception sponsored by prominent Pakistanis in the capital area. Some guests praised my article, but others pounced on me angrily, suggesting I had insulted their country and religion, and demanding that I write a similar article about honor crimes in India or Turkey or Egypt.

I encountered the same defensiveness back in Pakistan. In one town where I accompanied a group of women's rights activists from Islamabad who were protesting the beating death of a young woman by her husband and in-laws, the local bar association held a special impromptu meeting, and its leaders nervously asked me not to smear their town's reputation. Honor, not justice, was what mattered most to the community. In some cultures it would be called saving face.

Eventually, Zahida's husband was convicted of assault and sent to prison, while she became a minor cause célèbre and was able to travel to the United States, with help from several Pakistani-American organizations, to undergo surgery on her nose. But she will never know what her little boy looks like, and her sightless eyes will never be able to convey the horror of what she endured.

When I think back on the weeks I spent following her case, two images stay in my mind. One is of Zahida the last time I saw her.

She was sitting on a cheap metal cot in a relative's hut in her village, staring emptily into space.

The other is of an older woman I met outside the courthouse the day of the hearing, with a veil pulled over her mouth and nose. I chatted with her for a moment and told her what I was doing. She let her veil drop, and I saw that the right side of her face was disfigured by an old burn. I started to ask her about it, but a man hurried up, perhaps a husband or brother, and interrupted. She tightened the veil and shook her head. "It was an accident," she said.

ᦕᦕ

The first Pakistani I ever met was Benazir Bhutto, the gracious, articulate, Oxford-educated woman who became her country's prime minister. It was years ago at a reception in Washington, before she had become embroiled in corruption charges, been forced from office twice, and ended her political career in exile. We spoke only briefly that evening, but she exuded both poise and power, and she seemed to epitomize the notion that Islam and women's emancipation are not incompatible.

Much later, when I began visiting Pakistan regularly, I came to know other women who were modern, educated professionals. Indeed, some of the most impressive Pakistanis I met were women — human rights activist Asma Jehangir, former senator Abida Hussain, newspaper editor Maleeha Lodhi. Like Bhutto, they wore headscarves and *salwar kameez* — the traditional long-sleeved tunic and baggy trouser ensemble — but moved confidently in male-dominated arenas.

A handful of Pakistani women worked as lawyers and advocates for women's causes, usually operating out of small offices with tiny budgets. Zahida Perveen was represented by two female lawyers from Rawalpindi, who were treated with respect by court officials, but who toiled until late at night in a sweltering cubbyhole piled with moldy files. Their decrepit office building had no bathroom, no air conditioning, and no lighting in the stairwells.

And yet the more deeply I probed into Pakistani society, the more I realized that such women represented only a tiny, privileged minority. A far greater number, especially in rural and tribal areas, led lives of virtual imprisonment. Girls were regarded as family property to be bought and sold, traded to settle disputes, and married off as teenagers to whomever their families considered a useful match — even if the groom was a toothless, seventy-year-old landlord with two other wives.

The emancipation of women, I came to realize, is at the heart of Pakistan's struggle to find a balance between deference to traditional culture and participation in the modern world. It is the single most volatile social issue in the growing conflict between moderate and fundamentalist versions of Islam. The Koran does not condone violence against women, but it emphasizes female modesty, chastity, and subservience to fathers and husbands — and it is often invoked by those seeking to justify the cruelties of a conservative, tribal, male-dominated culture.

Pakistan has a modern constitution and laws, but in many rural areas, the codes and taboos of tribal custom govern community life. Male village and clan leaders have unquestioned authority over the schooling, marriage, and ultimate fate of local women. By law, religion, and international convention, Pakistani girls have equal rights to education as boys, but in practice, millions never attend school, often because their families will not allow it. In elections, some local leaders refuse to permit women to vote, considering it a shameful public activity.

In many parts of the country, tribes constantly feud over land and other issues, and hostilities may continue for decades. Grassroots assemblies called *jirgas*, composed of men from each clan, dispense summary justice based on barter and crude punishments. Police are often reluctant to interfere, arguing that tribal issues are best resolved by traditional means. Jirgas may arrange for a murderer's teenaged daughter to be married off to the victim's elderly uncle, or order the public stoning of young couples who try to elope. Illicit lovers, known as *karo* (the male) and *kari* (the female) may be murdered with the consent of their own families to avenge the disgrace.

In one notorious incident in 2002, a thirty-five-year-old woman in northwest Pakistan was gang-raped by four men on the order of a village council to settle a dispute between two tribes. The fight, which began when a teenaged boy and girl were overheard talking in a field, led to an escalating exchange of violent acts — including the group sodomy of the boy and gang rape of a female relative — to avenge each clan's "honor." Although local police knew about the events, no charges were filed until weeks later, after numerous press reports had appeared, because the rape victim's clan had less political influence.

In a second case that year, four men were sentenced to death for murdering two others in a land dispute, but then set free after negotiations with the victims' families. Under the bargain, they agreed to pay $1.3 million and hand over eight unmarried daughters as brides. Two teenaged girls were paired with a seventy-seven-year-old and a fifty-five-year-old man related to the victims, until the press got word and the police interrupted the weddings. Three others under age eight were to be handed over once they reached puberty.

Even under normal circumstances, virtually all marriages in Pakistan are arranged between families, and often the match is made within the same extended family. Such "cousin marriages" can produce birth defects from crossed eyes to blood disorders, yet even well-educated Pakistanis—like many in Afghanistan, Saudi Arabia and other conservative Muslim societies—continue to prefer them, sacrificing genetic variety for financial and social consolidation.

Upper-class weddings are opulent, three-day affairs at which mountains of food are consumed, men reinforce political relations, and women compete to appear in the most glittering costumes—but only for each other. The functions are segregated by gender, alcohol is never served, and there is none of the flirtation that enlivens Western social gatherings. Weddings are accepted venues for marriage proposals—but only between fathers. Teenagers do eye each other from behind ballroom pillars—but they are almost always blood relatives.

Grooms can feel as trapped as brides. I had a friend in Lahore, a young engineer and sports enthusiast who was in no rush to marry, but his father had died and his family kept pressing him to get engaged. I urged him to stand firm, take his time, enjoy life. But one day, after several months' silence, I received an e-mail greeting from him with a sheepish postscript: "By the way, I got married. My mother was getting lonely and needed someone at home. They found a girl for me. She seems OK, and she gets along well with my mother. Also we are going to have a baby. I don't spend too much time on sports these days."

Pakistan's classical poetry and song—most famously evoked in the works of Faiz Ahmed Faiz—are rich with images of flowing wine, yearning glances, heaving breasts and beating hearts. But in real life, romantic love is rare, frowned upon, and carefully hidden. Anyone with a satellite dish can watch romantic comedies from India or steamy Hollywood dramas from America—but all the intimate scenes, every hug and kiss, are blocked from view behind a grid of flashing digital dots.

No respectable unmarried woman lives alone, and few live apart from their parents. A college girl who engages in sex with a boyfriend may be literally unable to find a husband. Couples who elope are ostracized by society; the man may be charged with kidnapping and the woman with *zina*, the Islamic crime of having sex outside marriage. Adultery is fairly common among men and has little impact on their reputations, but in women it is considered a major family disgrace.

The double standards of sexual behavior, and the social acceptance of honor crimes, are not limited to rural, uneducated Pakistanis. Over the past several years, several courageous women have stepped forward to expose abusive male behavior and honor crimes in high places. Tehmina Durrani, the glamorous wife of a prominent politician, published a sensational autobiography in 1994 detailing years of beatings and forced confinement by her philandering husband. Asma Jehangir and Hina Gillani, two human rights lawyers in Lahore, launched a campaign against honor killings that gained startling focus from an incident that occurred in their office.

In April 2000, Gillani was in her office, consulting with a twenty-nine-year-old woman named Samia Sarwar who sought a divorce. A gunman burst in and shot the client dead; her own parents had ordered the killing to prevent the shame her divorce would bring on the family. The Sarwar case—and the condemnation it aroused from human rights groups abroad—touched an extremely sensitive nerve in Pakistani society. It was like lifting a rock off a pit of serpents that everyone knew about and tiptoed around. It exposed the primitive codes that superceded both law and reason, even in relatively affluent and urbanized families.

It also made a mockery of women's rights in a country that had twice elected a woman as prime minister. The government of Gen. Pervez Musharraf, who had seized power in October 1999 with a vow to bring justice and legitimacy to his country, was stung by the negative publicity. At a conference on human rights, Musharraf strongly condemned honor crimes, asserting that "such acts do not find a place in our religion or law. Killing in the name of honor is murder," he vowed, "and it will be treated as such."

But both law and religion have played a major role in reinforcing the misogynistic male culture that prevails in much of Pakistan. For years, conservative Islamic clerics have been agitating for the full adoption of *shariah*, or Islamic law, over secular precepts of justice. So far they have not been successful, but during the regime of Gen. Mohammed Zia ul-Haq, a fervent anticommunist and Islamic zealot who ruled Pakistan from 1977 until 1988, a series of puritanical shariah ordinances were enacted that included harsh punishments for sexual crimes.

Under these ordinances, both men and women who commit zina can be ordered stoned to death or whipped one hundred times. The punishments are rarely invoked because the standard of proof is extremely high—four male witnesses to the sex act itself—and because the cruel, Taliban-like spectacles of public whippings during the Zia years still rankle. But women's advocates in Pakistan say such charges are brought almost exclusively against women—frequently by their own families—and that often they must spend several years in jail awaiting trial.

A separate, Islamic-based legal concept that was adopted as law in 1990, known as *qisas* and *diyat*, legalizes the kind of personal vengeance traditionally meted out by tribal councils—literally an eye for an eye—and places the rights and responsibilities of justice in the hands of the victim's relatives. They may choose to press formal charges or pardon the crime, to demand money or inflict an identical injury on the criminal or a relative without fear of legal prosecution. Thus, while Pakistani law does not explicitly condone honor killings, women's activists say it sends a signal that murder within families, such as Samia Sarwar's, is not necessarily the business of the state.

To extremist Islamic clerics, whose influence has grown steadily in Pakistan over the past two decades, the control of women is a major obsession, and fear of European-style women's liberation is a major factor, ranking only slightly below U.S. support for Israel, in the growing anti-Western clamor from Pakistani pulpits. The issue resonates deeply with men, especially those from impoverished, illiterate backgrounds, and it has helped swell the ranks of adherents to religious parties and leadership cults.

In Karachi, a controversy erupted several years ago over whether women should be allowed to take jobs as ticket collectors on public buses. Crusading mosque leaders insisted it was shameful and dangerous to have women interacting with strange men—as if the brief exchange of a ticket could instantly lead to uncontrollable passion, rape, and pregnancy.

"Islam says women should stay at home, under the veil, looking after their children," explained Abdul Rehman Salafi, an Islamic cleric who took an active role in the crusade. I found him in his mosque office, bent over a copy of the Koran. "If men and women are allowed to mix freely, it leads to crimes, and unmarried women become mothers. Islam gives full freedom to women," he declared earnestly, "but only within four walls."

In the minds of many Pakistani men, Islam's constraints on women are a convenient cover to exercise absolute control over them, while its emphasis on mercy and self-restraint may do little to rein in men's violent impulses. It struck me as significant that Zahida's husband flew into his jealous rage after coming back from praying at the village mosque, presumably with his male friends. Perhaps someone had remarked on her pretty face or coy nature, and had goaded him to teach her a lesson. Outside the courthouse, when he was put back on the prison bus, I saw several men come up to shake his hand through the window bars.

One of the most appalling aspects of a society obsessed by male "honor" is that it turns the victims into criminals. A girl who runs away from abusive parents or an elderly husband is breaking the law and can be sent to jail. Often, young women who seek a divorce but are not living with their parents, or who have been accused of zina, are sent to government homes, known as *darulamans*, while awaiting court decisions. They are closely watched, forbidden to leave or to receive unrelated visitors. In theory this is to protect them from society, but it is also to protect society from them.

I visited one darulaman in Rawalpindi, a shabby city twenty miles from Islamabad, where twenty-eight young women were confined in a locked, school-like building with bars on the windows and doors. Only relatives and lawyers were allowed to visit. The residents spent their days studying the Koran, sewing, and watching TV. Some of them were precocious and outgoing—qualities that would make them popular in an American university, but suspect in a society like Pakistan. All of them were victims of entrenched double standards, and many had been subjected to cruelties that in the West would have been crimes in themselves.

One girl of twenty had been forced to marry a man more than twice her age; she then eloped with a boy, and her family filed police charges against her. A mother of five said she tried to divorce her abusive husband, but was then kidnapped by her own brothers, who threatened to disfigure her face. A third detainee, older than the rest, said her husband beat her and began sleeping with another woman, but her own parents forced her to return to him; she had now been confined for a year while awaiting judicial proceedings.

"My parents say it is shameful for me to want a divorce," she told me. "They say it will ruin their reputation and that no one will marry me if I am secondhand." She looked so desperate that I felt like grabbing her and spiriting her out of the building. I felt so lucky, and so guilty, to have been born in a country where I could make my own choices. This woman was thirty-five and had borne several children, but legally she was still a child. "I don't want to go home," she burst out. "I don't want to get remarried. I just want to be free."

❧

A foreigner landing for the first time in Islamabad, the Pakistani capital, would be impressively deceived. The wide boulevards are free of trash, potholes, and donkey carts. There are traffic police on every manicured corner, ATMs and cell phone stores on every commercial block. Gleaming marble and stone monuments to democracy house the parliament, the Supreme Court, the treasury. On dozens of leafy side streets, modern mansions with rooftop satellite dishes bespeak worldly sophistication as well as new wealth.

Many of my Western colleagues found Islamabad hopelessly boring; there was no nightlife, no bustle, no tension. There were no real people, either, only politicians and bureaucrats. But I was grateful for the boredom. For me, the city was like a Swiss spa: a safe, sanitized sanctuary in a region where daily life was dirty, desperate, and unpredictable. During dozens of visits over four years, my home there was the Chez Soi, a private guest house on a quiet street. There, I could soak in a hot bath after another exhausting drive from Afghanistan, watch HBO until dawn if I was too wired to sleep, and leave my door unlocked when I took my dog for a walk.

At the same time, I was also aware of being watched by the intelligence police. They probably knew I had nothing to hide, but they were obsessively suspicious of anyone who often traveled to Pakistan from India. Sometimes an officer who called himself "Mr. Khan" (the Muslim equivalent of Jones or Smith) would call me up to chat, casually hinting that he knew what my appointment schedule was for the day.

Often I would glimpse a nondescript sedan following me at a distance, or catch someone murmuring to my driver and then slipping away. I tried not to become paranoid, but it was easy to find dark meaning in every casual question, every mysterious nod between strangers. Once, I saw two men in a car parked near mine, and on impulse I pulled out a business card and walked over to hand it to the driver. As I approached, the two agents looked sheepishly startled and hurriedly drove away.

Another time two men drove up to the Chez Soi in an unmarked car, demanded to see me and refused to identify themselves. The receptionist, a woman, was terrified and started to call the police until I came out and assured her I was safe. The men had arrived to escort me to the intelligence service headquarters for an interview, but their cloak-and-dagger culture was so entrenched that even on an official errand, they couldn't bring themselves to behave normally.

The Chez Soi was often full of foreign journalists, and we formed the sort of floating friendships that are both intense and unreliable. Planning was impossible, reunions were serendipitous, and dinners were bouts of drunken decompression at the United Nations Club, the only foreigners' bar in town. Sensational news like the U.S. bombing of Afghanistan drew reporters from all over the world, and sometimes we recognized each other from very different times and places.

At first I was incensed that the club did not allow Pakistanis, but gradually I came to appreciate what it meant to have a private, Westernized niche in a conservative Muslim society—a place where I could sip wine, order a steak sandwich, read the *International Herald Tribune*, and count on running into at least one old friend. I shot a game of pool with a man I had last seen in Mexico a decade before, met another colleague I had not seen since Haiti, and picked up friendships with other Delhi-based reporters that had been hurriedly dropped months before.

There was little time or opportunity for love; the word was not a part of the local vocabulary, and all substitutes were hopelessly rushed and shallow. Instead I found another outlet for my affections, adopting various stray cats and dogs I encountered and providing them with what sustenance and shelter I could in my transient condition. Every time news snatched me away, I left a supply of pet food in the Chez Soi kitchen and crossed my fingers that they would still be hanging around the porch when I returned.

One bedraggled white cat was always waiting to greet me on the porch, no matter how many months had gone by. On one visit I noticed she was pregnant, but then she vanished for several days. A tropical summer storm sprang up, and I was falling asleep around midnight when I heard a meow outside. I opened the door, and there she was, matted with mud and holding a half-drowned kitten in her mouth. To my astonishment she trotted inside, deposited it on my bed, and returned to the storm to bring back three more. I dried them off with a towel and she began nursing on my bed, purring with pure contentment. I don't believe I have ever felt as trusted by anyone in my life before or since.

I made a few good Pakistani friends, mostly journalists and academics, who invited me partway into their lives and culture. I shared my first *iftibar*, the sunset meal during the fasting month of Ramadan, with a professor at a campus snack stand, waiting for the signal from the nearest mosque and then hungrily attacking bowls of dates and yogurt. I heard my first recording of Faiz Ahmed Faiz at the home of the Chez Soi manager, who sometimes invited me over for a discreet bottle of Bordeaux. I bought my first salwar kameez with a friend who guided me through a maze of narrow shops. When I tried it on before a mirror, I realized I had finally found a clothing style that flattered me. Over time I also came to like wearing a *ᵭupatta*, the Punjabi scarf that loosely frames a woman's face and shoulders. After a long stay in Pakistan, when I was back in Western-hip New Delhi, my head always felt naked for the first few days.

Yet usually, there was a certain distance and formality to my relationships in Pakistan, partly because I was trying to remain objective, and partly because, as an unattached woman, I was a social anomaly. People were accustomed to dealing with female professionals, but they could not understand why I would travel alone, and I was constantly asked whether my husband or parents had given me permission to do so. People were also flummoxed to learn I had no children, and doubly so when I said it was by choice. In Pakistan, there was simply no such thing as a female free agent; the very idea was unacceptably subversive.

Often I interviewed generals and professors and politicians in their front parlors, without ever glimpsing their wives. Professional men who spoke English often had wives who did not. Sometimes I was included in political dinners or other social functions, but the men usually went stag. I attended several receptions at the modern, gilded mansion of a suave hotel owner and cotton baron who enjoyed entertaining foreigners. But I always felt uncomfortable at such soirees, as if I were dining on ill-gotten wealth with a roomful of people who were all part of a game I knew nothing about.

∾

Just a few miles in any direction from Islamabad lies an entirely different country. It is a vast, hot, dry land of 140 million where most people live in villages, speak only Urdu or a regional dialect, cannot read or write, travel by donkey or horsecart, live by immutable unwritten codes of debt and honor, labor for pennies an hour, have little access to public services or political rights, and know of the world only what their imams tell them at the mosque on Fridays.

In the air-conditioned drawing rooms of the capital, professionals scoff distastefully in manicured English at the "fundos," the fundamentalists who preach *Shariah*, the Islamic law of a stern and unforgiving God, and *shahadat*, the graced state of those who die in defense of Islam. But in the countryside, where government tends to be synonymous with extortion rather than service or rights, millions of people have been increasingly drawn to a fervent, reactionary brand of Islam.

In the past several years it has become fashionable to describe Pakistan as a "failed state." (Najam Sethi, the Lahore newspaper publisher who coined the phrase, was briefly jailed on charges of subversion; he had made his critical comment while speaking to an audience in India.) But to me, Pakistan has a larger, deeper problem than dysfunctional institutions: it is a society struggling against itself, trying to define its religious ethos and its place in the world, pulled toward the technified, global future and dragged back into the feudal, parochial past.

Pakistanis have a pronounced love-hate relationship with the West. They are enamored of its technology, comforts, and entertainment, but suspicious of its decadence and freedom. I have waited in line with hundreds of men outside the American embassy in Islamabad, desperate to secure tourist visas so they can vanish into the illegal immigrant workforce and send home $100 a month. But a few blocks away, I have stood outside mosques where hundreds of devout Muslim men listened raptly to fiery jeremiads against Western pornography and prostitution, and I have seen chanting mobs stomp on burning straw dummies of President George W. Bush.

I have opened a daily newspaper and seen these two items on the front page: One is a news report describing tens of thousands of mourners at the funeral of Aimal Kasi, a Pakistani man sentenced to death in America for shooting two CIA employees in 1993. The mourners praise the man as a "hero of Islam," and Parliament is halted for a special prayer. The other item is an advertisement for a bank, with a photograph of a happy, modern Pakistani family (veilless mom, beardless dad, two kids in jeans) playing with computers and planning to "reach for their dream" with borrowed money.

Pakistan was created as a Muslim nation and safe haven, but in the country's short fifty-five-year history, Islam has often proved more a volatile, divisive force than a unifying sanctuary. It has pitted Shiites against Sunnis and moderates against extremists, spawned domestic terrorism and exacerbated tensions with foreign neighbors, especially India and Afghanistan. The true clash of civilizations is occurring within the borders of Pakistan itself.

Pakistan was also founded as a parliamentary democracy, a concept dear to its founder Mohammed Ali Jinnah, but it has been failed by its elected leaders ever since. Its two major parties have been guided by narrow self-interest; its political heroes have proven corrupt or inept. Its armed forces have intervened repeatedly in politics, staging three coups and engineering other regime changes when the civilian system bogged down in power struggles or corruption, and thus keeping the country frozen in a permanent state of political immaturity.

On the surface, Pakistan appears to be a free country; there are no troops on the streets, no prisons full of dissidents. But the military establishment exercises a more subtle form of control, using a large network of intelligence agents to keep tabs on political parties, religious sects, and journalists. Their purported job is to ferret out foreign skullduggery, but they also function as agents of domestic political control. There is no need to be swaggering about the streets with assault rifles; one call from someone's uncle or cousin is enough to solve a problem, and the implied threat of force is enough to keep a largely impoverished and illiterate populace in a state of passive submission.

In many ways, the "state" of Pakistan is impressive. In addition to a large and professional military establishment, it has a sophisticated bureaucracy and a pampered science community that has placed Pakistan in the exclusive club of nuclear powers. The problem is corruption, institutionalized and ubiquitous. International agencies rate Pakistan as one of the most corrupt countries in the world; credit card fraud is so frequent that overseas charges are routinely blocked. (I went to the same travel agent in Islamabad for years, but both Visa and American Express repeatedly refused to approve my plane tickets.) Officials siphon off vast amounts while teachers go unpaid, public hospitals have no medicine, roads are never paved. The police and civil service extend corrosive tentacles into every aspect of life, and the most mundane of transactions—from getting a phone installed to searching a land title—require a bribe. Even menial jobs go to those who have a relative on the inside. Being a health inspector or tax collector means having the opportunity to strike deals; being a policeman means having the power to demand fees for filing charges or freeing prisoners. In a society where only corruption pays, only a fool tries to be honest. Everyone becomes vulnerable to pressure and extortion, and every weakness becomes an opportunity to take advantage.

A hefty chunk of Pakistan's economy is entirely illegal: the smuggling trade. Hand-woven carpets and opium sap from Afghanistan, stolen Japanese TVs and car parts from the Gulf States, antibiotics from India and tires from Iran—all follow ancient smuggling routes across Pakistan, avoiding duties and taxes with the collusion of customs authorities. Drug trafficking is a way of life in the semiautonomous tribal territories that border Afghanistan, where foreigners are not allowed to travel without a police escort and armies of tribal gunmen protect vast mud-walled warehouses.

Pakistan is a country of enormous legitimate economic resources: millions of acres of fertile farmland that produce high-quality sugar and wheat, cement and munitions factories, textile mills that export sheets and towels to dozens of countries. But most farms and factories, and the wealth they produce, remain in the hands of a tiny elite: the feudal barons of rural Sindh and Punjab, and the industrial families of Karachi and Lahore.

The first group has long dominated power in the countryside, with about 2,000 families retaining vast land holdings despite laws limiting them to 150 acres, and using private guards to keep hundreds of thousands of laborers in illiterate, bonded servitude. Benazir Bhutto came from a feudal family, as have many of Pakistan's parliamentarians and ministers. In many ways, Pakistan is still a country of landed elites, and those without land are forever insecure.

The second group, consisting of some twenty-two major industry-owning families, has more modern aspirations, but it has long thrived at the state's expense, dodging taxes and loan repayment on a massive scale while the government's foreign debt soared to $32 billion by 1999. Phantom enterprises have been created by wealthy industrialists to do nothing but borrow money and then declare bankruptcy. Monopoly and siphoning-off of profits have drained the industrial sector of productivity and the state of revenue, while further enriching business owners.

For foreign journalists, it was difficult to gain access to Pakistan's reclusive economic elite. Aside from those receptions at the cotton baron's mansion, my only glimpses of real wealth were at society hotel weddings, where women wafted through lobbies wreathed in pearl-studded, gold-threaded saris and salwar kameez that must have cost thousands of dollars. I often drove through the posh districts of Islamabad or Lahore or Karachi, passing houses hidden behind high walls, the entrances adorned with faux pillars, the roofs covered with satellite dishes. And every time I wondered the same thing: Where did it all come from?

As is so often the case, my first guided tour of this rarefied world came after the tycoon in question was behind bars. It was in late November 1999 when I was invited to visit a fanciful, 450-acre estate just outside Lahore. The grounds were bordered by thousands of eucalyptus trees. Green lawns and gardens surrounded half a dozen luxurious bungalows and a modern, twenty-two-room mansion with twin stuffed lions guarding the marble foyer. There was a fleet of Mercedes Benzes and an exotic animal farm with pure white horses, prized buffalo, grazing deer, and two enormous camels that strutted about, poking their heads through the trees.

The compound, known as Raivind, had been built as a personal playground and status symbol by Prime Minister Sharif, scion to one of the country's largest industrial fortunes. By the time I saw it, the estate was abandoned except for a handful of caretakers and army troops guarding the entrance. Sharif was in jail, deposed in a military coup, his assets confiscated. Official investigations into his multiple family businesses would reveal a pattern, typical of Pakistani business practices, that included unsecured crony loans, heated speculation, phantom projects, and false bankruptcies.

My guide, an official from the Ministry of Information, was as intrigued as I was as we tiptoed around the grounds, peeking a little guiltily through drawing room windows. "You build a palace thinking you will stay there a long time, and then suddenly you are gone," he mused.

∾

By mid-1999, Pakistan was in the grip of deepening economic and political malaise. People were tiring of Sharif's autocratic governing style and self-indulgent habits. He had won office on a platform of economic reform and prosperity, but during his tenure the country sank further into poverty, corruption, and foreign debt, while Sharif helped his family businesses prosper at state expense and built himself the showpiece estate at Raivind, his ancestral village.

Sharif was inarticulate and press-shy, leaving most of the talking to his spokesman, a former journalist and scholar named Mushahid Hussain. I often engaged in verbal sparring matches with Hussain, who had an unctuous manner, a well-fed paunch, and an airy answer for everything. He always insisted that everything was fine, that the critics were self-serving hypocrites, that the army was loyal and the mullahs were under control, and that the foreign debt was being renegotiated.

The last time he repeated this mantra to me, talking on three phones and tossing off quotes with barely concealed impatience, was at an interview in his official residence in early October 1999. Tensions had been building between Sharif and his army chief, Gen. Musharraf, ever since the abrupt reversal of the Kargil adventure. In recent weeks, rumors of a military coup had been building, but Hussain brushed them aside with his usual laugh.

Six days later, on October 12, the army seized power in a dramatic but bloodless coup. Sharif, in a dramatic but clumsy attempt to fire Musharraf, had his retirement announced on the evening news while the army chief was in mid-air, flying home from a meeting in Sri Lanka. Army officials acted to cut off the TV broadcast, but Sharif ordered all airports shut down so Musharraf could not land. There followed a frenzy of confused instructions, anguished cockpit messages and tense showdowns between military officials. Finally army units loyal to Musharraf seized Sharif's home in Islamabad and the airport in Karachi. The plane landed there at 7:47 p.m., with less than fifteen minutes of fuel left.

Sharif, arrested with a group of relatives and aides, would be confined in Pakistani prisons for fourteen months, convicted in court of hijacking and conspiracy, and then forcibly exiled to Saudi Arabia. Hussain, the loquacious spin doctor, would spend eighteen months under house arrest, cut off from speaking with anyone except his immediate family and the squad of army troops camped on his lawn.

The coup was sweeping and decisive, replacing the upper echelons of executive power with a cadre of crisp, uniformed men with a mission to clean up the mess. It was a familiar story for Pakistan, one that dismayed foreign advocates of South Asian democracy (principally the United States and Britain) but that was not unwelcome to a populace repeatedly let down by its civilian leaders. While the West frowned in disapproval, the nation heaved a collective sigh of relief.

I was in southern India when the coup occurred. By the time I reached Islamabad again two days later, Parliament had been suspended and sealed off, a state of emergency had been declared, and Musharraf was fully in control. I had no idea what to expect, or even whether I would be allowed to land. But to my great surprise, there were no troops in the airport, shops were open and traffic was moving normally. This was not like any military coup in my experience. Except for soldiers guarding the gates to Parliament, it was hard to tell that anything had happened at all.

On October 17, I got my first good look at the man who had taken over the country, and I was frankly impressed. Musharraf appeared on national television, dressed in crisp khakis and seated beneath a portrait of Pakistan's revered founder, Jinnah. He spoke with somber resolve, saying Pakistan's civilian leaders had betrayed Jinnah's vision and created a "sham" democracy that benefited only the rich. Now, he said, it was the army's patriotic duty to step in and save the nation from chaos and corruption. "This is not martial law," he promised, "only another path toward democracy."

As I listened to the speech, I realized I had heard it before, on another continent and in another phase of my life. Twenty-six years earlier, Gen. Augusto Pinochet had seized power from the elected socialist government of Chile, vowing to restore order to a politically convulsed society, to modernize the economy and to "give form to a new democracy." Like Musharraf, Pinochet was the product of a proud, disciplined military establishment who had a messianic view of his role in history, and many Chileans had initially welcomed the coup in hopes that strong medicine would purge their country of multiple ills.

But in the years I had spent following the Pinochet regime, I had seen noble military intentions perverted by absolute power, economic reforms imposed at the cost of suffering and humiliation for millions, and political participation quashed for years in the name of political cleansing. I had seen how a single military ruler, with no checks and balances, could force necessary changes on a resistant system — but also how he could succumb to the cruel temptations of dictatorship and become tragically convinced that he was irreplaceable.

At the time of the coup in Pakistan, I did not know enough about the country to understand the dynamics of what was happening, or the intractable nature of the challenges facing Musharraf. But despite my antipathy to military rule, I instinctively liked the man. Musharraf seemed honest, unpretentious, and determined to do the right thing. He was fifty-three, tough but modernistic, both a highly trained commando and combat veteran and a literate, traveled diplomat's son who wore spectacles and spoke flawless English.

Pakistanis, for their part, seemed to have no misgivings at all. In the days and weeks after the coup, I interviewed as many people from as many walks of life as I could, from academics to shopkeepers, from civil servants to mosque leaders. Virtually everyone said they had become disillusioned with politics and that military intervention had become Pakistan's only hope for reform and recovery.

Sharif's family and supporters protested, but almost no one was listening.

Maleeha Lodi, the poised and elegant newspaper editor who had once been Benazir Bhutto's envoy in Washington, told me she thought Musharraf was "the last chance for my country," and promptly agreed to accept the same post in his regime. Two days later, in a dingy shoemaking workshop in Lahore, the owner told me he had laid off seven workers and had no money to pay the electric bill, but had high hopes that the new government would revitalize the economy. "Allah has finally answered my prayers," he said.

Musharraf set off with an astoundingly ambitious agenda, eager to correct every social injustice, reform the cronyish political system, punish financial scofflaws, and jump-start the economy. One of his first targets was wealthy businessmen who had avoided paying billions of rupees in taxes and bank debts, and Pakistanis who struggled to feed their children every day were treated to the gratifying, televised spectacle of prominent fat cats being hustled off to jail by squads of army troops.

In Lahore, I managed to arrange an interview with several relatives and associates of a wealthy businessman, Naseem Saigol, who had just been arrested by army troops at his mansion and hauled off to a military jail. We sat in his elegant parlor, sipping tea and nibbling pastries on china laid out by silent servants. Everyone spoke polite, perfect English. We could have been at an estate in Sussex or Santa Barbara. It was not the kind of place one dispatched a squad of scruffy soldiers to arrest the resident peer.

Saigol's family agreed that the economic system needed to be reformed, and they acknowledged that his textile-based conglomerate had defaulted on $9.6 million in government loans. But they insisted the money was in the process of being paid back, and they were spluttering with indignation at the arrest.

"We think they wanted to pick up a few big household names to satisfy the public thirst for blood," said one of Saigol's colleagues. "We all had a lot of hopes for the army when they came in. I agree things in Pakistan need to be cleaned up, but you don't have to use terror tactics."

If anything, though, the new regime was not tough enough. The roots of corruption were thickly laced through the economy, and critics remained skeptical that Musharraf could yank them out. A financial witch-hunt grabbed headlines, but experts warned that only a major structural overhaul of the banking and tax systems and a massive purge of the bureaucracy could make a serious dent in the corruption that cost the nation nearly $2 billion a year.

Musharraf's effort to collect taxes also met with stiff opposition. Less than 2 million out of 140 million Pakistanis paid taxes on income or profit, and the army chief proposed to levy a 15 percent sales tax and undertake a nationwide tax inventory of retail businesses. But traders' groups balked with strikes and protests, arguing that the tax collection system was corrupt and that little revenue was given back in public services such as health and education.

"This is a huge litmus test for the new government," a loan recovery officer for Habib Bank told me shortly after Musharraf announced the crackdown on loan defaulters. "If it works, perhaps we can create a new culture of repayment in Pakistan. But if it fails, the military will not be able to show its face to the nation, and it will not be able to tackle the really hard targets, such as terrorism and religious fundamentalism."

Musharraf's most difficult challenge was to curb the growing power and popular influence of the Islamic fundamentalist groups who had first flourished under Gen. Zia. As a moderate, educated Muslim anxious to see his country progress, Musharraf knew these groups were holding back Pakistan from both domestic emancipation and international credibility, producing a generation of young men who knew nothing but the Koran, holding back women from becoming literate, fomenting sectarian conflict at home, and promoting controversial anti-Western crusades abroad.

Here too, however, the general discovered that "reform" meant challenging powerful groups who could easily marshal the religious fervor of the masses. He pledged to vigorously prosecute "honor killings," but found police and judges unwilling to cooperate and sympathetic to defendants who felt their masculine honor had been threatened. He attempted to bring the Koranic academies under government control, offering state subsidies and computers to those that adopted a broader academic curriculum, but many rejected the proposal as an infringement on their religious independence.

Musharraf's Achilles heel was Pakistan's foreign policy, long-dominated by muscular religious defensiveness rather than practical alliance-building. This in turn led to an unfortunate interdependence between the state and the very religious groups that were fomenting violence and extremism inside Pakistan. Musharraf needed these so-called jihadi groups, the advocates of an Islamic holy war, to prosecute the covert insurgency in Kashmir. And he could not afford to abandon his controversial support for the Taliban regime because of its close ties to Islamic groups and segments of his own security forces.

Within a year in power, Musharraf had been forced to tone down or abandon many of his initial crusades, and his reformist star had lost its luster. In person, he remained charming and straightforward, often meeting with journalists and disarming them with self-confident candor. I interviewed him several times and watched him perform on several dozen occasions, and after each encounter I found myself privately rooting for him. Here was a general with a powerful army at his command, I found myself thinking, but he was in way over his head.

Ayaz Amir, my favorite Pakistani newspaper columnist, had initially welcomed Musharraf as a breath of fresh air in a stale and stifling society. After the coup, he abandoned his customary cynicism and welcomed the general with relief, especially his vow to bring honesty and accountability to government. "The clouds have lifted," Amir wrote. "This is thundering music. . . . March on in this fashion, great chief, and troops of angels will speed you on your way."

But after a year of watching the army chief take one false or faltering step after another, Amir joined the chorus of disappointed fatalists. He described the beleaguered Musharraf as a military Sisyphus, trying like previous Pakistani strongmen to roll a heavy stone up a steep and slippery hill. Military intervention, no matter how benign and progressive, he wrote, "only ends up blocking political evolution and adding to the sum of popular frustration. How many times are we fated to walk the same road?"

∽

The pace of political events in Pakistan was often so swift and dizzying that I became its prisoner, rushing from ministry briefings to political teas to sessions with academic analysts, churning out story after late-night story that included the word "yesterday" in the first paragraph. But the stories that I really cared about, the ones I considered it both a privilege and a responsibility to research and write, were the ones about the daily struggles of people who lived in the other Pakistan.

To me, it was a luxury to spend an entire afternoon in a refugee camp or a brick factory or a used-clothing bazaar. I learned more about the country in a few hours at a shoemaker's workshop or a school for street children or a clinic for drug addicts than I did at a dozen news conferences by men in suits and uniforms. I was much happier wandering on my own with a translator among the bazaars of Rawalpindi or Peshawar than shouting to make myself heard while squeezed among a dozen TV cameras in an Islamabad ballroom.

What I learned in the neglected corners of Pakistan was the way things really worked: how people became trapped for life in debt and poverty; how merit earned nothing and connections meant everything; how tradition and obligation and fear substituted for law; how the concentrated power and privilege of the few affected the lives of the many. I learned why no one trusted the system or bothered to vote, and why people with no hope turned to a religious vision that burned with belligerent conviction.

If wealth was hard to track down in Pakistan, poverty was everywhere I looked. In the alleys of Karachi, boys bent over carpet-weaving looms or glued on sandal soles in dim, dank rooms. On the streets of Rawalpindi, armies of young garbage scavengers set out each morning with empty sacks, and returned at dusk with the day's loot dragging behind them. In the fields outside Peshawar, entire families of bonded laborers baked bricks all day, falling deeper into debt and permanent servitude to their employers. Animals fared no better: tiny donkeys staggered along the roads, loaded with mountains of bricks or wood; emaciated horses pulled passengers in wooden-wheeled tonga carts until they sometimes dropped in their tracks from exhaustion.

One of the places that drew me back, again and again, was the Data Shrine in Lahore, a park-like religious sanctuary that permanently teemed with a Dickensian frieze of humanity. There were legless and armless beggars lining the pathways and drug addicts sprawled unconscious on the stone patios or huddled in twos and threes around tiny tin-foil opium pipes. There were sharp-eyed children shadowing pilgrims for alms and hundreds of ragged people lined up for free nan and soup, which was ladled from huge vats into their outstretched bowls.

Across the street from the shrine, a nonprofit organization called New Life had set up a drug rehabilitation clinic. Addicts wandered in and out all day, arguing woozily over nothing, dozing on mattresses, exchanging old needles for new. One day I watched two men carry in a boy of seventeen, emaciated and covered with sores, and drop him like a sack of bones on a chair. I watched a counselor explain to blank, uncomprehending faces how dirty needles could spread something called AIDS. I watched men bow in prayer inside, then slip into the alley outside to inhale cooked opium from their homemade foil pipes.

Occasionally, though, someone escaped from this hopeless panorama and actually found a new life. I met such a man through the clinic, a wizened fellow of about forty with a scarred face and an impish grin. His name was Muzamil Hussain. He had spent more than a decade living on the streets around the Data Shrine, panhandling and stealing and doing odd jobs. At one point he had been injured in an accident and developed gangrene in his legs. Both had been amputated at the knee.

I first encountered Hussain at a residential workshop operated by New Life in the piney hills surrounding Islamabad. He was very busy that morning, stumping around on leather kneepads that were strapped to his waist. The light filtering through the pine trees was pale and ethereal. I watched in awe as Hussain filled the coffee pot to heat, fed his pet chickens, put on a gauze mask and expertly spray-painted a stack of ceramic bowls, which would be sold to help support the retreat. When he finished, he sprayed a giant pine cone with gold frost, stumped over and handed it to me. "This is the first home I have ever known," he said. He was the happiest man I had met in a long time.

∞

Interlude

Amsterdam——It is the week before Christmas, and I am frantically scribbling cards in an airport café, planning to mail them as soon as

I land in Washington. Along with each one I am enclosing a photograph taken on the porch of the Chez Soi. I am sitting on the ground
in jeans and a tee-shirt, hugging a small, shepherd-like dog with a
plaster cast on one foreleg.

A few weeks ago, my taxi hit her on the highway from Peshawar
at dusk. I heard the unmistakable thud and jumped out. She was
staggering across a field, and I chased after her. When I reached the
spot where she lay, she was limp and shivering with shock. I carried
her back to the cab, rushed to my vet in Islamabad and laid her on
his metal table. Both her leg and jaw were broken. I held her while
he plastered her leg and wired her jaws together. There was blood
everywhere, but I was concentrating too hard to notice.

By the time the dog was well enough to move from the clinic to
the Chez Soi, we were friends for life. She was small but feisty, and
within weeks she was digging up bones and sprinting madly across
the flower beds, plaster cast and all. I named her Rafi, short for the
Arabic word meaning "friend," and I made a hundred copies of that
photograph to send out with my Christmas cards. I especially liked
it because I looked so happy, and I hoped people wouldn't peer too
closely and notice that my shirt, a gift from a waggish colleague, said,
"Long Live Osama."

I know when I reach home tomorrow, I will find a stack of other
people's Christmas cards in my parents' parlor. They will be smiling
portraits of couples surrounded by children and pets, snapped outside a beach house or posed in front of a fireplace. They will look like
the cards from previous years, with the proud addition of a new son-
in-law or granddaughter and scribbled notes about vacations and
graduations. They will communicate a message of growth and ac-
complishment, based on foundations that grow more solid and sure
with time.

For a few hours, I will feel jealous of these settled lives and emotional certainties, of friends and relatives who have been steadily
adding accoutrements to their comfort and generations to their tree.
I will wonder briefly what is wrong with me, why I have never really
wanted to settle down and raise children, why I keep shedding possessions and relationships when others are accumulating them.

I will think about the photographs from my first wedding, more
than twenty years ago: my father beaming as he escorted me into
the church; my mother fussing over the chiffon and lace gown she

designed and sewed; my new husband and me posing happily under a wisteria arbor. I remember feeling relieved that day, thinking I had finally merged the two halves of my personality. I was marrying a Japanese American photographer I had met in Peru, a man who seemed to echo my dreams of adventure and creativity and concern for the world. But the day's events followed a different script and reflected my parents' traditions: refined tastes, subdued wealth, exclusivity. For years I had grappled with this internal dichotomy; perhaps my marriage would finally resolve it.

Instead, I soon grew restless. My husband began working his way up the American ladder; I wanted to plunge into distant struggles and terrain. When the chance came, an offer to become a newspaper correspondent in Latin America for the *Boston Globe*, I immediately accepted. My family was worried but proud, and it never occurred to them to try and dissuade me. I had been raised to think, to dream, to make a difference. Children would be nice, but I was not obliged to produce them. I was legally, constitutionally free to undertake the "pursuit of happiness," a phrase I would take completely for granted until two decades later, when I landed in South Asia and discovered that millions of women lived and died without ever being told they had the right to be happy at all.

I spent the 1980s wandering across Latin America and the Caribbean when the terrain was hot with guerrilla wars and drug trafficking and military coups. I was especially drawn to Haiti, a place of dazzling light and reptilian evil, and Chile, a culture of wine and poetry where students were braving tear gas and fire hoses to bring down a military dictator. By the time the decade was over, my marriage had evaporated and I had fallen in love with a Chilean American scholar. We drank cabernet, listened to protest music and interviewed people whose dignity and dreams had been crushed by dictatorship. He too seemed the perfect reflection of my two halves; romantic but respectable, drawn to revolution yet careful never to let the flame consume him.

Eventually we married, moved to Washington and wrote a book together. I became an editor, he became a diplomat. But as we acquired more adornments and anchors, I began to feel stultified by success. I stayed out too late, I drank too much wine, I found excuses to fly back to Santiago and Port-au-Prince. One day, I moved into a tiny apartment with a mattress on the floor, quit my office job, and plunged into a gloriously grubby new beat, writing about Hispanic immigrants and Third World refugees for the *Washington Post*.

Many of the people I encountered on this beat were struggling to overcome violent and impoverished pasts and to find a solid niche in America. There was an illiterate janitor from El Salvador who had crossed the desert from Mexico with his wife and eight children, a shy girl from East Africa who had escaped ritual mutilation by her tribe, a dignified editor from Honduras who had been tortured by the American-backed army.

But there was one character whose tormented odyssey was in reverse, and I immediately recognized it as an extreme version of my own struggle. His name was Guillermo Descalzi, and he had once been a dashing, impeccably dressed TV newsman in Latin America. By the time I met him in Washington, he was a half-mad vagrant and crack addict living in an abandoned attic. Most of his addled philosophical ramblings made no sense, but sometimes he struck a pure, painful chord in me, especially when he talked about the emptiness of celebrity and the need to pare away everything—possessions, personality, pretensions—to the bone.

"I am trying to set an example for myself," Descalzi explained to me one day, his face covered with stubble, his eyes piercing. "I am trying to erase my ego and to find communion with the spirit of God. There are some things you must say with your life, not with words, and it's come to that. In the past, I spent a great deal of time saying very little." I knew Descalzi had hurt and betrayed many people in his self-absorbed, downward quest for the primordial truth. I knew he was in the grip of powerful drugs. But I also knew he was right.

Like Descalzi, I have been determined to shed the trappings of a privileged life, to free myself from the bonds and burdens that sap energy and empathy and outrage. Like Descalzi, I have forsaken a normal life in a quest for something I still find difficult to define and have glimpsed only at rare moments. I have neither risen nor fallen as far as he did, my pretensions have not been as lofty nor my indulgences as degraded. But I have done damage, I have abandoned people who loved me or kept them waiting far too long, while I set out on yet another pilgrimage that some might consider as selfish, and as hopeless, as his.

At an age when most sane, successful people measure time and progress by annual raises and Christmas cards, I am still living for these few, fleeting moments of inspiration and insight and raw emotion, for brushes with near-death and impossible love. I am still out looking for fragments of grace in the desert, *buscando flores en la basura*, as Guatemalan songwriter Ricardo Arjona put it, instead of building a home and cultivating my own garden.

Sometimes, when one of those moments occurs, I am certain it has all been worth it. If I were snugly settled in a New England nest, would I have met Zahida Perveen and been able to expose the evil of crimes committed against thousands of women in the name of honor and religion? If I were car-pooling to soccer and tending delphiniums and editing others' words, would I have met Muzamil Hussain and been able to describe an unexpected glimmer of hope in a Muslim society that many Westerners have written off as a corrupt failure?

I have not always made wise choices, and there are some that still make me wince to remember. I may very well live to regret the larger choices I have made, especially the decision not to have children. I may eventually discover that a succession of intense experiences and epiphanies add up to nothing, that I have lost more than I have gained by rushing off to another distant revolution or earthquake instead of leading a quieter but more cumulative life, closer to those I love. In the end, though, the choices were mine, both the mistakes and the redemptive moments. That in itself is a privilege that my sojourn in South Asia has ensured I will never take for granted again.

CHAPTER FIVE

The Wrath of Allah

*"And fight in the cause of Allah
against those who wage war against you,
but do not commit aggression,
for verily, Allah does not love aggressors.*

—Holy Koran, Shura 2, Verse
190

*"How big is a rupee when you spend it in the name of Allah,
and how small when you take it to the mall."*

—Fundraising slogan, Jamaat-
I-Islami Party

 THE call of the muezzin is one of the most haunting, seductive sounds I have ever heard. Many times, the first call, *fajr*, has woken me from half-sleep in Peshawar or Lahore before dawn, almost pulling me toward it, and I imagined following the notes through the misty air and twisting alleys of a sleeping city to a cavernous, vaulted sanctuary where old men bowed and murmured in the warm, familiar gloom. Many times at dusk, hearing the first notes of *isha*, the evening call, I have flung open my hotel window in Srinagar or Kandahar and leaned out, closing my eyes and listening until the last echo died away.

Hazan is both lullaby and awakening, a call to worship that slowly builds to an irresistible crescendo. First a single, quavering voice rises from one minaret; then a second, gravelly one joins in a few blocks away. The voices multiply, blending into an endless, cacophonic hum, neither in harmony nor in competition. It is like a joyous chorus of the deaf who can hear only God and sing only to Him. These are the sentinels of a faith that moves to timeless rhythms and unchanging beliefs. God is great, there is no other God, awake, arise, come and worship Him.

The call has gone out for centuries, and I am far from the first Westerner to feel or describe its lure. Islam is not my religion and never will be; I have seen far too much hatred and bloodshed and oppression perpetrated in its name, and I could never accept the limits it places on women. Even the mosque itself, the source of the siren song that beckons me so, is off-limits to women in most countries. Yet there is something appealing in the simple message—especially to someone caught up in frantic, modern pursuits—that says we should distill life to its essentials, slow down, set aside worldly things, put God first.

Mosques are like cathedrals. They bring back the austere, echoing stone churches of my childhood, the hush of vespers, the rustle of prayer. They are places for contemplation, meditation, feeling the presence of God. All my life I have sought out such places, especially old cemeteries, to sit and write and think. Years ago, in summer, I liked to study the old New England tombstones of ship captains and educators and preachers, especially ones with Biblical names like Obadiah and Ezekiel, of the wives who outlived them and those who died in childbirth, and to imagine an earlier time when life was hard but faith was unshakeable. I drew solitary sustenance from these reveries; I imagined myself enduring great trials to perform great deeds.

So in a way, I think I understand the powerful attraction of Islam, with its quiet sanctuaries and purifying ablutions and rigorous striving for perfection, that has drawn hundreds of thousands of boys and young men, mostly poor and illiterate, to fundamentalist mosques and *madrassahs*, or Koranic academies. To memorize a sacred book in a mysterious language, to imagine dying a glorious death in defense of one's faith, to become a soldier of God and be assured of a place in Paradise—how potent that elixir must be to someone with no money, no education, and no prospects for success in this world.

During my travels in Pakistan, I met hundreds of these religious students—the cannon fodder of foreign proxy wars, the dupes of manipulative religio-political bosses, the raw material of an extremist movement that has sought to impose the punitive dictates of Islam on a moderate, modernizing Muslim society and to block out the threatening temptations of modern Western culture.

I watched them gleefully smash effigies of President Bush and President Musharraf, cursing one as an infidel aggressor and the other as his pawn. I watched them reverently chant the name of Osama bin Laden and vow to die defending the Taliban regime in Afghanistan from foreign intervention. I watched them sit cross-legged for hours, bobbing and nodding as they memorized aloud verse after verse of the Koran, while a stern turbaned teacher listened with a switch laid across his desk. I watched them listen in rapt attention to streams of vitriol pouring from mosque loudspeakers, and then stream into the streets with a roar, ready to explode the "Islamic bomb" and slay the first Western infidel they encountered.

And yet I was also struck by how innocent they seemed, how malleable and excitable, how yearning for certainty and inspiration, how churning with hormonal energy for which they had no socially permissible outlet. In the West, they would have been tackling each other on playing fields, emulating Hollywood action heroes and competing for the attention of girls they saw every day in class. Here, all that youthful drive was channeled by their elders into a straitjacket of piety whose only outlets were fantasies of revenge and martyrdom.

My first visit to a madrassah was in Peshawar in 1998. The white-turbaned mullah in charge of the school offered me tea and cookies and offered to answer any questions I had. I was ignorant and confused about Islam then, and my queries were sincere. *Why should Muslim men wear beards?* "Because that is the way of the Prophet." *Why memorize the Koran in a language you don't understand?* "Because it is a holy book."

The man spoke automatically, with suppressed impatience, as if lecturing a child. But it suddenly dawned on me that he had no real answers and no analytical basis for them; the educator was merely repeating what he had been taught. When I asked if he had any message for American readers, his reply was blood-curdling. Western countries were "the true terrorists," he declared. The world must be "Islamized," by force if needed. He politely passed me the plate of cookies, and added one more point: If any Christian missionaries dared to come to the area, "we are going to start shooting them."

What I remember most vividly about that astonishing encounter, though, was not the mullah but one of his students, a slender boy of perhaps fourteen, who was summoned to perform a brief Koranic recitation for me. He had been sitting on the steps nearby with two or three friends, during a break between classes. They were holding up a pocket mirror to their smooth chins and searching in vain for a wisp or two of hair—the sign, I learned later, that they would soon become formally eligible to fight in a holy war.

After he finished chanting several Arabic verses, the boy took a deep breath and declared in Pashto, the Afghan dialect that is widely spoken in northwest Pakistan: "It is my daily prayer that one day I will be in Afghanistan so I can become one of those killed in the way of Allah." He glanced at the turbaned director, who nodded his approval, and then darted away to rejoin his pals.

∾

This fanatical crusade did not spring from the spiritual needs of Pakistani society; from the beginning it was a creature of larger political ambitions, foreign funding and international disputes. Its main intellectual birthplace was New Delhi in the 1860s, when Muslim scholars founded two schools of conservative Sunni thought known as Deobandi and Brelvi. In the 1940s, during the tumultuous subcontinental campaign for a Muslim political revival or homeland, two religious parties were formed in Delhi that have now become the largest in Pakistan—Jamaat-I-Islami and Jamiat-e-ulema-Islami. They disagreed on the preferred path to Muslim power, but they both sought to build a society where Shariah, or pure Islamic law, prevailed over secular law.

In 1947, Pakistan was founded as an "Islamic republic," both a haven for Muslims where governance was to be based on Islamic principles of social justice, and a parliamentary democracy that protected the rights of religious minorities. The trail of bloody massacres and massive forced migration that accompanied the forcible Partition of India galvanized the new, radical Islamist groups, but they remained small, marginalized from political life and weakened by sectarian splits.

In 1970, under left-leaning Prime Minister Zulfiqar Ali Bhutto, the two major religious parties won only eleven seats in Parliament. But Bhutto tried to woo the groups by banning alcohol and gambling, and during his tenure a new constitution was drafted and enacted whose opening paragraphs stressed the authority of Allah, not man-made laws, over the nation.

When Gen. Mohammed Zia ul-Haq seized power in 1977, the fortunes of Pakistan's religious parties rose rapidly, and several of their leaders were elected to the Senate. Zia, an Islamist dictator who shared their vision of a puritanical religious state, enacted numerous provisions of Shariah law, including one that made blaspheming against Islam or the Prophet Mohammed a capital crime. He was also a shrewd Cold Warrior who needed Islamic fighters in the U.S.-backed crusade to resist the Soviet invasion of Afghanistan. Pakistani mosques and madrassahs, many of whose students were Afghan refugees, sent them eagerly back into battle.

After Zia's death in 1988 and the Soviet withdrawal from Afghanistan the next year, some Islamic guerrilla groups were rerouted by Pakistani intelligence agencies into the burgeoning Kashmir insurgency, while others trained more cadres to serve and fight for the Taliban militia that seized Kabul in 1996. All together, the "jihadi" or "holy war" groups based in Pakistan are believed to have given military training to half a million youths in the 1980s and 90s, many thousands of whom lost their lives fighting in Afghanistan and Indian Kashmir.

In the process, fundamentalist Islamic thought and institutions sent deep roots into Pakistan itself. In 1971 there were only an estimated 900 madrassahs with 180,000 students, mostly small schools connected to neighborhood mosques in areas along the Afghan border. By 1997, there were at least one million students studying at nearly 7,000 madrassahs across the country, many of them sent by families who could not afford to educate them any other way. They received free room and board, and they were taught that Islam was the only true guide to life, that women were to remain at home and raise children, that modern distractions were sinful, and that the West was the enemy of their faith.

At the same time, the growth of religious fervor and militarization led to increasing sectarian violence among Sunni and Shiite Muslim groups in volatile cities like Karachi, where gunmen periodically sprayed rival mosques with rifle fire during prayer services and vanished. There were also sporadic terrorist attacks in public places, such as bus stops and bazaars, with grenades or bombs. As the number of religious groups and agendas multiplied, so did the potential for violence in a country already swimming with weapons.

But Pakistan's civilian leaders, preoccupied with a see-sawing power struggle between the People's Party of the Bhutto family and the Muslim League of the Sharifs, tried to placate or co-opt the Islamists rather than rein them in. Benazir Bhutto was anathema to them as a woman prime minister, and during her first term they worked with the intelligence services to undermine her, so once she reached power again, she turned a blind eye to their cross-border jihads in Kabul and Kashmir. Nawaz Sharif did the same, introducing a Shariah law bill and keeping himself largely aloof from Islamic guerrilla activities beyond Pakistani borders.

Pakistan's deepening economic woes also contributed to the growing strength of its religious parties. In the 1960s, the country appeared to be moving toward steady growth and modest prosperity, with poverty levels dropping to about one-third of the populace. But over the next three decades, the trend sharply reversed itself, and by the late 1990s, more than two-thirds of Pakistanis were living in poverty. Desperate with their earthly lot, and alienated from a corrupt, stagnant system that seemed to reward the rich and punish the poor, people turned toward Islam with its ethos of social justice and its promises of paradise.

The extremist parties, capitalizing on this alienation, offered struggling Muslims a home, a cause, and a reason to live. Westernized experts and intellectuals in the drawing rooms of Islamabad and Lahore continued to dismiss the extremists as "fringe" groups, while secular politicians, many of whom were well-fed beneficiaries of feudal wealth, assumed they could never win an election. Meanwhile, in another world of neighborhood mosques, shabby bazaars and free madrassahs where poor and disaffected Muslims gathered, the religious parties were steadily gaining influence.

By the time General Musharraf took over in 1999, the jihadists were enjoying unprecedented popularity, and they were becoming a political force to be reckoned with as well as an embarrassment to a country trying to present itself as a forward-looking member of the world community. Their vision of religion was not shared by a majority of Pakistanis, but they were close allies of Islamists in the army and intelligence services. As such, they essentially dictated the controversial foreign policies—covert insurgency in India, formal recognition of the Taliban—that made Pakistan a pariah in the developed and democratic world.

Three years later, after Musharraf had sided with the West in the war on Islamic terrorism and held elections that restored a multi-party Parliament and provincial assemblies, Pakistan's six major religious parties made an unprecedented popular showing at the polls. Nowhere was their victory more clear-cut than in Northwest Frontier Province, the heart of conservative Pashtun culture, where families kept their daughters in purdah, named their newborn sons Osama, and sent their older ones off to fight jihad.

∾

To enter the old quarter of Peshawar is to step into a scene from the Bible or a verse from the Koran. Endless twisting alleys are lined with stalls selling hand-woven carpets, brass teapots, dusty silver jewelry, multicolored mountains of spices, birds in cages, knives in leather scabbards. The gracefully carved bulbs of white and green minarets rise from mosques on every corner. Men in robes and turbans sit astride tiny donkeys, veiled women bargain over vegetables, elders sip tea in the carpeted shadows. Turn a corner at prayer time, and the entire lane before you may be filled with symmetrical rows of barefoot men on scraps of cloth, all bent simultaneously to touch their foreheads to the ground.

Sometimes, when I wander through these bazaars, I am seized by the irrational wish that time would stop and keep this muted, unhurried tableau of history from turning into a frantic, honking, polluted copy of Third World urban development. And yet it is just such a yearning, to halt the inevitable course of progress and cling to the primitive virtues of a 1,400-year-old religion, that has made Northwest Frontier a fervid hive of the most obscurantist forms of Islamic ideology.

This is virtual Taliban territory, a microcosm of conservative Afghan tribal culture, where every mosque echoes with fire-and-brimstone sermons on Friday, every block echoes with boys' voices memorizing Arabic verses, every woman's face is covered and every man wears a beard. Official power may lie 150 miles east, in the granite federal ministries of Islamabad and the manicured military compounds of Rawalpindi, but the mullahs of Peshawar look heavenward for guidance and well beyond Pakistan's borders for holy wars to fight.

One of the oldest and largest madrassahs in Pakistan is Darul

Uloom Haqqania, a thirty-minute drive from Peshawar. Its brochure describes lofty-sounding goals: "To spread the light of knowledge in the world . . . to provide the society with scholars . . . to preach the message of Islam . . . to safeguard Muslim culture and civilization from corrupting influences."

The director of Haqqania, Sami ul-Haq, is a bespectacled mullah and a shrewd former senator who has spearheaded legislative drives to make Shariah the law of the land. Ul-Haq, who welcomes foreign journalists to Haqqania, is proud of his 28,000-volume library and sensitive about being labeled an extremist. Yet he has also been an outspoken backer of the Taliban, pointing with pride to the thousands of students his madrassah sent to fight in Afghanistan, and to the smaller number who became officials in the extremist Kabul regime.

Despite his worldly air, ul-Haq occasionally revealed a startling, Taliban-like myopia. During one of our chats in his office, I mentioned that I considered it an especially needless and tragic error for the Taliban to have prohibited music, a crucial element of culture and historical memory in Afghanistan's pre-literate society. In the Taliban's defense, ul-Haq complained about the vulgarity of Western pop music. In retort, I referred to the spiritual splendor of Beethoven—and received only a quizzical frown. The learned mullah had never heard of him.

In many ways, Peshawar has always been more an Afghan city than a Pakistani one, with Pashtun tribes straddling the border and Pashto spoken far more widely than Urdu. More than two million Afghan refugees fled to Northwest Frontier during the Soviet occupation and the civil war, and Peshawar became the nerve center of plots and intrigue among numerous exile and refugee groups. The area's refugee camps have long grown into full-fledged communities, and their leaders replicate the tribal, political, and religious complexities of their homeland. Even ardently anti-Taliban groups can be deeply conservative, as I discovered through one embarrassing incident.

One day in Islamabad, I was called by the information ministry and asked to meet a new official. When I entered, he informed me politely that the elders of one refugee camp had filed a formal complaint, accusing me of appearing there in "indecent and provocative" clothing. I was stunned. I had been wearing my usual sack-of-potatoes dress and scarf, and I couldn't imagine how I had offended anyone. Then I realized the elders had probably confused me with another American woman who visited the camp around the same time, a hip young photographer who insisted on wearing jeans and tank tops. The ministry official laughed sympathetically and told me not to worry, but it took weeks for my indignation to fade.

The faithful of Peshawar's many mosques and madrassahs are easy to whip into an emotional frenzy over any perceived threat or insult to Islam, whether from at home or abroad. One especially volatile issue is blasphemy, a crime loosely defined as "offending the religious sensibilities" of a Muslim. Under the Islamic statutes enacted by Zia, blasphemy has been punishable by death since 1986. Such charges are often misused to harass religious minorities such as Ahmedi Muslims or to exact vengeance against personal enemies. An accusation of blasphemy can also set off lynch-mob hysteria among devout Muslims.

In 2001, the *Frontier Post* newspaper in Peshawar mistakenly printed a letter to the editor that insulted the Prophet Mohammed, the most sacred figure in Islam, describing him as a womanizer and a Jew-hating "Nazi." The newspaper immediately issued an apology, but the next day five members of the editorial staff were arrested on charges of blasphemy. After a provincial branch of Jamaat-I-Islami circulated the offending text in its newsletter, an outraged crowd attacked the newspaper's office, vandalizing the building and setting fire to the presses while police watched impassively. Even more tellingly, government officials and national press associations cautiously criticized the mob attack — but vigorously condemned the blasphemous publication.

Two weeks after this incident, I visited the shaken journalists in Peshawar's dilapidated central jail. One was an eighty-year-old feature writer, another a frightened-looking editorial assistant who had physically inserted the e-mailed text into the paper. He confessed that he had a recurring drug abuse problem and had not read the entire letter first. He was clearly horrified at what he had done. "I am a Muslim," he explained miserably. "I would never abuse our prophet." The man was eventually sentenced to life in prison.

Most of the religious groups' wrath, however, was directed at foreign attacks on Islam, and Friday mosque sermons often railed against the pro-Israel, pro-India, anti-Taliban policies of the United

States and its Western allies. On at least a dozen occasions between 1999 and 2002, I drove to Peshawar from Islamabad to cover street protests staged by various mosque leaders. The ritual was always the same: fire-breathing speeches inside the mosque, followed by an eruption of excited young men into the streets and a boisterous march that lasted for several hours.

I was always nervous and tense during these rallies. There were usually rows of police guarding the route and plainclothes agents mingling in the crowd, but the mood was agitated and the potential for violence high. Usually I ducked inside an alley or storefront with several other reporters, waiting for the crush to pass and thankful I was not a TV cameraman whose job was to wade into the mob and film. If the atmosphere seemed relatively calm, I would beckon one or two boys out of the mob and try to make conversation, with inter-preting help from a local journalist. Often they were eager to explain how they felt—and to reassure me that, even if they were carrying posters saying, "Long Live Osama" and "Death to President Bush," they meant no harm to me as an individual.

In some ways, their banners were the local equivalent of "Go, Steelers!" or "Tar Heels Forever." The young men who exuberantly hoisted them were adolescent and college-age products of cloistered boarding schools; bolder in groups, pumped up by their coaches, and eager to outshine their rivals. They had been taught to hate the same enemy and worship the same heroes, while being cut off from access to knowledge that might have given them a different perspective on the world. The tragedy was that instead of being inspired to excel and compete in life, they were being programmed to pick up a rifle, charge across the Afghan or Indian border, and die.

Not all of the young devotees were poor and illiterate, either. I met one medical student from a tribal area near Peshawar, bright and articulate, who proudly told me he had just abandoned his studies to join a religious party that was organizing volunteers to fight on be-half of the Taliban. His parents were disappointed at first, he said, but he felt his duty as a Muslim was more important than his profes-sional career. He had covered the walls of his father's metalwork shop with posters of bin Laden, and his new party membership card was embossed with a slogan about vowing to sacrifice everything for Islam. "Now I am just waiting for them to give me the order," he said, with a smile.

Some of the clerics who ran Peshawar's madrassahs seemed open to change, especially the introduction of computers and modern academic subjects into curricula that had long been strictly based on dusty Islamic texts. They were protective of their independence but not secretive about their work, except that most did not openly admit their students might be sent off to fight a holy war. A few were willing to let foreign journalists visit and even photograph classes, eager to dispel the perception that they exploited children in the name of religion.

"Madrassah students are human beings, and they should be studying human things," Mufti Ghulam ur Rehman, the director of a Koranic academy for 270 boys, told me. His tiny office was filled with reclining cushions, and he worked cross-legged at a low writing table, but there was a new computer monitor and keyboard next to it. "We want to make each student a perfect man and a perfect Muslim, but the world is modernizing," he said, adding that the school offered elective courses in law, math, English, economics, and word processing, "while keeping within purely Islamic values."

But in some cases, even when their elders realized the value of good public relations, religious students had been so thoroughly isolated and indoctrinated against Western moral corruption that they were visibly uncomfortable in my presence. During one of my first visits to Pakistan, I arranged an interview with a group of religious students and arrived wearing what I thought was modest dress: a loose blouse, long skirt and headscarf. When I sat down, there was a flurry of whispers and the students looked disconcerted. Finally someone brought in a blanket and wordlessly handed it to me. "Your calves are showing," my interpreter explained.

Several years later—long after I had learned to cover myself completely in such situations, and long after I had become inured to hearing rote recitations of the holy war mantra—a sadder, more startling encounter gave me a new understanding of the perverse power of Islamic brainwashing on gullible minds. It was in a prison in Afghanistan, where dozens of Pakistanis from the Northwest province and border tribal areas were being held. Incited by their imams, they had crossed the border to fight for the Taliban, but instead had been arrested almost immediately. There were perhaps fifty men in half a dozen large cells, huddled in blankets and dozing or reading. I poked my head inside one doorway and asked through my interpreter if anyone wanted to talk to a foreign journalist.

One prisoner with piercing, kohl-rimmed eyes sat up and started to make a speech about jihad, but another one immediately backed into a corner and drew up his knees, covering his eyes and chanting loudly in Arabic. I asked the guard if he was mentally ill. "No, he's trying to pretend you are not here," the man replied. I felt insulted and embarrassed, but I also felt a stab of sympathy. To this poor man, I was not a journalist, or even a person. I was a dangerous contagion that had entered the only private space he had. I backed out of the cell immediately, apologizing for the intrusion.

∾

Despite their growing numbers and headline-grabbing notoriety, Islamic extremists still represent only a fraction of Pakistani Muslims. The region's far more dominant religious tradition is a form of Sufism: mystical, superstitious, iconic, and often bizarre, but never violent or aggressive about imposing itself on anyone. There are shrines to Sufi saints in every city, and they attract an astonishing parade of humanity. Some are pitiful pariahs like the beggars and addicts of the Data Shrine in Lahore; but others are families in their Friday best, bringing babies or lambs and goats to be blessed, or young wives unable to conceive and hoping for a miracle.

At the shrine of Bari Imam in Islamabad, the saint's annual birthday is a raucous religious celebration, not unlike the Easter carnivals in Rio de Janeiro. There are transvestite dancers, people who chant for hours in trance-like states, swarms of pickpockets and squads of police. But the strangest Sufi phenomenon is the so-called healing power of *chuhas*, or children with tiny deformed heads, who are placed at the entrances to shrines so they can "bless" petitioners. I have heard reports that unscrupulous gangs take orphans from shrines and force them to wear iron skullcaps, keeping their heads from growing so they can earn shrine donations, but I have no idea if this is true.

Most educated Pakistanis practice a moderate, voluntaristic form of Islam in which culture plays as important a role as liturgy or law. Men attend weekly mosque prayers on Fridays but do not necessarily drop everything to pray five times a day. Women dress modestly but do not cover their faces with veils, and many work outside the home. People fast from sunup to sundown during Ramadan, but they may not set their alarms at 3 A.M. to cook the prescribed pre-dawn meal as well. If they can afford it, they travel to Saudi Arabia once for the hajj pilgrimage to Mecca, but the resulting social status (and permanent honorific of becoming a "hajji") is just as important as the ritual of faith. Most Pakistanis do not drink alcohol, at least outside their homes, but they are not uncomfortable mixing with Christians and foreigners who do.

As Pakistan began to acquire a terrorist label in the late 1990s, many Muslim leaders and scholars were chagrined and embarrassed, and they took pains to point out to visitors like myself that "jihad" was a widely misunderstood word: a call for personal striving toward the perfection—and, if necessary, the defense—of Islam, but not for a war of armed aggression against the world. At the same time, many devout Pakistanis remained suspicious of Western culture, viewing it as vulgar and licentious, and bitterly opposed to American policy toward Israel, Bosnia, and other regions where they saw Muslims as being oppressed.

"We are not against the Western way of life, but we do not want any interference in ours," the leader of a mainstream mosque in Islamabad told me one Friday after a crowded prayer service. "Islam does not teach hatred, it teaches love, but it is the love of a mother and child, of a husband and wife, not this free love and sex of the American and British kind. We do not want to destroy America, we only want to save and defend our own culture."

While the hate-filled harangues of extremist Sunni mullahs attracted only a relatively small minority of poor and disenfranchised Pakistanis, the subtler and more strategic approach of the largest religious party, Jamaat-I-Islami—combined with widespread public disillusionment over the performance of successive secular leaders—contributed to its quiet, steady growth. By 2000, the party claimed to have five million members. Jamaat's goal was as radical as the other Islamic parties—a full-fledged Islamic state—but it was in no hurry to take over. Its longtime leader, Qazi Hussain Ahmed, constantly declared that the group sought to bring about this change by "peaceful, democratic means."

I met and interviewed Qazi numerous times, and I found him one of the shrewdest political leaders I had ever met. He was one of the few conservative Pakistani clerics who spoke English and was knowledgeable about Western civilization. He was a pragmatic chameleon who could give a rabble-rousing, anti-Western speech to a rally of emotional supporters one day, then turn around the next and reassure American visitors that Jamaat would always operate within the law, had no aggressive designs, and sought only to bring social justice and the full benefits of Islam to the nation.

The keys to Jamaat's phenomenal growth were political organization and social work. Through a network of charities, it operated schools, low-cost clinics, literacy programs, widows' aid funds, and farmer assistance programs. Its cadres were everywhere, offering condolences to the dead, dispensing help to the needy, and weighing in on every important local issue. They were clean-cut, low-key, and austere, and unlike Pakistan's secular political leaders, they practiced what they preached.

In Lahore, near the party's headquarters, I visited a clean, efficient Jamaat-run hospital where patients paid a dime for each medical prescription and the staff spread out tiny rugs in the front lobby five times a day to pray. I also visited a large, coed state university, where members of the Islamic Student Union, a Jamaat-backed organization, welcomed freshmen with reminders that popular music, movies, and mixed-gender socializing were immoral. Their immediate goal, they told me, was to steer their classmates away from the temptations of Western culture. Their ultimate dream was to have entirely separate campuses for male and female students.

"Our values are different from those of Europe and America, where the family system has been destroyed because there is nakedness and women and men are allowed to mix freely," one earnest student leader told me, offering his cell phone number in case I had any other questions. He looked and sounded like a scrubbed, self-confident acolyte of the Moral Majority, but there was no way I could explain the irony to him. "Our society is strong because its religion and its family system are strong," he declared. "We are here to preserve and protect it."

∞

To a certain extent, I secretly empathized with the concerns of the Islamists' anti-Western message. As a beneficiary of women's liberation, an educated world traveler who had abandoned marriage and avoided parenthood to pursue my dreams, I could hardly endorse the notion that women should be sheltered behind a curtain for life. And yet whenever I returned to the West, I was appalled and saddened by the increasingly vulgar, titillating spectacle of popular culture — the talk-show confessions and slugfests, the six-year-old sex-goddess beauty pageants, the demeaning rap lyrics.

I was also revolted by the American cult of profit and excess — the ever-larger meal portions and clothing sizes, the tyranny of brands, the rush to sue. I had been raised in a privileged world, but I had been taught modest and egalitarian values. I hated to think of a younger generation addicted to sugar and fat, credit and consumption. When an angry mob in Karachi attacked a Kentucky Fried Chicken outlet in October 2001, I knew their wrath was directed against a symbol of U.S. military might, but I secretly hoped it might slow the burgeoning American export of junk-food cravings to a rice-and-lentil populace bedazzled by foreign fads.

If the Islamists were obsessed with honor and shame, it sometimes seemed as if the West had entirely forgotten what they meant. At one madrassah in Peshawar, the director told me he was opposed to the regional tribal practice of bartering girls to settle disputes, describing it as cruel and un-Islamic. There was little difference, he went on to explain, between such primitive customs and the degrading commercial exploitation of Western women in television and films. I thought for a moment, and I decided the mullah had a point.

But there were other times, when trying to maintain a professional demeanor and observe the decorous dictates of a Muslim society left me exhausted and depressed. I never felt persecuted or reviled in Pakistan, as I had been during my visits to Taliban-ruled Afghanistan, but I was often anxious and frustrated. My job required me to listen politely to grossly distorted, anti-Western rants without responding or showing offense. During many interviews, I had to keep my headscarf from slipping and my feet tucked under me, even when my legs were falling asleep. During religious street rallies, I had to show respect for another religion and culture while mine were being insulted.

I suppose I could have protested or argued back, but I never did. As a guest in a foreign country, I was loath to fulfill my hosts' worst stereotypes of Westerners as obnoxious and immoral, and determined not to give them an excuse to discredit my work. And even though I could not avoid attracting stares as soon as I stepped outside the Westernized bubble of Islamabad, I also believed I should try, as much as possible, to blend into my surroundings and absorb events, rather than attracting attention, making demands and becoming part of the story.

Many Pakistani Muslims told me they were pleasantly surprised by my attempts to dress modestly, learn conversational phrases in their languages, and understand their culture. Many aspects of Islam appealed to my contemplative, humble notions of religion: I never failed to feel awed by the silent beauty of mosques, and I always felt a bit safer when I heard the Koranic prayer crackle over the intercom as each Pakistan International Airlines flight taxied for takeoff. But I was a tourist, not a pilgrim; an observer, not a convert. In Pakistan's Islamic world, I was politely received but permanently out of place.

Sometimes I would wake up early on a Sunday with nothing to do, wondering why I had traveled so far to explore an alien faith and wishing, as I listened to the jumble of muezzins' voices start to rise, that I could hear bells pealing across the morning mist. I knew there were Roman Catholic churches throughout Pakistan, and that upper-class Muslim families often sent their children to Catholic schools because of their high academic quality. But there was no parallel history of Protestant missions, and I had the vague, distasteful impression that the few Christian charities in the region were connected to evangelical sects. As a liberal Methodist, I was spiritually homeless in a society where all available religions were formal, conservative, and ridden with taboos.

Then one day, in a completely unexpected corner of Pakistan, I found a first connection to my faith. It was in a shelter for abused women in Rawalpindi, where I was conducting some interviews for my story on Zahida Perveen. Up a narrow flight of stairs was the attic, a carpeted room with barred windows, through which a soft afternoon light filtered. There, huddled together on a mattress, were a woman and her five children. She was an Afghan refugee named Fawzia who had run away from an abusive husband, taking her two teenaged sons and three younger daughters. The children were eager, bright, and bored to death in the attic, but their mother was too nervous to let them leave. We quickly became friends, and on

A member of the Taliban militia guards the door to the National Museum in Kabul, Afghanistan, in March 2001. The museum was sealed for years by the Taliban regime, which regarded many objects in its historical collection as un-Islamic.

A young girl and her older female relatives wait in line for food in Kabul in 2002. Even after the fall of the extremist Taliban regime, many Afghan women continued to wear full veils in public, largely because of tradition.

A widow begs outside a Hindu temple in the Indian state of Tamil Nadu in 1999

A devout Hindu woman prays at a festival in New Delhi, India, in the fall of 1998, where effigies of the goddess Dirga were paraded to the Yamuna River and then toppled into the water.

A Hindu pilgrim sits serenely in a densely packed crowd at the Maha Kumbh Mela, a mammoth Hindu festival that attracted millions of devotees to the confluence of the sacred Ganges and Yamuna rivers in 2001.

A woman and her family in rural Gujarat State in northeast India feed bread to their cow in 2001, days after a massive earthquake struck the region, leaving thousands of people crushed to death in village huts and urban buildings.

A temporary pontoon bridge crosses the Ganges River, where it was constructed to accommodate millions of Hindu pilgrims who thronged a tent city near Allahabad, India, for the Maha Kumbh Mela festival in 2001.

The Pandey family in New Delhi; Ashok, his wife Asha, and Ravi, 4. The Pandeys, a family of Hindus from Uttar Pradesh State, taught me a great deal about their religion and society, especially during a trip we took to baptize Ravi in the Ganges.

A woman begs at a Hindu temple in southern India, lighting incense and seeking alms.

A Kashmiri Muslim man bows his head in spiritual contemplation outside a shrine in Srinagar, the summer capital of Indian Kashmir.

A woman and her child wait at a refugee camp in Kashmir, India, in the spring of 1999, during the ten-week conflict in the nearby Kargil Mountains between Indian security forces and Pakistan-based guerrillas.

A family of Kashmiri Muslims sits disconsolately with their burned belongings in the fall of 1999. Their village, Khargam, was allegedly torched by Indian troops in retaliation for an assault by Muslim separatist guerrillas.

An Afghan refugee peers through a window in a waiting room at the Khyber Pass checkpoint at the Pakistan-Afghan border. Since the 1980s, Pakistan has accepted several million refugees fleeing war and drought in Afghanistan.

A derelict man, probably addicted to drugs, sleeps in the doorway of a shoestore in the old walled section of Lahore, Pakistan. The maze of alleys and shops is also a haven for addicts and crime.

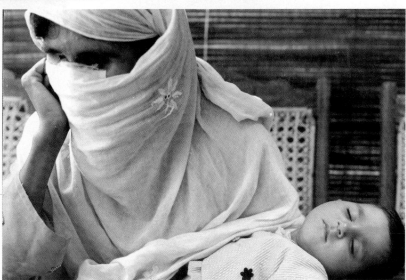

Zahida Perveen, a Pakistani woman whose eyes and nose were gouged out by her jealous husband, waits outside a courthouse during his trial for assault in May 2000. Thousands of women are maimed or killed in "honor crimes" in South Asia each year.

An elderly woman with her grandson in a remote village in central Nepal in 2001. The village is in a region controlled by communist rebels who bring both social services and political terror to neglected areas.

A group of apprentice Buddhist monks in an ethnic Sinhalese village in Sri Lanka that was attacked in 2001 by the Tamil Tigers, a secretive guerrilla army that seeks a separate homeland for the Tamil ethnic minority.

Two students at an Islamic academy in Peshawar, Pakistan, during a street demonstration in the fall of 2001. Its leaders called for U.S. forces to leave Afghanistan and proclaimed Osama bin Laden, depicted here in a religious newspaper, an Islamic hero.

A girl wearing a traditional Afghan veil shops in a vegetable bazaar in Peshawar, an ancient city in Pakistan near the Afghan border where Afghan customs have long prevailed.

A bride at her wedding in Kabul, Afghanistan in 2002, one year after the collapse of the Taliban regime. Afghan brides wear modern gowns but all music and dancing at weddings is strictly segregated into male and female sections.

An Afghan boy in Jalalabad, a prosperous but deeply traditional city in eastern Afghanistan. Many school-aged boys there work driving donkey carts, ginning cotton, and performing other hard labor.

Afghan refugee children wait for food handouts in the Shamshatoo Refugee Camp in northwestern Pakistan in the summer of 2001. Thousands of refugees fled across the border that year from drought and fighting between Taliban and opposition forces.

An Afghan refugee woman with her baby signs up for
food rations at Shamshatoo Refugee Camp in northwest Pakistan in the summer of 2001.

An old woman and her grandson living in abandoned ruins in Kabul,
Afghanistan, in the fall of 2002. Thousands of families poured into Kabul
after the collapse of the Taliban, many finding only primitive shelter in the
war-ruined city.

An Afghan refugee in northwest Pakistan holds an old Afghan identity card of himself, wearing a traditional pakul cap, from the days of the armed anti-Soviet resistence in the 1980s.

An Afghan boy at a parade in Kabul in the summer of 2002 holds photographs of Afghan fighters killed in the armed resistence to Soviet occupation during the 1980s.

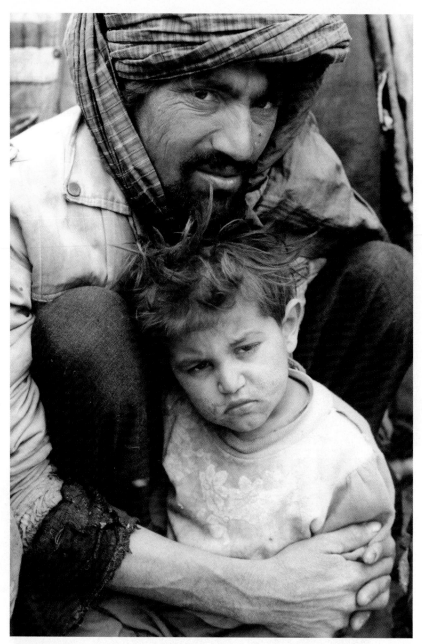

An Afghan man holds his son outside their tent in a sand-swept refugee camp near the southern border with Pakistan. They are ethnic Pashtuns who fled from persecution in northern Afghanistan by ethnic Tajik and Uzbek militias.

weekends I began bringing them books to practice their English. After a few visits, they unlocked a metal trunk and shyly showed me another book they kept carefully hidden. To my astonishment, it was a Bible.

In Afghan society, converting to Christianity was anathema; under Taliban rule it was also a capital crime. Fawzia had fled a repressive regime, a violent marriage, and a traditional religious culture that sided with men like her husband. She was a pariah who could never return home, and she was pinning her children's future hopes on a religion to which she had only recently been introduced. When I asked her why, her reasoning was simplistic but unassailable. "What did Islam ever give me but cruelty?" she said to me one day when we were sitting in the attic. "I like Christianity because it always talks about love."

Still, I was skeptical of conversions, and suspicious of converters. When the family introduced me to Cindy, a young Protestant missionary from Indiana who had been teaching them English and Bible studies, we were instantly wary of each other. I smelled fundamentalism; she smelled sensationalism. I was always asking questions and taking notes; she was always praising God and thanking Jesus. It occurred to me that we were both using these vulnerable refugees; in my case to sell newspapers, in her case to save souls. But we both cared about them too, and we enjoyed plotting ways to sneak them out of their cloister for picnics in the hillside parks overlooking Islamabad.

The family had applied for asylum in the United States, but after months of hiding in the shelter, there was still no word on their case. The children looked forward to our outings, to a few hours of freedom when they could breathe fresh air and pretend to be normal. Sometimes, as we chugged up the Margalla Hills road in Cindy's van, she would start singing their favorite hymn, "He's Got the Whole World in His Hands," and the children would join in, giggling at the words they could not yet pronounce.

But Fawzia, often depressed and teary when I saw her in the shelter, was also terrified of being seen in public. She never dared go shopping, and whenever the children went out with us, she made the boys wear dark glasses and the girls cover carefully with scarves. On the night she had run away from her husband, he had tried to strangle her with a rope. Despite all her precautions, Fawzia was convinced he would track them down through the large and incestuous Afghan refugee network in Pakistan, which included many Taliban sympathizers. "If he finds us, he will kill us all," she predicted with grave certainty.

Ironically, church was the last place Fawzia could have felt safe; her exploration of Christianity was perforce a clandestine, furtive one. But I knew Cindy attended Sunday services somewhere in Islamabad, and one day she asked me if I'd like to go with her. I was feeling especially lonely and far from my roots, so I agreed. To my surprise, we pulled up in front of a plain brick building, on the same quiet street as the American embassy, which I had driven by dozens of times. It was called Protestant International Church.

Inside, the sanctuary was painted white, with rows of folding metal chairs and an old piano in one corner. There were perhaps fifty people gathered there; some European, some Pakistani, some Asian. As I sat with closed eyes, listening to the familiar liturgy and the chords of familiar hymns, I felt my muscles relaxing, my mind wandering, my resistance yielding. I felt secure and serene, and I wished Fawzia could feel it too.

After that morning, whenever I happened to be in Islamabad on a Sunday, I attended the ten o'clock service. Sometimes the preaching was a bit too zealous for my taste, and some of my favorite psalms and hymns rang with a new, militant fervor that seemed to echo the fiery sermons ringing from fanatical mosques in Peshawar and Karachi and Lahore. But most of the congregation members seemed kind, tolerant, and well-intentioned. They taught English to refugees, they distributed food to the poor. They had Muslim friends as well as Christian, and they had chosen to live in an impoverished country where they thought they could do good.

The only church member I came to know well was Cindy, and in time we overcame our mutual reserve and developed a strong friendship. Sometimes we were invited to Sunday lunch and the home of the pastor and his wife, and before the meal everyone would join hands and give thanks. At one luncheon, I mentioned I was about to leave for another trip into Taliban-ruled Afghanistan, and someone offered a prayer for my safety. I blushed and shrank into my chair, but I was secretly touched. This congregation was the only true sanctuary I had found in South Asia, and it was the only place that reminded me of home.

My other spiritual retreat was Fawzia's attic: a secret carpeted room where I was always welcomed with unabashed joy, where I too could hide from the world. Whenever I returned to Islamabad from another lonely reporting trip, it was the first place I headed. The children gave me crayon drawings of lambs and crèches from Bible coloring books, and I taped them to my bedroom walls back in New Delhi. I needed this little refugee family as much as they needed me. I knew they were desperate to leave the shelter and escape from Pakistan, but I didn't want to lose them.

In the summer of 2001, a form letter arrived from the United Nations refugee agency. It said the family's asylum application had been rejected with a check mark in a box that said they did not "meet the criteria." There was no further explanation. Fawzia was devastated, but she was also tired of being afraid. Resolved to rebuild a normal life, she moved into a tiny rented house, enrolled the kids in school and found a job as a housemaid. I was traveling a great deal at that time and lost touch with the family for several months. They had no telephone, so the next time I returned to Islamabad I drove to their house unannounced.

I found Fawzia and the four younger children sitting in the front room, looking grave and frightened. Then the oldest boy came out of the bedroom. There were bloodstains on his shirt and bruises on his arms. One week before, the family told me, had been kidnapped at gunpoint by a group of men while he was shopping in a market. He recognized several of them as his father's relatives. They drove him to Peshawar, tied him up in a barn, burned him with cigarettes and questioned him for hours. His frantic family back in Islamabad had no idea where he was.

"They kept asking me where my mother was, and where we had gotten the book," the boy recounted. His captors were talking about the Bible. "They were wearing beards and turbans. They said I had become an infidel and deserved to be hanged. They said they would kill me if I did not tell where my mother was. I was very scared and screaming in pain, but I kept saying I didn't know anything and praying that God would show me a way to escape."

Somehow, the boy slipped away at night when his guard fell asleep and managed to board a bus heading back to Islamabad. By the time I happened to arrive the next day, Cindy had already taken him to a hospital and helped the family write a letter to the UN refugee agency, asking that their asylum case be reopened. In the anxious days that followed, she kept reassuring Fawzia and the children that God worked in mysterious ways, that the boy's ordeal was part of His plan. I was far more pessimistic; I knew that thousands of Afghans had filed asylum claims, that some had concocted elaborate horror tales to strengthen their cases, and that jaded bureaucrats might simply not believe the boy's story.

I should have had more faith. Barely two weeks later, a letter arrived saying their asylum application had been accepted. And three months after that, Cindy and I drove the family to the Islamabad airport, where a man from the UN office was waiting with six passports and six tickets to Los Angeles. The boys were wearing new jeans and sneakers; the girls' long hair had been bobbed. We exchanged tearful hugs and promised to keep in touch, but I knew I was probably seeing them for the last time. Fawzia trembled a bit, but she smiled broadly as she pushed her brood through the metal detector. On the other side, she turned for a final wave, sweeping off her headscarf and stuffing it into her purse.

I never did meet Fawzia and her children again, though the boys occasionally sent me e-mails reporting that their grades were okay or their mother was learning to drive. But I often thought about our times together, reading in the shelter and munching chicken in the Margalla Hills. I thought about the love I had received from such an unexpected source, and about the fragments of grace that had filtered in through the windows of a sunny attic. Once, on the way to an interview, I happened to drive by the shelter, but it looked dark and silent. I felt a sharp pang of loneliness, and on the way back, I asked the driver to take another route.

Interlude

How strange it feels, and yet how familiar. Once more I am alone, wedged into a window seat, sleepless at dawn, floating between continents and commitments. Far below, civilizations rise and fall, forest fires rage and die out. A child cries and no one picks her up, a spindly burro totters along a road under a mountain of bricks, a man watches a shadow creep across a cell wall. These images touch me, but they cannot hold me. I jet in and out of other people's sealed fates, I devour their pain and transform it into prose and move on, clutching a passport from the most powerful nation on earth.

Once more I have adopted and abandoned, held out my arms and then pulled back. I always knew the moment would come for Fawzia and her family to leave their secret nest and take wing, and that our time together was more precious for it. I felt sorry for them and yet I envied them, for they were united by flesh and blood. In contrast, I remained an honorary aunt, an ephemeral presence, a temporary crutch on their permanent journey.

The pattern was not a new one in my life. In the 1990s, I "adopted" the family of the Salvadoran janitor who lived in Washington's Latino community. I spent months accompanying them on picnics and weddings and baptisms, doing homework with the kids, helping the parents cope with legal forms and bureaucracies. Once, I even flew with two of the girls back to visit their native village in El Salvador, an astonishing odyssey in which I learned a great deal about the moral murk of war and had the unforgettable experience of watching and hearing a pig being castrated.

But once their story was published and I moved on to a new assignment, I inevitably lost touch, visited less and less often, neglected to keep track of the children's birthdays, forgot phone numbers I had known by heart, learned belatedly of minor crises in school that once would have brought me running. Our lives, once tightly tangled, disentwined.

It happened again in Santiago, where I lived alone for many months, working on the book about Pinochet. I spent almost every Sunday afternoon in the parlor of a gracious, erudite diplomat and his wife, sipping tea and nibbling cake and discussing politics, but mostly feeling at home. Then one day I finished my research and left the country. We corresponded for a while, and once we met briefly in Vienna, where they were posted after the return of democracy. But then the man's wife died, and he retired, and we lost touch. I have no idea if he is still alive, but I can still close my eyes and feel the cozy welcome of his parlor, and I hope he knew how much it meant to me.

In Haiti, I once had a close friend named Renal, a tailor and community activist in the largest slum in Port-au-Prince. Through his eyes, during many visits, I learned about the suffering and stoicism of ordinary Haitians, their dreams and disillusions. Partly thanks to him, I became deeply attached to Haiti for nearly a decade. Its extremes of beauty and cruelty were overpowering; its people were astoundingly resilient amid crushing poverty. After my last assignment there in 1994, I missed Haiti greatly, and I was thrilled when Renal wrote and asked me to become his new baby's godmother.

Just after New Year's in 1998, I flew to Port-au-Prince to attend the baptism, carrying a frilly white baby dress from J.C. Penney. It was a glorious day, a simple ceremony that affirmed life in a country far too accustomed to death, where 86 babies out of every 1,000 died before their first birthday. Being part of it was a way to cement the bonds of a long-distance friendship, to give one child an edge in a precarious existence, to make a small personal investment in a forsaken place. When my friend Renal handed me his daughter, he gave a small formal bow and said, "Now she is yours, too."

But like so many things in Haiti, the marriage crumbled and the baby's mother moved away. I had promised to send schoolbooks and start a savings account, but I was no longer confident they would end up in the right place. After a while there were no more letters, and once my sights shifted to South Asia I lost touch with the family completely. The vows we made that morning, to protect and uphold a child with God's blessing, quickly came to naught.

When I think of those families now, I feel deep gratitude and deep regret. Both the gift of knowing them, and the pain of losing them, came to me only because I was a lonely traveler. I know the value of the support and sanctuary they gave me, but I am less sure of the value of the fleeting attention and fame I gave them. In large measure, the energy and passion I poured into these temporary families was a substitute for something else, something I was always in too much of a hurry to look for closer to home.

Years ago, when I was first heading overseas, an older journalist warned me not to go. "Being a foreign correspondent means catching planes with no one to see you off, and landing in airports with no one to welcome you," he said. "Are you sure that's what you want?" My friend was right. Time after time, over the last twenty years, I have landed in a strange place with no one to meet me, only instinct to guide me, and a natural disaster or political crisis to deconstruct by midnight. It is the truest essence of what a foreign correspondent does, the highest use of our skills and senses: to start from scratch.

I am very good at starting from scratch. I am like a door-to-door salesman, a perennial barfly. I can talk my way into private offices and "do not enter" zones, ask weeping strangers intimate questions, turn chance encounters into debates that last all night and friendships that last for months. But I am a terrible failure at following through. I always seem unable to make the leap from romance to love, from glibness to wisdom, from frantically meeting deadlines to taking a deep breath and writing what I really mean. Is one quality the necessary cost of the other?

Sometimes, in an airport bar or a window seat somewhere over the Atlantic, suspended between worlds with time on my hands, I suddenly behold a panoramic view of the life I usually keep in neat, separate boxes, and I can make no sense of it. If I have had enough wine, I find myself weeping. I think of the people I have left behind and of those who await me, and somehow both parts of my life seem equally unreal and impermanent, both seem to reinforce my own ephemeral state rather than offering solid ground.

Still, I keep repeating the same patterns. I keep shying away from permanent commitments and making temporary new ones, keep adopting dogs and cats and other people's children. I am constantly lugging satchels of Meow Mix and mittens, vitamins and ABC books, to Kabul or Islamabad or Delhi. The simplest explanation is almost too obvious: Having no children of my own to nurture, I am constantly seeking substitutes; being a professional vagabond, I am constantly tossing out anchors to give meaning to my drift.

But there is another, more complicated issue behind the transient, sporadic nature of my efforts at making bonds that never seem to last. I myself was an adopted child, taken in as an infant by two people who loved me but did not look like me, who raised me in an atmosphere of care and privilege and purpose but knew nothing about my genealogy. In a profound sense that is no reflection on them, I do not know who I am, and I am not connected to anyone. I know the magic access codes and mannerisms of the American aristocracy, but I am much happier among the anonymous wretched of the earth.

Perhaps it is all of a piece: My peripatetic career in a profession where today's epiphany is tomorrow's trash, my magnetic attraction to people that suddenly deadens, my tendency to collect strays rather than pedigrees, my emotional attachments that end with the last line of a story, my intense serial involvements that never add up. Perhaps the qualities that make me a good journalist (a light traveler, an empathetic observer, a quick study, an emotional extruder) are exactly the same ones that make me a flawed person, that keep me from making the transition from hotel to home, from passion to commitment, from child to parent. Perhaps I am searching, in a thousand exotic places and faces, for clues to the puzzle of myself.

CHAPTER SIX

A Country Without Faces

*All statues that are present in different
parts of the country should be destroyed.
These idols have been shrines of infidels.
Even now they are respected, and maybe
in the future they will become shrines again.
The only true object of worship is God,
and all false gods should be destroyed . . .
so that in the future no one will
worship or respect them.*

—Decree issued by Taliban
authorities on 4th Zilhaj 1421
(February 26, 2001)

IT was late on a frozen winter night, and my
deadline was fast approaching. My fingers,
glued to the metal receiver of my satellite
phone, were too numb to feel. Behind me loomed the dark, heatless
stone terminal of the Kandahar airport. Ahead was the runway
where a hijacked Indian jetliner, with 155 hostages aboard, had sat
for the past three days, surrounded by gunmen, while Afghan and
Indian officials held tense negotiations over the passengers' release.

The airport was crammed with foreign journalists, exhausted and
numb with cold. Some were sneaking sips from miniature airline
whiskey bottles. This was high drama—a terrorist hijacking on Taliban turf—and many of us had cut short winter vacations to rush to
the spot. In thirty-six hours, I had air-hopped from Connecticut to
New York, Amsterdam, Delhi, Dubai, Peshawar, and Islamabad,
where Taliban diplomats, normally recalcitrant and vague, were issuing instant press visas. By the time I landed in Kandahar on a small
United Nations jet, my brain was functioning on pure adrenaline.

For hours, we squinted at the ghostly airliner at the far end of

135

the tarmac, waiting for a miracle. Photographers with telephoto lenses tried to make out the shapes and gestures of the masked gunmen who lounged on the tarmac. One tall man, presumably a Muslim militant, was incongruously dressed in plaid pants. We knew there were talks going on, that the hijackers had demanded the release of certain Kashmiri guerrillas from Indian prisons. The Taliban authorities were behaving with uncharacteristic hospitality, offering us blankets and coffee, acting as go-betweens with Indian officials, trying to appear statesmanlike.

There was no sound from the plane. The details of the passengers' invisible, eight-day ordeal inside the commandeered Indian Airlines jet would trickle out later, from survivors and crew members: the honeymooning couple saving scraps of food for each other, the nervous gunman smashing a passenger in the head, the terrible stench from the toilets. Those of us outside, kept far from the plane by Afghan soldiers, could only imagine, and wait.

Then suddenly, in a frenzy of afternoon activity, it was all over. The Indian foreign minister's plane was landing, a convoy of dark-glassed utility trucks was racing for the hijacked jet and then racing away again, the hostages were emerging from one plane and climbing into another. At a surreal joint news conference in the frozen terminal, Minister Jaswant Singh, the haughtiest of Indian Brahmins, was clapping the back of his black-turbaned Taliban counterpart, Mullah Wakil Muttawakil, and thanking "your excellence" for helping to resolve the crisis, before boarding his plane back to Delhi.

None of us knew exactly what had become of the hijackers and released Indian prisoners. There were rumors that they had been driven to the Pakistan border and set free, but no confirmation. For the moment, all we knew was that a miracle had indeed occurred: all the hostages except one had survived and were heading home.

The night grew colder and darker as I typed madly on the terminal floor, then rushed out to the tarmac to set up my telephone satellite and call the office. I was halfway through dictating my story when the editor on the other end interrupted and said, "Happy New Year!" I looked up, startled, and saw several journalists touching their styrofoam coffee cups together in a toast. In the frenzy of meeting my news deadline in a bleak and isolated corner of the world, I had nearly forgotten.

It was midnight, December 31, 1999. The millennium was turning, the *Post* was printing a special edition the next morning, and my story, "Afghan Hijack Drama Ends Peacefully," was going on the front page. For me, this was more thrilling than being invited to the most glamorous New Year's gala I could imagine. I was drinking cold coffee and wearing a snowsuit, but I might as well have been sipping champagne in a sequined gown. Instead of dancing until dawn, I rolled myself up in a blanket on the floor of a heatless, empty airline terminal. But I was far too excited to sleep, and I wanted the night to never end. It was the best New Year's Eve of my life.

∾

The eleventh-hour rescue of the hostages afforded the Taliban regime a rare moment of international praise and gratitude. Few people realized then that several of the freed prisoners and hijackers were notorious Islamic militants. No one could have predicted that two of them—Maulana Masood Azhar and Omar Sheikh—would later become involved in major terrorist attacks, including suicide bombings in Kashmir and the gruesome beheading of an American newspaper reporter in Karachi.

At the time, the Taliban's diplomatic role in resolving the crisis— and its surprisingly efficient arrangements for foreign press coverage—seemed to be sending a new, more accommodating signal to the world. For the first few months of the new year, officials in Kabul and other cities became more open to interviews, more willing to grant requests, more eager to display their accomplishments. They were still awkward and inscrutable, but they seemed to be trying harder.

One blustery, sand-swept day in March, I found myself standing in a patch of desert a few miles outside Kandahar City, surrounded by clouds of acrid smoke that billowed from a small mountain of burning burlap sacks and charred cans. A squad of sullen, baby-faced militiamen guarded the flaming pile, Kalashnikovs slung casually across their shoulders. A black-turbaned mullah chanted verses from the Koran, while a cluster of other Taliban officials, who had alighted from their luxury four-wheel-drive vehicles, listened soberly. The desert wind tugged at their robes and whipped the oily fire westward.

The ceremony was a formal, symbolic incineration of narcotic drugs—10,000 pounds of hashish and 800 pounds of heroin, to be exact—which had been confiscated by the Taliban. The authorities were clearly proud of themselves: UN anti-drug officials had been invited to witness the torching, and journalists were allowed to take photographs. I was the only reporter at the scene, though, since the authorities had fumbled in translating the date (by their solar calendar, the year was 1420, not 2000) and informed the press the ceremony would take place on a Thursday instead of a Tuesday.

The event was remarkable, and not only because I came away with my first-ever close-up photos of Afghan militiamen in their enormous turbans. It also marked the first time that Taliban leaders, who had resolutely defied world criticism of their severe religious agenda, used their absolute domestic power to do something aimed at pleasing the international community and winning its economic support.

For the farmers of Afghanistan, opium poppies and hashish were traditional, highly profitable crops; their ultimate destination and use was of no concern. Poppies grew in tough, dry soil that would support few other plants, and they had a guaranteed market through drug traffickers in Iran and Pakistan. Cultivation flourished in the lawless atmosphere of the civil war, and by the 1990s, Afghanistan was producing 75 percent of the world's heroin.

During the first four years of Taliban rule, poppy production continued to rise, with a record 4,600 metric tons of opium paste produced in 1999. Taliban officials also collected a hefty tax on opium production, one of the few sources of revenue in a decimated economy. Although Islam banned the use of intoxicants, and the Taliban severely punished alcohol users, they continued to draw a convenient distinction between consuming and producing drugs.

But in early 2000, at the persistent urging of UN anti-drug officials, who promised to help farmers grow substitute crops, the Taliban suddenly decided to curb the production of poppy. A national decree was issued that all farmers must immediately reduce their crop by one third, then gradually eliminate it. Officials also banned the collection of taxes on hashish and heroin. The decrees were greeted with enormous skepticism by foreign officials, but the Taliban seemed to mean what they said. It was only later that another motive emerged: soon after the ban, the price of opium had skyrocketed.

"This is not just symbolic. It is something we take very seriously," a Taliban anti-drug official told me during the desert torching ceremony. The Kandahar governor, Mohammed Ahsan Rahmani, went further, ordering a 50 percent crop cut in his province. "When a person is intoxicated, he cannot worship God, so it is completely forbidden under Islamic law," he said. "Poppy growing has continued because of our weak economy, but it is the policy of the Islamic State of Afghanistan to ultimately eradicate its cultivation and use."

Over the next two days, I drove across the desert to several parched villages where the UN had been trying to persuade farmers to grow apricots and almonds instead of poppy. The region was being choked to death by drought. Millions of sheep and goats had died, and herders wandered forlornly across rock-hard plains, searching for a few thorny bushes. In these villages, the UN had donated seeds, opened a health clinic and helped farmers dig irrigation wells. The local elders said they were grateful, but they admitted frankly that poppies were the only crop that made sense for them to grow.

"We don't like poppy, but we are poor, and we have to grow it to feed our families," said a twenty-four-year-old man I found hand-weeding his field full of new emerald poppy greens. His name was Mullah Janan; he was illiterate but he had studied the Koran enough to be made imam of the local mosque. He said poppies gave work to many people, especially at harvest time, when they lanced bulbs with curved knives to gather the sap that made opium paste. There was no need to cross the desert to sell it, he added, because men on horseback came to collect it. "Wheat gives us food, but poppy gives us money to buy tea and medicine and other things we need," Janan said. "Without it, the people would not survive."

Taliban authorities also made sporadic efforts to persuade foreign visitors that they were making "progress" on the volatile issue of rights and opportunities for girls and women. In every interview, they insisted that restrictions on women's activities were "temporary" and would be lifted once the country was peaceful and the government could afford to build work and school facilities that were segregated from men. I didn't believe them for a minute, but as with the anti-poppy decrees, I was impressed at their attempts to improve their image abroad.

In Kabul, I was invited to visit several mosques where young girls attended early-morning classes to memorize the Koran. The rooms were dark, the students sat on stone floors, and the teachers were stern graybeards who paced back and forth with long sticks in their hands, while tiny girls wearing white kerchiefs took turns standing up and nervously reciting Arabic verses. It was a poor substitute for math and spelling, I thought as I watched this grim scene from a corner, but it was better than being forced to stay home all day, sewing and sweeping and staring out the window.

In the fall of 2000, I was among a group of journalists who accompanied Sadako Ogata, the UN high commissioner for refugees, on a trip to the city of Herat. Ogata was a retired Japanese political scientist, a tiny woman of seventy-three with a determined personality. She was the highest-ranking UN official to visit Afghanistan since the Taliban had seized power, and her official mission was to promote the return of 2.6 million Afghan refugees from Iran and Pakistan, but she quickly steered the focus to women's rights.

On the first evening, Ogata was received at the palace of Gov. Khairullah Khairkhwa, who was known as a moderate by Taliban standards. For three hours she met with provincial authorities behind closed doors, while we slumped on a stone terrace outside. It was midnight when the meeting ended and we were ushered into the room. Ogata and Khairkhwa sat stiffly beside each other. Later, UN aides told us she had politely browbeaten her astonished hosts on the subject of women's rights, calling it the major obstacle to the return of refugees.

The governor was clearly on the defensive. He said there were several schools and colleges for girls in Herat, and he invited us to visit them. He said he had issued decrees banning such tribal customs as bartering virgins to resolve disputes and forcing widows to marry their brothers-in-law. He said he wanted to do more but was held back by conservative rural traditions in the region. Ogata smiled coolly. "Our talks were extremely frank," she said. "They talked about traditions, and I said, 'okay, you have tradition, but this is the twenty-first century. Come up with concrete results.'"

The next day, we were taken to visit the provincial nursing school, where about 120 young women were being allowed to study, and a privately supported "home school" for young children, which the Taliban allowed to operate under strict rules. The nursing students were nervous and cautious about answering our questions, but a few revealing comments managed to slip out.

"We are so few, and we have so many friends who want to be studying with us," said one girl of about nineteen. "Our greatest desire is to have a medical faculty, but there is none for women." She started to say more, but the class teacher, an elderly man in a turban who had been listening closely, suddenly rapped his knuckles on the wall. The girl fell silent, and we were ushered out of the classroom.

Having failed to impress their esteemed UN guest, local Taliban authorities made matters worse by arresting a European TV camera crew from our group while they were trying to film the scene outside Herat's historic central mosque. The team knew they were taking a risk, and they apparently made no effort to be subtle: two tall blond men in jeans, setting up their equipment on a boulevard filled with people and filming unhurriedly while a crowd gathered.

The rest of us were already at the Herat airport, waiting to fly back to Pakistan. We doubted the camera crew would be mistreated, but we were worried and exasperated, and several journalists refused to board the UN plane as long as their colleagues were detained. There were shouts and swearing. Our luggage was lined up on the runway, but no one budged. My heart was pounding and I had to force myself not to dash to the plane.

Then a walkie-talkie crackled, and the tension broke. The governor had ordered the crew released, and they were en route to the airport. As soon as they arrived, we all scrambled onto the plane as fast as we could, holding our breaths until we saw the ground zoom safely away. The farewell tea and cookies sat untouched in the airport VIP lounge, and a couple of turbaned officials waved forlornly from the tarmac. Within five minutes, I had fallen dead asleep.

In spite of everything, in spite of the drought and the war and the burqas and the religious police, Afghan refugees longed to go home. Many older ones in Pakistan had been away for twenty years; many younger ones had been born and raised in refugee camps. Yet even though their clans and language and religion straddled the border, they never felt entirely welcome. Officially, Pakistan offered them sanctuary and support; unofficially it blamed them for a host of social ills and kept them in legal limbo.

The UNHCR also wanted the Afghans to return, to relieve the burden on their host countries and foment a spirit of rebuilding in their native land. The agency could not force them back, but it could offer modest incentives: three sacks of wheat, a blue plastic tent and $100 in cash awaited each family once it crossed the Afghan border. Taliban authorities had no objections; they were eager to prove that the country was now stable enough to accept them, and they promised a secure if far from luxurious welcome to any Afghan who accepted their conservative Islamic creed.

And so it happened that I found myself, one scorching hot and dusty day in the summer of 2000, bumping along in a taxi behind a brightly painted, hopelessly overloaded cargo truck as it crept down a nearly-invisible desert track toward a dust-colored Afghan village called Chinar. The truck was piled with bundles of bedding, metal trunks, sacks of wheat, several tethered chickens and an extended family of twenty-four exhausted people.

Their journey had begun three days before in Haripur, a rural area in northwest Pakistan that was home to thousands of Afghan families. More than a hundred of those families had signed up to join a convoy of twenty-eight trucks that would carry them, their animals and their worldly goods some 250 miles: past Peshawar and across the Khyber Pass, stopping in Jalalabad to collect their wheat and money, following the main highway toward Kabul and then fanning out onto dirt tracks that led back to their native villages.

I had arranged with UN officials to follow the convoy from start to finish, but that proved more daunting than I had imagined. Three times I drove from Islamabad to Haripur, only to find the departure repeatedly delayed. Each family had to be interviewed by UN workers, and their homes inspected, to make sure they were genuine returnees, not opportunists planning to pocket the cash, sell the wheat and scurry back to Pakistan. Leaving a roofbeam in place or a teapot behind could signal that the departure was temporary. Even after all the families were approved, not enough trucks could be found to ferry them, and the send-off was delayed one more day.

While I waited, I wandered through Haripur, ducking into huts surrounded by wheatfields, asking who was ready to go home and who wasn't. Some people were afraid of landmines exploding or armed conflict breaking out again; others said they wanted to make sure their daughters could go to school. Some said their villages had been destroyed by rockets during the civil war; others said the more recent drought had baked their fields as hard as granite.

What I did not find, however, was anyone who objected to the Taliban regime. After the first few conversations, I realized I had been wrong to assume that all Afghan refugees were like the educated, urbanized exiles I had met from Kabul and Herat. These were villagers from the same Pashtun ethnic group as the Taliban — conservative, traditional and devout. The women covered themselves with veils when they stepped outside their huts. The men had never been to school, and some did not want their daughters to be educated. It was not the Taliban these Afghans had fled, it was the ravages of war. Now, after years of bloodshed and upheaval, they hoped to go home to an orderly, peaceful Islamic state.

Shortly before dawn on June 9, the convoy finally got underway. There were 528 people on board twenty-eight trucks, including a farmer named Mohammedullah and his family. He was only thirty-six, but his face was as wizened as a man of sixty. He had been a teenager when Soviet rockets bombarded his village about an hour's drive southeast of Kabul, sending everyone fleeing in the middle of the night with only the clothes they were wearing. Now, after fifteen years in exile, he had decided to come home.

At noon, the precariously piled trucks crossed the Khyber Pass and were waved into Afghanistan after a cursory inspection of their papers. By dusk the families were lined up outside the UN office in Jalalabad for their money and wheat, some of which they confessed they would sell right away. I spent the night in a UN office; the families slept on their sacks in the trucks. The next morning the caravan chugged off again, swaying heavily. The heat rose, the dust swirled, the sun beat down on the travelers. Babies cried, and mothers tried to shelter them beneath pieces of cloth tied to poles.

By late afternoon, the truck carrying Mohammedullah's family had turned off the highway and was heading for Chinar. The dust was so thick I couldn't see the road ahead, but suddenly I heard dogs barking and boys shouting. The truck slowed and stopped. We had arrived at our destination. Children jumped off and women were handed down over the tailgate, clutching their veils around them. I shook the dust out of my hair and scarf and looked around. *There is nothing here*, I thought to myself — just a jumble of mud-colored walls and a cluster of dirt-streaked children. Nothing at all.

Several men began unloading sacks and trunks, but Mohammed-ullah reached into the cab of the truck and took out a leather book wrapped in faded blue cloth. On a hunch that it was a family trea-sure, I followed him as he carried it up a path to a mud house, still scarred and cracked from Soviet rockets. The house belonged to his brother-in-law, who had returned from Pakistan in an earlier con-voy. Several women and children peeped out from a curtained door, giggling.

The farmer unwrapped the book, kissed it and pressed it to his forehead. Then, standing in the dirt patio, he opened his Koran and began to read. "It says that at times a Muslim must leave his home and travel abroad to escape the rule of infidels," he said. "Now that time is over for us. Now we have a government that is on the side of the people and on the side of Islam. I have been gone fifteen years, but I have come back to rebuild my house and my garden and my country."

I was touched by this man and his faith, and I could only wish him well. There was neither water nor electricity in his village, no school or clinic. Most of the houses still lay in ruins and the rest were barely habitable, but his determination was firm. We were only an hour's drive from Kabul, but the repressive urban reign of the Tali-ban seemed utterly irrelevant here—and my own feelings of horror at the regime's excesses suddenly felt like misplaced Western bias.

After the truck was unloaded, the men gathered in the brother-in-law's front room for a meal. The women and children remained hidden, but I was invited, along with my translator, to join the men around a single, large metal bowl filled with potatoes and meat grease. I watched queasily for a few moments as everyone tore up pieces of bread and began eagerly sopping up the mush. After forcing down a few mouthfuls to be polite, I busied myself taking notes. Sev-eral men spoke worriedly of the difficulties ahead, but Mohammedul-lah said he was pleased to see someone had already put up a new mud-walled mosque.

"We had a good life here once. I never forgot my home and my country," he said after the meal was done, leaning back happily against the wall. He was eager to get to work plowing his long-aban-doned fields, perhaps planting some almond and apricot trees. "This is my soil and this is where I want to stay."

∞

The Taliban's sporadic efforts to win international approval—whether by welcoming refugees, reducing poppy cultivation or opening a few girls' schools—never amounted to much. They had few friends, they were terrible at public relations, and their few laudable deeds were quickly lost amid a much longer list of oppressive ones. Most foreign criticism focused on harsh punishments and mandatory veils, but my two personal favorites among Taliban rules, for their sheer stupidity, were the bans against playing chess and raising songbirds as distractions from religious worship. What creature sings God's praises more gloriously than a lark?

The regime's other problem was Osama bin Laden. The renegade Islamic leader had been living in Afghanistan since 1996 as a guest of the Taliban, and after the 1998 suicide bombings of the U.S. embassies in Kenya and Tanzania, American officials began demanding that the Kabul regime turn him over for prosecution. The Taliban repeatedly refused, arguing that they could not betray a Muslim guest. As the impasse deepened, it increasingly dominated relations between Kabul and the rest of the world, forcing the regime deeper into defiant isolation.

Throughout 1999, American officials pressed the UN Security Council to squeeze the Taliban into giving up bin Laden. That November, the council froze all Taliban financial assets abroad and grounded Ariana, the national airline, from foreign flights. One year later, after intermittent negotiating overtures and pledges that both sides claimed were insincere, bin Laden was still at large. This time Washington pushed through harsher, more sweeping UN sanctions, imposing a lopsided arms embargo that applied to the Taliban but not to their armed domestic opponents, the Northern Alliance.

Some Afghans in Kabul, struggling through another harsh winter and a third year of severe drought, admitted privately that they wished bin Laden would leave the country and spare them further suffering. But the mounting foreign pressure only hardened the Taliban's stance. Bin Laden was an honored guest, officials said over and over; both Afghan and Islamic tradition demanded that he be shown hospitality and shelter. As a government, the Taliban had few resources but enormous pride. Bin Laden had helped bankroll the anti-Soviet jihad, trained Taliban fighters, and commissioned the construction of new mosques. To surrender him to a Western adversary would be an unthinkable humiliation.

After the first set of sanctions was imposed, I was granted an interview with the foreign minister, Mullah Muttawakil. We sat in his official receiving room, a once-ornate chamber with threadbare carpets and shabby brocade furniture. The walls were hung with oil paintings of landscapes—snow-capped crags and a dark, brooding forest scene that made me think of Gaspar Friedrich. They had been substituted for portraits of Afghan leaders, in keeping with the Taliban's belief that all human images were idolatrous.

Outside, in an untended formal garden, rosebushes drooped in the midwinter frost. In the streets beyond, the Afghan capital was freezing. Ragged children scavenged for firewood, and men lined up at dawn for free bread at UN-sponsored bakeries. At home, coughing families huddled around tables covered by blankets, with a metal bucket of hot coals placed underneath. Muttawakil spoke softly and looked down as he answered my questions.

"The United States wants us to tie Osama bin Laden's hands and send him to them as a gift. We have offered to have him tried here, or to have other Muslim countries judge him. But how can we give them a human being as a gift, especially when his crime has not been proven?" he protested. The minister said he believed Washington had singled out bin Laden as a new Islamic demon to replace Saddam Hussein and Muammar Qaddafi. But in the Muslim world, he said, "the United States has made him into a big hero."

As for the sanctions, Muttawakil added, the United States was trying to destroy Afghanistan "with missiles and hunger," but it was bound to fail because Allah "hears the prayers of the innocent and defends those who are trampled upon." This was the same chilling, rote refrain I had heard from other Taliban officials: the world might turn against them, but God would provide.

Despite the Taliban's assertions of divine deliverance, many UN aid officials who worked in Afghanistan were extremely concerned that the sanctions would harm the struggling populace more than the regime. They also feared a backlash from the public, even though UN programs fed hundreds of thousands of Afghans, sponsored polio vaccine campaigns, and operated home schools for girls. How could people be expected to distinguish between UN agencies that fed them and others that were trying to asphyxiate them?

Immediately after the first sanctions were imposed, angry crowds demonstrated outside UN offices in six Afghan cities, throwing stones or setting fires. The UN withdrew its foreign staff members several times from the country, resuming operations only after Taliban authorities promised to provide better protection. But relations remained tense, and a new source of friction began to threaten foreign aid programs and services: the regime's puritanical priority of keeping women separate from men.

With Afghan women barred from most employment, foreign nonprofits had become one of their few available sources of income, skill-building, and socializing. The Taliban tolerated this at first, but over time they began to impose ever-more-rigid restrictions and ever-more-cumbersome logistical barriers to prevent men from coming in contact with female coworkers or clients. In the spring of 2001, Taliban religious police raided an Italian-sponsored hospital after hearing reports that male and female staff members were mingling in the cafeteria, and the hospital was shut down in protest.

Meanwhile, a popular program of low-cost bakeries operated by the World Food Program came under a sustained Taliban attack. The bakeries, operated in Kabul and several other cities, were a multi-level hearth for Afghan women. They fed tens of thousands of families headed by war widows. They provided baking jobs for hundreds of widows and village refugee women with no skills, and office jobs for younger educated women with no other opportunities.

At a time when most Afghan women were forced to remain at home, idle, isolated, and often depressed, each WFP bakery was a warm, chatty refuge. I visited several of them and was cheerily welcomed by a dozen women with flushed faces, flour-dusted clothes, and heat-reddened palms, working around open, wood-fed ovens. As they pounded dough balls and slapped them against the hot mud walls, the women made jokes, talked about their children's illnesses, and reminisced about pre-war life. Outside, a Taliban guard often stood vigil to make sure no men entered.

In a way, though, the bakery program worked too well, and Taliban authorities became suspicious. When WFP officials announced they planned to conduct a household survey to check on complaints of fraud in the program, especially ration-card selling, the regime found an excuse to crack down on its operations.

First the authorities forbade men from interviewing women, so the agency hired 700 Afghan women to survey the housewives. Then, in a devastating blow for international efforts to keep at least a few women occupied and earning income, the regime suddenly banned all Afghan women from working for foreign aid organizations. Officials said the WFP should bring in women from abroad to conduct their survey. The UN agency refused, protesting that this was both impractical and unfair, and the bread project was suspended for months while the negotiations stalled.

At the same time, Taliban authorities issued an edict requiring all aid workers from other countries, whatever their religion, to abide by strict Islamic rules on personal conduct. They banned foreign women from driving vehicles and required all ex-patriates to sign contracts agreeing not to drink alcohol, eat pork, engage in unmarried sex, or meet Afghan women.

The repressive measures on foreign assistance programs, which seemed self-destructive on the surface, were a direct response to an escalating series of punitive steps taken by U.S. and other Western governments, including the forced closure of Taliban diplomatic offices in New York as well as the UN sanctions. The more isolated the authorities became, the more defiantly they lashed out at the only foreign targets within their reach. The more they were punished by the secular "infidel" world, the more obsessively they focused on their narrow religious agenda, turning ever more inward and backward.

Beyond the official crackdown, foreign aid workers complained that they were being harassed by Arab fighters, the freelance Islamic militant "guests" who lived in cities like Kabul, Jalalabad, and Kandahar. Arab money and support had long been crucial to the Taliban's success, Arab religious influence in Pakistan's madrassahs had formed the basis for Taliban theology, and Arab fighters by the thousands had joined the Afghan militia. For the most part, though, the Arabs remained segregated in their own compounds and villages, uncomfortable and unwelcome among local Afghans.

In Kabul they seemed to live more openly and freely, eating in local restaurants and staying in middle-class homes that were sometimes located on the same streets as foreign agency compounds and guest houses. One male UN employee complained that when he went jogging in the morning, a group of Arab neighbors in a utility truck tried to run him down several times. Several foreign women complained that when they passed a group of Arabs on the street, one would make a throat-slitting motion and leer at them.

My own encounters with Arabs in Kabul were few but hostile, and one was unforgettably chilling. I was browsing in an antique shop one morning, and I sensed the boy behind the counter suddenly stiffen. I turned around, and a large, grizzled, heavily-armed man stood in the doorway. He inspected several antique daggers, turning them over and peering at the sharp blades. Unable to resist, I nudged my interpreter to ask where he was from.

"Iraq," the man answered. His hair was wild and matted, his eyes were bloodshot, and his manner was nervous, like an addict or a thief. "The Americans killed my mother and my brother. Now I am here to kill them." I told him I was an American, and he guffawed, keeping his hands on his rifle. "I guess I won't kill you," he said, snickering at his joke. I laughed too, but the hairs on my neck were standing up, and the boy behind the counter had shrunk into a corner. When the Iraqi gunman turned and left, we all exhaled in relief.

∾

Whenever I needed a respite from the relentless tension of being a Taliban "guest," I ducked into another antique shop on Chicken Street, where a man named Ahmed offered me green tea in cracked Chinese porcelain cups. He spoke a little English, and we would sit on his carpet for a while, chatting about Afghan history. I was always the only customer, and occasionally I bought something from one of his dusty shelves—a small lapis lazuli box, or a carved animal figure—although I always had great difficulty persuading him to let me pay.

One day, Ahmed said he had something special to show me. He shut the door and turned around the sign to "closed," vanished into the back of the shop and re-emerged with a dusty leather album. Carefully, he pulled out several paper packets and opened the contents. They were postcards, faded photographs and old drawings that depicted long-dead kings and generals in their full formal regalia.

I was momentarily stunned. Here were the most important figures of Afghanistan's history, its tyrants and heroes, its conquerors and defenders. And yet here was my friend Ahmed, as sly and nervous as if he were offering me illegal hashish pipes or erotic tribal statuettes. "We have to be very careful of the religious police, you know," he said with an apologetic shrug.

Afghanistan, under the Taliban, had become a country without faces. Like the contraband postcards and the portraits removed from the Foreign Ministry, even dignified historic countenances were deemed sinful to behold. Postage stamps showed nature scenes, and the official currency featured engravings of mosques and shrines. In the bazaars, open-air stalls were hung with posters of Mecca's holy site in a hundred different angles and styles, but there was not a single human face. In the official newspapers, articles were accompanied by maps or photographs of fruit stands or Islamic artifacts.

The regime took its cue from the most revered Islamic figure of all, the Prophet Mohammed, whose face was described but never depicted in Muslim literature. In its zeal to create the perfect Muslim society and render complete deference to God, the Taliban movement sought to erase all temptations of human narcissism and idolatry and replace them with self-effacing humility.

The Taliban's top religious leader, Mullah Mohammed Omar, set the supreme example of this policy. A reclusive village cleric, he was believed to have lost one eye in battle, but only one or two photographs of him existed, he almost never appeared in public, and virtually no one in the country had ever seen his face. There were no published photographs of any other officials, no commissioned portraits, no record of what they looked like. The Taliban ruled invisibly, died in battle anonymously, left no legacy of heroic monuments or memoirs. They were secretive and shy, but they were also remarkably faithful to a concept of divine power that brooked no human rivals.

Most photos of faces were not permitted, and family portraits were confiscated from people's homes, forcing them to hide wedding albums, children's snapshots and even mementos of dead parents. For passports and official ID cards, Taliban rules dictated that headshots be no larger than a postage stamp, men must pose in beards and turbans, and women must show only their eyes. Modern cameras were banned, but wooden box cameras were set up outside certain ministries. Like magicians, their operators ducked under dark cloaks, swished bits of paper in chemicals and waved tiny, blurred images in the air to dry.

Once, when I was waiting at Kabul's airport, a Taliban policewoman entered the female waiting room and began searching everyone's purse. I had no idea what she was looking for, but finally she extracted a forbidden item and held it up with a grimace. It was a packet of snapshots showing several men and women posed in a group. The passenger, a middle-aged teacher, leaned over to me. "My brother," she murmured with a sigh of resignation. "My husband." The other waiting women smiled sympathetically but said nothing. The policewoman stuffed the photos into her own purse and wordlessly left the room.

The Taliban's ban on graven images extended to animals, living or dead. Inside the presidential palace, militiamen broke off the heads of marble fish in a fountain and scratched out the heads of peacocks in royal tapestries. The prohibition also applied to statues and artistic objects of the human figure, which the Taliban viewed as idolatrous. The smashing of statues and idols from other religions figured prominently in their version of Islamic history, and one legendary Afghan figure, the Sultan of Ghazni, was known as the "idol-breaker" for having decimated Hindu statuary during his military conquests of what is now northern India.

For centuries, Afghanistan was a crossroads of world culture. Explorers from Marco Polo to Alexander the Great passed through it. A dozen civilizations camped there for a century or two, leaving behind priceless relics for archeologists to unearth. The Kabul Museum, which opened in 1919, was renowned for its collection of statues and objects: carved Greek coins, landscaped Nooristani screens, miniature clay Buddhas, a bronze Hercules statue from the first century and Oriental goddess figurines from 3000 B.C.

The most renowned historic treasure, though, was a pair of giant Buddhas, 120 and 175 feet tall, carved into the sandstone cliffs of Bamiyan in north-central Afghanistan during the sixth and seventh centuries. Soon afterwards, Buddhism passed out of Afghanistan with the coming of Islam, but the majestic Buddhas remained an awe-inspiring sight for visitors well into the 1970s.

Upon seizing power, the Taliban sealed off the Kabul Museum, but the regime promised to cooperate with foreign agencies to restore and preserve the country's historic heritage. The Buddhas remained untouched. By early 2001, however, regime hardliners were pressing for full-scale destruction of non-Islamic icons. In early February, a dozen Taliban officials entered the Kabul Museum and smashed fifty-four objects. Three weeks later, authorities issued a decree ordering that all statues throughout country must be destroyed. "Only Allah deserves to be worshipped," the decree stated. "These statues have been used as idols by infidels before. . . . They could become idols again."

As it became clear that the Taliban intended to destroy the Bami-yan Buddhas, governments and organizations across the world expressed outrage and begged the regime to reconsider. Officials from Iran, Pakistan, Egypt, and other Muslim countries joined in, asserting that such statues inflicted no harm on Islam. But the Taliban, stung by the new UN sanctions, refused to budge. In early March, military demolition teams assembled with hammers, axes, assault rifles, and explosive charges. No one was allowed to observe, but officials in Kabul issued brisk progress reports as the massive carvings were blasted away. After ten days, they announced that the deed was finally done.

I spent that entire time in Kabul with a dozen other foreign journalists, begging for permission to travel to Bamiyan. Every day officials promised to arrange a trip, but every day it was postponed. Minister Muttawakil met with us several times, dutifully defending the attack, but we sensed that privately he was embarrassed. When the BBC reported that ordinary Afghans were distressed by the demolition, its correspondent, Kate Clark, was instantly deported. One man I spoke to, a former tour guide, expressed sadness and shame. The Buddhas "showed that Afghanistan was on the highway of civilization," he said. "Now our own government is destroying our heritage."

At the time, Taliban officials pointed out angrily that the world was far more concerned about the Buddhas than about the drought and destitution that afflicted millions of Afghans. My own initial reaction was similar. For five years, the regime had treated its human subjects with cruelty and indifference. It had chopped off thieves' hands, stoned lovers to death, and put half the population under house arrest. And yet the world's civilized countries had largely limited their response to diplomatic ostracism. Suddenly, a huge burst of international outrage had erupted over an assault on objects that, as Information Minister Qudratullah Jamal noted dryly, were "only made of mud and stone."

With every new indignant quote I saw in the newswires, every pompous lament about the annihilation of Afghanistan's priceless heritage, I shook my head and wondered: *Isn't flesh and blood more important?* It wasn't until several years later, when the Taliban were gone, that I finally stood at the foot of the sandstone cliffs of Bamiyan, gazing up at what was left of the Buddhas. I thought about the extraordinary effort it had taken to carve them into solid rock, and I felt their enduring power as a symbol of faith. I realized then why the Taliban had seen these great stone figures as an insult to their God—and why the world had grieved so deeply at their loss.

The destruction of the Buddhas marked a fatal turning point for relations between the Taliban and the world—and also for any prospects of religious moderation within the regime itself. Like the crackdown on foreign charities whose help was desperately needed by the populace, the smashing of "idols" which the government had previously left unharmed signified the triumph of hardline, inward-looking Islamists over moderate, more worldly officials in a behind-the-scenes conflict that had been building for months.

Everything the Taliban did was cloaked in secrecy, but Afghans and foreigners who had regular contact with officials in Kabul said they had sensed that the struggle was intensifying and that the "pure" Islamists—generally found in the defense ministry, the judiciary, and the Virtue and Vice apparatus—were gaining ground over more moderate officials in the ministries of information, finance and foreign relations. As UN sanctions increasingly froze out the regime, the hardliners argued, there was no longer any reason to placate the world by preserving idolatrous objects or allowing women to work.

In another sign of their increasing religious intolerance and obliviousness to world opinion, the Taliban suddenly turned against the small communities of religious minorities, Afghan Hindus and Sikhs. These close-knit enclaves had existed for generations in Kabul, Jalalabad, and other cities, trading in cloth and spices from abroad and worshipping quietly at their temples. Their numbers had shrunk greatly during the Soviet conflict and civil war, and thousands had fled to India and elsewhere, but hundreds remained behind when the Taliban seized power and had coexisted peacefully with their rule.

In April, I visited several Sikh temples in Kabul and met their leaders. They were easy to spot because of their brightly colored turbans, but their strict behavioral code was similar to the Taliban's; both eschewed alcohol and tobacco, both kept their women veiled and apart from men; both worshipped from a single holy book. In

deference to the Taliban, they told me, they had put away all portraits of their gurus. In turn, they said, the Taliban respected their
views and left them alone. "We like Afghanistan," one temple leader
told me. "The Taliban don't bother us, and they have told us we can
worship according to our religion."

But in May 2001, while world outrage over the demolition of the
Buddhas was still fresh, the Taliban suddenly issued a religious de-
gree that ordered all non-Muslims to wear distinctive signs on their
clothing when appearing in public. The state news agency said this
was to protect groups such as Hindus and Sikhs from harm, but to
human rights groups and foreign governments it smacked of Nazism.
Critics immediately invoked the humiliation of European Jews in the
1940s, forced to wear yellow Stars of David on their sleeves. Officials in India, the homeland of Hinduism and its Sikh offshoot, de-
plored the order, calling it further evidence of the Taliban's ideological backwardness.

The Taliban's sudden harassment of Hindus seemed as inexplica-
ble and bizarre as their physical assault on the 1,500-year-old Buddhas. It was possible, as one Taliban diplomat insisted, that the religious elders in Kabul "did not know about the Star of David and the
Jews," and had no discriminatory intent. But coupled with the attack
on the Buddhas, it seemed the Taliban were trying to provoke conflict with religions that posed no threat to them, to humiliate the
country's few un-Islamic remnants in a frenzy of religious purifica-
tion.

To me, what was even more mystifying was the authorities' flat
rejection of the sober, dignified pleas to spare the Buddhas that came
from fellow Muslim leaders in Pakistan, Egypt, and the Gulf States.
According to the decree, the decision had been made by unnamed
senior Islamic clerics and judges. I decided to find out, if possible,
who they were and what their thinking was. The foreign ministry
wrote several helpful letters on my behalf, but I was turned away
from every door. After I waited several hours at the Supreme Court,
watching turbaned elders with long gray beards sign papers and vanish behind doors, an official came out and summarily dismissed me,
saying I should "listen to what was announced on the radio."

If the ministries were impenetrable, I thought, perhaps I could
find the answer in a more public forum of Taliban thought: the
mosques. I approached several in Kabul, and was finally received in

the office of the Pul-e-Khishti Mosque, a magnificent blue-domed building where Taliban officials often worshipped on Fridays. The imam, Maulvi Shujauddin Haddam, said he was happy to answer my questions. When I asked him about the destruction of the Buddhas, he expressed unabashed joy and relief, as if a deeply offensive sore had finally been cut away from society.

"We sacrificed 200,000 lives to install an Islamic government," he said. "Now that we have destroyed the idols, we hope it will bring the blessings of God on us." What about the views of other Muslim leaders, I asked, the clergymen who had come from Egypt and Pakistan to beg for the Buddhas to be saved? Didn't their opinions deserve respect? The imam waved my question away, his face showing obvious contempt. "We don't have to follow any other kind of Islam. The real Islam is only in Afghanistan now," he said. "The farther the international community gets from us, the more we are convinced of the truth of our religion."

I sat there in stunned silence, absorbing the implications. This was not humble, God-fearing devotion; this was the blind arrogance of utopians, the self-righteous hubris of the Khmer Rouge and the Shining Path. There was no way it could be sustained indefinitely, not even by force, in a country of 25 million people that was deliberately being cut off from the world. I thanked the imam politely and left, but a startling new thought was repeating itself in my head. *They're doomed. The Taliban are doomed.*

Interlude

Peshawar——It is a chilly evening in April. I am standing in the back of an open pickup truck, racing down from the Hindu Kush mountains of Afghanistan. Behind us the jagged hills are receding in the sunset, turning into a soft mauve blur. We have safely crossed the Khyber Pass into Pakistan, and the tension and isolation of working in Taliban territory are fading with every mile.

The road ahead is empty, and the driver is going much too fast for the sharp curves, but I don't care. The wind is whipping at my face and cotton scarf, and a stranger is standing beside me, a man I have just met who seems to share some of my own intense compulsions and haunted dreams. I have no idea what will happen next or where my next assignment will take me, but I am seized with such intoxicating joy and relief that is suddenly occurs to me, with stunning force and clarity, that I would be quite happy to die right now.

In the days and weeks after that first encounter, I shared a dozen extraordinary conversations with this kindred spirit, a Polish journalist my age who somehow survived communism and martial law with his compassion and idealism intact. Our lives had taken parallel tracks without ever touching, our epiphanies and yearnings and sacrifices had been the same. He told me about Africa and Eastern Europe and the Afghan civil war; I told him about Haiti and Chile and El Salvador.

We had both seen revolutions crumble, heroes become co-opted, poverty breed cruelty and power create sycophants and spies. We had both survived long nights of loneliness and fear and self-doubt. And yet we both still believed in a search for what was dignified and noble in human nature, in the power of the written word to move people, in the same gods that had inspired us twenty-five years before.

As inevitably happened, our paths diverged as abruptly as they had collided, the intense conversations dwindled to sporadic e-mails between continents and eventually stopped. The last time I saw my Polish friend was in a crowded hotel conference room in Kabul, in a scrum of cameras and wires and bodies scrambling to cover some event. We stared at each other through the crowd without speaking, months flashed by in a few seconds, and then he was gone.

What will always remain of the relationship, what no one can ever steal or edit or adulterate, is the memory of that exhilarating ride down from the Khyber Pass, two strangers talking a mile a minute as we braced ourselves in the back of a truck, leaving a bleak, oppressive winter behind and laughing into the spring wind ahead.

There was one essential difference between us, though. My friend went back to his home and family, perhaps a bit restless and nostalgic but essentially unchanged. I kept on going, mentally clinging to the back of that truck until I could leap onto the next one. Like most of the memorable moments I have experienced in my travels, this one involved someone I barely knew and would eventually lose.

Like most of my journeys, this one was over too quickly to acquire real meaning or fill lonely nights. I was always moving too fast to allow my memories to accumulate, always rushing my experiences into print instead of savoring them and learning from them, always writing for strangers who could erase me just by turning the page.

I have been a writer for more than three decades. I have written a million words, but what have they added up to, where have they gone? How often did they move a reader to laughter or anger or tears, or at least to put down the newspaper and stare into space for a moment, lost in thought? Maybe thirty times, in as many years, have I received a letter from a reader who was deeply touched or disturbed by something I wrote. Usually the people who bothered to write were the ones with petty or pedantic complaints, sometimes singling out a word or phrase to criticize from a long, carefully crafted tale I had slaved over for days.

When I think about it, the stories that have meant the most to me, and to readers, were the personal ones, the rare first-person columns I wrote about how it felt to turn thirty, or get married, or survive an earthquake, or watch my grandmother slowly dying in a nursing home. I was part of a profession whose members were relentlessly trained to keep ourselves out of the story, while readers were eager to know what we thought and felt, whether we reacted like human beings or robots when we confronted grief and gore and death.

Over the years, I have become so proficient at projecting dispassion that it frightens me, so accustomed to delivering a third-person version of history that sometimes I'm not sure what I think anymore. If I don't slow down, stop typing, switch off the programmed part of my brain and allow my thoughts to wander along unfamiliar paths — including the dark and bramble-filled ones I have assiduously avoided entering — I'm afraid the chance will be gone forever.

I am haunted by that thought, by the inevitable fading and forgetting of even the most powerful experiences, by what happens to memory when we die. I have met so many people who are refugees from memory; who never owned a photograph of their parents; whose homes and belongings and heirlooms and mementos were wantonly destroyed; who witnessed horrors or endured hardships they cannot bear to mention. It is my job to appropriate their memories, to coax them out of hiding and into the consciences of distant readers.

But what about the family tales I missed back home while prodding strangers for intimate details? Why did I never take the trouble to ask my own grandparents about their lives and times? When my parents are gone, who will keep their memories alive? Do I have the right to become their self-appointed curator, and what vicarious memories would they wish me to enshrine in these pages?

I think of my mother's father, a refined old gentleman from Boston who wore a mustache and a monocle, who smelled like pipe tobacco and sent me whimsical notes in the mail with drawings and stories of animals. I called him "grand-père," but I only saw him at Christmas and occasional family reunions, and he died before I was old enough to know him. But I know that my mother worshipped him, and that when she was a young girl, before the Depression had swept away so much, leaving behind the family's rose-patterned silver and iron-willed pride, he would promenade with her along Commonwealth Avenue and she would feel like a pampered princess. I also know that the worst experience of her life was the night he died of a heart attack, only a few hours away but alone, without his only child at his side, because the doctors had mistakenly reassured her he was out of danger.

I think of my father's father, a genteel Baltimorean from a family of lawyers and judges, named after a man who had saved his father's life from highway robbers. He was stern and old-fashioned, devoted to his wife but given to lecturing his sons on their grades and his grandchildren on their table manners. But I also remember the twinkle in his eye, the jaunty green bow tie he wore, and the joke he always told about Justice Holmes and Justice Brandeis, watching a cute girl walk by and "wishing we were seventy again." (I tried that one out on the Chief Justice of the Supreme Court in Kabul, who was not at all amused.) I remember Granddaddy standing in front of the fireplace, swaying with his eyes closed, and humming along to a scratchy recording of "Madame Butterfly." And I remember him at his wife's funeral, thirty years ago, clinging to his tiniest granddaughter for dear life.

Now that they are both gone, all I have left is their pictures to bring back the smell of Virginia tobacco and the melody of a Verdi aria, to preserve the fading legacy of a gentler, more upright generation. Robert Remington McCaffrey will always be there, with his waxed mustache and his foulard tie, in an old red leather frame on the bureau. William Pepper Constable will always be there, with his green bow tie and his faded red boating cap, hanging on the library wall.

How would I feel if an armed police squad suddenly stormed into the house and tore up those pictures, ranting about idolatry and graven images? What happens to a family, and to a society, when sentiment and memory and continuity are deliberately snatched away in the name of a higher, abstract belief? If there is nothing to inherit or pass on, does not the present become meaningless?

I may convince myself I have been living for moments, I may be a rootless and restless person by biology, profession and temperament, but without a history to cling to, without the faces of earlier generations to reflect upon, I think I would be truly lost. The Taliban may have thought they were glorifying God, but instead they stole a fundamental part of humanity, the right to remember the past, and that is what sealed their fate.

CHAPTER SEVEN

Tropic of Terror

A revolution is not a dinner party, or writing an essay,
Or painting a picture, or doing embroidery.
It cannot be so refined, so leisurely and gentle,
So temperate, kind, courteous, restrained, magnanimous.
A revolution is an insurrection, an act of violence
By which one class overthrows another.

—Mao Ze-Dong, 1927

THE highway meandered along the coast of Sri Lanka, through lush countryside that grew wilder and more beautiful by the hour. Monkeys scampered across the road. A herd of elephants grazed serenely in the distance. Further north, the pavement parted shimmering lagoons where egrets picked their way daintily among the reeds. Coconut palms and thatched huts lined the way, the breeze tasted salty, and we could catch glimpses of the sea—white surf rolling onto smooth white sand, fishermen hauling in a net, the azure mantle glittering beyond.

Our destination was Batticaloa, the scenic, seaside setting of a guerrilla war in paradise. Schoolgirls pedaled along on bicycles, holding up parasols. Leathery men sliced coconuts with machetes and offered the juice for sale with a straw and a smile. But every few blocks there was another army bunker, surrounded by sandbags and scrolls of razor wire. Every bus stop was a military checkpoint where passengers and their bags were searched.

And just inland, beyond the placid lagoons and swaying palms, lay Tiger Territory, a region controlled by a fanatical guerrilla army known as the Liberation Tigers of Tamil Eelam, or LTTE. The Tigers had built a parallel, "liberated" society in the villages and forests of northeast Sri Lanka, so fortified that no army patrol dared enter after dark. But despite seventeen years of fighting and tens of thou-

160

sands of deaths, the insurgents' mission—to create an independent homeland, or "Eelam," for the country's ethnic Tamil minority— remained an elusive dream.

At first I was stunned by the untouched beauty of Batticaloa. There was not a footprint or scrap of litter on the beach, not a hint of human investment in a waterfront as splendid as any I had ever beheld. War had stopped time and human progress dead, leaving only nature behind. I thought of other regions where I had covered vicious, protracted guerrilla wars: Guatemala, with its emerald high- lands and brilliant swirls of indigenous costume; Peru, with its mist- shrouded valleys and tile-roofed churches; Kashmir, with its lily-cov- ered lakes and alpine vistas. *It's really true,* I thought to myself. The cruelest conflicts do come to the loveliest places on earth.

It was January 2000, my first visit to Sri Lanka. I was there to chronicle the latest chapter in the endless conflict between the army and the LTTE. Hundreds of journalists had been there before me, and I was sure many more would come before the war ended. I needed to keep the story alive for faraway readers, to find new phrases and images that would give acute poignancy to a tragedy as chronic, and as grimly repetitious, as Kashmir's.

For years the LTTE, with perhaps 5,000 fighters, had relent- lessly harassed government forces ten times their size. Their weapons were mystique, mobility, and martyrdom. Led by a reclusive ideo- logue named Velupillai Prabakharan, the Tigers had built a disci- plined, youthful militia—including boys and girls as young as four- teen—who were conditioned to die for their cause. They fought ferociously and swallowed cyanide capsules if caught. The govern- ment's forces, in sorry contrast, were infamous for corruption and desertion. For one side, military service was a sinecure and an oppor- tunity for graft; for the other, it was a crusade.

The sensational signature of Prabakharan's army was the suicide bomb. LTTE cadres slipped into crowds at political rallies or air- ports, disguised as ordinary children. Then they detonated explosives strapped to their bodies, blowing themselves, their targets, and by- standers to shreds. One month before I arrived, a suicide bomber injured President Chandrika Kumaratunga, aged fifty-four, who was campaigning for re-election. The attacker, a man disguised in a wom- an's sari, reached out to embrace her at a rally and then blew himself up. The explosion left 14 people dead, 110 wounded, and Kumara-tunga nearly blind in one eye.

"These are the wounds of sheer, naked, and unadulterated ha-tred of man for man," the president declared three days later, appear-ing with her right eye heavily bandaged after winning a second term by 51 percent of the vote. "To all those who have ever doubted my resolve to lift the curse of hatred and death that has fallen upon our land, I offer the challenge to look into my face now."

At the time, this speech seemed a bit melodramatic to me, but the more I learned about Sri Lanka's tortured political history, the more it truly felt like a curse. This was one of the world's balmiest spots, a verdant island of 18 million with a democratic government, a high literacy rate, and enormous potential for tourism and trade. All the ingredients were there to transform Sri Lanka into another Hawaii or Singapore, except one.

The country's two major ethnic groups—the Buddhist Sinhalese majority and the Hindu Tamil minority—were consumed by mutual hatred. Their grievances were rooted in the colonial era, when the British had favored Tamils with jobs and educations. After indepen-dence in 1947, the tables slowly reversed, with the Sinhalese coming to dominate national life. Their dialect was made the national lan-guage in 1956, and many Tamils were relegated to second-class citi-zenship and menial labor in rice paddies and tea plantations. After the outbreak of anti-Tamil riots in the 1980s, the bitter divisions hardened further.

Yet the Sinhalese remained a "majority with a minority com-plex," as one analyst explained to me. Most members of the Sinhalese elite I met refused to acknowledge that any anti-Tamil discrimination existed; they quickly noted that the constitution protected minority rights and that Tamils were regularly elected to Parliament. They tended to view Tamil grievances as a result of caste and economic sour grapes, and to dismiss the Tigers as an isolated terrorist phe-nomenon, a military problem to be handled by the army.

After I had spent some time in Colombo, the capital, it was easy to see how this sense of denial could be so pervasive. The boulevards were lined with gleaming skyscrapers; the nightlife districts bustled with cafes and casinos; the ocean breezes blew. The Hilton Hotel, where I usually stayed, was a serene, disguised fortress built around an artificial pond of gliding carp and sunning turtles. Across a caged footbridge was a spa where I could jog in the gym or float in the pool for an hour before heading out—past the armed guards and anti-terrorist roadblocks—for another day of interviews about a civil war raging 150 miles away.

In the poorer Tamil districts, though, the war seemed palpably close. There was a permanent feeling of tension and sullen anger on the streets. Many city Tamils were refugees from the conflicted north, living in shabby rooming houses that were frequently raided by police. Emergency anti-terrorist provisions allowed the police—invariably of Sinhalese origin—to question and detain any Tamil and to search homes at any hour. Most Tamil men I met said they had been arrested at least once.

"Tamils come here for security, but their presence is seen as a threat to national security, so they are harassed," a human rights advocate told me. "There is a terrible fear psychosis. [Sinhalese] people live with the daily thought that anything can happen, an explosion, an attack. They used to look at every Tamil and see a garbage collector or a tea plantation worker. Now they look at every Tamil and see a suicide bomber."

Few Tamils would dare say so aloud, but many clearly felt the LTTE had given them a kind of self-respect. The Tigers' ruthlessness had inspired fear in a larger and more powerful ethnic group and made the world aware of the Tamils' plight. Yet even ordinary Tamils were afraid of the Tigers as well as the army, and despite the hostility they faced in Colombo, few dared risk returning north and becoming trapped in the armed conflict.

In a compound of rented rooms, where laundry was strung across the yard and children wailed from every curtained cubicle, I met Anton Singayaga, a laborer in his twenties. "I want to go home to my wife and children, but I am afraid," he told me. "If the army doesn't arrest me, the Tigers may think I am being too friendly to them, and they will threaten me too." His dream, he said, was to find a way to get to Europe or England, where many Tamils have relatives. "I have a passport, but no way to leave," he said. "All I can do is hope and wait."

One of the places I often visited in Colombo was a human rights agency called the Forum for Human Dignity, a rundown pair of rooms crammed with moldy files. The director, Maheswary Velautham, showed me dozens of court petitions she had filed on behalf of

Tamils looking for missing relatives, seeking the release of prisoners, or complaining of harassment. One client was a fifty-seven-year-old Tamil woman who had fled from the north. Tearful but poised as she sat in her tiny urban hut, she listed the grim highlights of her family history for me. Her home had been bombed by soldiers. Her oldest son had been shot dead by the army. Her second one had been tortured until he vomited blood. And three weeks ago, her youngest son had been picked up by the security forces and vanished.

Suddenly, as I sat in that steamy rented room, I was back in wintry Kashmir, listening to an old Muslim woman wail over the disappearance of her sons. Once more I was torn between pity and suspicion, asking myself the same questions: Were these boys guerrillas, innocent victims, or something in between? Was their mother telling the truth or playing a role in a larger, historic drama of competing lies, in which all Tamil or Kashmiri boys were potential terrorists and all Sinhalese or Indian forces were their persecutors? The terrain was different, but the game was depressingly familiar.

From the outside, the world of the Tamil Tigers seemed like that of the Taliban: a hermetic, utopian movement whose young disciples, impoverished and impressionable, were given a sense of order and belonging, a moral mission, a dream to kill and die for. But it was a difficult world to penetrate. The Sri Lankan military authorities did not permit foreigners to enter the conflict zone, and the Tiger leadership was notoriously reclusive.

Prabakharan, the movement's commander, had been hiding in the northern jungles of Sri Lanka for years, and he had emerged to meet the press only once, in 1990. Photographs showed a stocky middle-aged man in combat fatigues, with a cyanide capsule on a chain around his neck. He made periodic pronouncements on the clandestine Voice of Tigers radio, usually stating his willingness to hold peace talks while repeating his demands for an independent Tamil state.

But nothing in his voice or manner reflected the messianic grip in which he held thousands of followers, inspiring them to carry out more than 150 suicide bombings. In 1991, former Indian Prime Minister Rajiv Gandhi was campaigning in southern India when a young

Tamil woman handed him a garland of flowers, then blew them both up. In 1993, a teenager on a bicycle pedaled up to the motorcade of Sri Lankan President Ranasinghe Premadasa and detonated a body bomb, killing the president, himself, and eleven others.

The most senseless attack of all was the one that killed Neelam Tiruchelvam, a moderate Tamil parliamentarian and Harvard Law School graduate who was one of the best-known Sri Lankans in the West. For years he had worked tirelessly to bring about peace, and to settle the conflict through constitutional reforms that addressed Tamil grievances. In LTTE propaganda, though, Tiruchelvam was portrayed as a traitor to the Tamil cause. And on July 29, 1999, a man walked up to his car in Colombo and detonated a bomb at his waist, killing them both. It was a stunning blow to Sri Lanka's prospects for peace, and a horrific reminder that the LTTE fanatics had only contempt for those who truly sought it.

"In their eyes, Neelam constituted a threat. He was working with the government so they saw him as the enemy," said Saravanamuttu Paikiasothy, a social scientist at the left-leaning Centre for Policy Alternatives in Colombo. "Their logic has always been simple and brutal. You're either with them or you're against them. They are calling the shots, and they will eliminate anyone who tries to find a solution that can be used to play them out of the game."

Every time I read of another suicide bombing, I wondered the same thing: What was this child thinking when she pushed the detonator? Of dying for Tamil Eelam? Of pleasing Prabakharan? Of saying good-bye to her parents? How had the LTTE transformed these tropical teenagers into robots who welcomed death? From the few clues available, the Tigers seemed to offer a radical version of summer camp, a secret club where poor young Tamils could find purpose and camaraderie. Girls, more submissive to authority, made especially malleable recruits. In return, these junior samurai pledged to be loyal and abstinent, competed to be tough and brave, and were swept up in a tide of peer pressure and military mystique that carried them toward death. They built their own coffins, buried their comrades and celebrated an annual "martyrs' day" with eulogies by Prabakharan.

In a handful of interviews, young "rehabilitated" Tigers told of being kidnapped, forcibly recruited, or simply volunteering because the LTTE promised them regular shelter and food. They described

being cut off from their families and undergoing intensive indoctrination. Promotional Tiger videos showed rows of slender young fighters, marching or saluting in uniform, their faces hidden by kerchiefs
but their eyes shining with conviction.

In a fundamental way, the adolescent Tigers were no different
from the madrassah students of Pakistan who became the religious
warriors of the Taliban movement—rescued from poverty, isolated
from the world, provided with a substitute family, praised for valor
and punished for disobedience, indoctrinated in a history of victimization, and imbued with a visionary myth. The Muslim teenager
who died blowing up an army post in Kashmir, dreaming of Islamic
paradise, could easily have been the Tamil Tiger cub who died blowing up an army post in Batticaloa, dreaming of Tamil Eelam.

Despite its near-invisibility and extreme ruthlessness, the LTTE
was backed by a sophisticated international support network. Nearly
one million Tamils lived in Europe, Canada, Australia, and Britain,
as well as southern India, the ancestral Tamil homeland. Sentimen-
tally attached to their ethnic cause back home, many contributed to
pro-Tamil front groups operating in South Asian neighborhoods
from London to Montreal, making the LTTE one of the best-
financed and -equipped guerrilla armies in modern history.

The Tigers also used websites to publicize their cause well before
the Internet had become a common global phenomenon. From the
Colombo Hilton's business office, my colleagues and I could log onto
pro-Tiger sites that kept faster track of election results or military
action than the international wire services, with a ready supply of
commentary and analysis. Although direct fundraising was banned
in the United States and other Western countries that had declared
the LTTE a terrorist organization, its foreign supporters funneled
large sums into sophisticated weaponry, such as long-range artillery
and rocket launchers, that enabled the LTTE to challenge Sri
Lankan forces with increasing success.

I was skeptical of all the electronic hype, though, and anxious to
get a firsthand glimpse of Tiger operations. But journalists were
banned from the conflict zone, and clandestine contact was nearly
impossible and highly risky. Merely obtaining government permission to enter northeast Sri Lanka by road was a tortuous bureaucratic process that required repeated visits to three ministries.

Finally, with my official Defense Ministry travel permit in my hand and a Tamil-speaking friend at my side, I set off in a jeep one glorious morning, heading toward Batticaloa. We reached the first army checkpost by noon and handed our documents to the guards, but they refused to let us pass. I spent the next three hours fuming in a tropical garden surrounded by barbed wire, while the post commander tried to reach his superiors. Finally, after a second permission letter was faxed from Colombo, we were allowed to drive on.

The coastal highway was dotted with sleepy Tamil villages, where clusters of curious people formed each time we stopped. They were reluctant to be identified but eager to talk. When I asked about the Tigers, some peasants were evasive but others spoke of them with unabashed reverence, hinting that their sons or nephews had slipped away to join the militia. Their own lives were a constant struggle to survive, they said, and the elected government had brought them little relief.

"They are our only champions. Their dream is our dream," one elderly peasant told me. He was sitting in an empty village market, with just a few piles of coconuts and fish displayed on wooden planks. I asked him why so many houses looked abandoned, their thatch roofs sagging and doors missing. "Everyone has run away, from the army, from the war, or maybe to join with them," he said cautiously. "You aren't going to put down the name of this village, are you? Those of us who are left here, we're too old to run away or fight."

As we neared Batticaloa, there were more army checkposts, more signs of tension. In one spot a line of men waited sullenly outside a church. An army squad had raided their village at dawn and rounded up every male for questioning. At another village, people complained they could not walk on the roads at night or they would risk being shot. "Even if you are bitten by a snake, you have to wait until the next morning to go to the hospital," said one rice farmer.

The city itself was under total military control, with troops on every corner. But they were visibly nervous and under strain. At one checkpost I tried to take a picture of three girls with parasols, waiting for their purses to be searched, but a soldier lunged forward and grabbed my camera, demanding the film. (I kept insisting it was a digital camera, and he finally gave up.) At another point, our driver swerved to pass a slow bus. Suddenly, dead ahead, was a soldier with an assault rifle raised and pointed at our windshield. I thought he was going to shoot us, and my heart stopped. After ten interminable seconds, his expression softened as he recognized foreign faces and lowered the gun.

Later, at a fortified military compound, an army intelligence officer explained to me why the soldiers were so nervous, why they searched schoolgirls and stopped buses and trusted no one. "This is like Vietnam," he said. "The LTTE wants to disrupt and destabilize. They are terrorists fighting a guerrilla war, but we have to follow international rules. They come in disguise, but we have to wear uniforms. If we do our jobs, people say we are harassing them. How can we win?"

Despite its tropical beauty, Batticaloa was dilapidated and forlorn, with little commercial or professional activity. There was an airport, but no civilian planes dared land for fear of missile attacks. The only beds available were in a decrepit motel-tavern with noisy drunks at the bar and two moldy, roach-infested rooms in the back. But before curfew, I was cordially welcomed for meals and conversation by Batticaloa's only resident politician, Joseph Pararajasingham, a member of Parliament from the moderate Tamil United Liberation Front.

Pararajasingham walked a delicate and dangerous line. He was one of the few elected leaders who dared to regularly visit the embattled zone, and he risked his life each time. He was critical of abuses by the army, and his job included helping local Tamils file complaints for detained or missing relatives. But like all moderate Tamil leaders, he was vulnerable to attack from the LTTE, who viewed such officials as sellouts and had assassinated several of them. "Most Tamil MPs just stay in Colombo. My friends have told me to leave, but people line up here every morning, asking for my help," he said.

I knew Tiger Territory lay just a short walk inland, past several shallow lagoons, and I was dying to make the trip. But no one was willing to accompany me, and everyone advised me against it. Local army officers described it as a jungle empire ruled by fear and fanaticism, where a Western intruder might be taken prisoner or even killed.

But other people who had crossed the lagoons on humanitarian missions or commercial errands painted a different portrait. They described a parallel world that was stern but orderly, with its own schools and police, where certain unarmed outsiders were allowed to come and go. Muslim merchants said the Tigers allowed them to enter on bicycles to sell necessities, as long as they paid a commercial "tax." A worker from the International Committee of the Red Cross said the guerrillas had allowed Red Cross teams to retrieve the dead bodies of Sri Lankan soldiers, and also to give talks on human rights to Tiger troops.

And under a coconut palm, outside an open-air seaside chapel, I met Father Joseph Mary, a Tamil Jesuit priest who was sympathetic to the Tigers and had crossed the lagoons many times. He depicted their world as a microcosm of extreme morality, where alcohol and cigarettes were banned and troops slept in gender-separated dormitories. "Their code of conduct is even stricter than the church," he said. He acknowledged that the LTTE punished recruits cruelly and extorted money from local residents, but he said they also respected Hindu culture and sent condolence messages to the families of fallen troops. "I had one altar boy who disappeared, he was fourteen. I found him across the lagoon several months later," Father Joseph recounted. "He was totally changed. They made a man out of him."

∽

If my visit to Batticaloa added a romantic sheen to my image of the LTTE, it was violently ripped off by the scene I beheld several days later, in a village called Gonagola. It was a thriving Sinhalese "colony" of rice, coconut, and banana plantations, one of many outposts established in Tamil areas by the government in the 1950s. Its nerve center was a Buddhist temple, attended by a coterie of adolescent monks with shaved heads and orange robes.

One night several months before, a squad of Tigers had slipped in, grabbing and butchering people as they slept. More than fifty people had died. On a table in the temple office was an album full of photos. They showed sprawled bodies, severed limbs, and bloodied jumbles of clothing. In one hut decorated with pictures of the Hindu elephant god Ganesha, an old woman told me her son had been hacked to death in his bed by uniformed men speaking Tamil. "They were not in a panic. They did these horrors in a casual way, and they even drank tea," she said.

The head priest, Siriwansa Thero, said he had no doubt the LTTE had carried out the atrocities. "We were living a peaceful life, we had paddy fields next to the Tamils. There were no problems until the 1980s, but now even the children are brought up with a spirit of division in their hearts," he said. Since the recent massacre, the village had been under twenty-four-hour army guard, and no Tamils were permitted to enter. "If they came here, people would get very agitated," Thero said matter-of-factly. "They would not be safe."

The Gonagola attack did not occur in a vacuum, however, and the capacity for gratuitous mayhem was hardly exclusive to the Tigers. It was closer to a way of life, a perverse tradition that had become entrenched in Sri Lankan society during two decades of relentless conflict. In the 1980s, a Maoist revolutionary movement had risen among poor Sinhalese in the south, unleashing a wave of punitive barbarism by counterinsurgency squads and paramilitary groups. Thousands of people were tortured and killed; tens of thousands simply vanished. Bodies were burned and dumped on roads, heads were severed and jammed on posts or delivered, like milk bottles, to their families' doorsteps.

In the northeast, meanwhile, the LTTE unleashed its jungle campaign against the army, gaining control of numerous Tamil areas. In 1987, India sent in 70,000 peacekeeping troops, but after two years of fruitless combat they were forced to withdraw. The progovernment paramilitary squads then turned their notorious anti-Maoist tactics against the Tigers, terrorizing entire Tamil districts. Even after a decade, the scars of this vicious urban guerrilla warfare are still livid.

In the coastal town of Kalmunia, a sad-eyed, middle-aged telephone company worker recalled the horrors of 1990, after a truce collapsed and paramilitary squads went on a rampage, hunting down LTTE leaders and sympathizers. "They put people under piles of burning tires, they put plastic bags of petrol over their heads," he said.

The phone company worker said he himself had been arrested, submerged in water until he fainted, and had his toenails pulled out with tongs. "I swear to you I am telling the truth," he added, pulling off his sandals to show his deformed toes. "I hated the gun culture. I wanted my sons to have an education. But even now, the army looks at us with suspicion. People are afraid of the LTTE, they send bills like the phone company. But people also support them. No Sinhalese government has ever done anything for the Tamils. All we want is dignity and self-respect."

By 1994, the public was deeply weary of war, and the government's repressive policies had brought the country no closer to peace. Kumaratunga, the main opposition leader, campaigned for direct negotiations with the LTTE, ethnic reconciliation and an end to the "culture of assassination," which had claimed both her father and husband. Her party won its first parliamentary election in seventeen years, and Kumaratunga was elected president. But the peace talks repeatedly bogged down, with Parliament paralyzed by political disputes and the Tigers convinced they could wear down the army on the battlefield.

The ultimate trophy for both sides was Jaffna, a northern city of half a million and a historic seat of Tamil culture and leadership. The gauntlet had been thrown down in June 1981, when Sinhalese police stormed the city's library and set it on fire, destroying nearly 100,000 books and a rare trove of Tamil literature that included manuscripts written on palm leaves. For next decade, both forces battled for control of Jaffna, and in 1990 the LTTE captured the city, setting up a brutally efficient parallel government. The army fought back and recaptured Jaffna in 1995, but by then the once-gracious city had become a scorched ghost town and the surrounding peninsula an isolated war zone.

In the spring of 2000, the Tigers launched a bold offensive that cut off the peninsula and left thousands of army troops trapped at a strategic spot known as Elephant Pass. The Kumaratunga government broke off cease-fire talks and declared "emergency war powers," a draconian move that increased police powers and banned all news of the conflict. Local newspapers appeared with whole sentences, paragraphs and even cartoons whited out. Some of the offending portions included war coverage, but the thin-skinned censors also erased one harmless cartoon of a bandaged soldier lying in a hospital, dreaming of playing cricket.

Like many foreign journalists in the region, I had rushed to Sri Lanka after the stunning LTTE victory. Already physically banned from covering the conflict, we could now neither rely on local press reports nor send our own stories abroad without line-by-line government censorship. One day I wrote a story about worried and angry Tamil refugees in Colombo, and duly faxed it to the censor's office. Several hours later I was called in to the office, where I found the government press officer, Ariya Rubasinghe, in an officious huff. My story was on his desk, with thick red lines drawn through it.

He began by saying that the government respected freedom of the press, but that for the moment, censorship was a "matter of national security." Then he proceeded to read my story aloud, pausing every few lines to accuse me of distorting the facts and making the government look poorly. I tried to be polite and discuss which words he found objectionable, but he grew exasperated and said the entire article was too offensive to appear in print.

I was furious, but also nervous. I didn't want to kowtow, but I also didn't want to have my visa revoked. That night, I reached an agreement with my editors: I would leave the country, and my original story would appear once I was back in India. The next morning I flew to New Delhi, sat down, and wrote another story about the censorship issue, mentioning the cartoon of the dreamy soldier in his hospital bed. The story revealed none of my private rage, but when I saw it in print a few days later, with a pointed headline and a photo of a censored newspaper, I felt just like I had poked the punctilious Mr. Rubasinghe in the eye with my pen.

∞

I finally made it to Jaffna, six months later, when the press was invited to observe an election there. The military tide had turned for the moment, the ban on press visits was temporarily lifted, and the army was eager to prove it could protect a democratic exercise in a war zone. But the experience was sad and surreal. We landed in troop planes and moved in a military convoy. The streets were deserted, the ballot boxes were delivered under armed escort and the polling places were surrounded by sandbags. The candidates, perfect Tiger targets, had not been allowed to hold campaign rallies.

The best-known office-seeker was a former guerrilla leader named Douglas Devananda, a middle-aged man with a pugilist's battered face. His party, the Eelam People's Democratic Party, supported Kumaratunga and spewed anti-Tiger vitriol. He lived in constant fear of bomb attacks, his Colombo headquarters was a fortified cavelike complex, and his Jaffna campaign office was an abandoned movie theater, guarded by grizzled men with submachine guns.

Devananda and his men were a spooky lot with a violent past, caught between two worlds and not safe in either. Yet his rhetoric was disarmingly democratic. "This is a war-torn area, but we have to start somewhere," he told me. Comparing Prabakharan to Hitler and Pol Pot, he said most Tamils "don't want either the army or the LTTE to control their lives, they want to choose their own leaders. We are patient optimists," said the half-blind, retired fighter. "We still believe there is a democratic way out."

But even with military protection, the operational space for democracy seemed hopelessly narrow. Half a mile from the city, an army colonel showed us a fortified farm compound from which the Tigers had relentlessly rocketed the city for months. Several days before the election, the army drove them out, leaving the compound a charred ruin of jumbled clothes and broken medicine bottles. But underneath the yard was a series of connecting tunnels and a ventilated, Viet Cong-style bunker with room for a large fighting squad. Even the colonel confided he had not expected to find such a solid underground fortress.

Later that day, we were formally briefed by the regional commander, Maj. Gen. Anton Wijendra, who proudly described the high rate of LTTE casualties—553 killed in action, 592 wounded—over the previous two months. He predicted that the Tigers would eventually negotiate in earnest, but he acknowledged it would be impossible to win "total military victory" over them. "Fighting a guerrilla war is never easy. There are many lessons in history," Wijendra told us somberly. "It is why the Americans failed in Vietnam."

That night, as our military plane took off for Colombo, every light was doused to minimize the risk of a rocket attack. We rose with a lumbering roar, the dense black forest menacing on all sides. I wondered how many Tigers were out there, watching and waiting to pounce. And I wondered how many lessons from Southeast Asia were being learned, or lost, in this new jungle war.

∽

When I finally managed to enter Tiger Territory, it was not in Sri Lanka at all. It was in Nepal, where a different guerrilla movement was fighting for a more ambitious, abstract dream: a Maoist revolution that would sweep away the corrupt structures of power—a bickering parliament, an ossified monarchy—and replace them with "popular" rule. This insurgency was even more mystifying than the LTTE; in the mid-1990s, it had abandoned political legitimacy to embrace an extremist ideology already discredited by most of the world.

If I could begin to understand one of these groups, I thought, it might unlock keys to the other as well. Both had built small militias of disciplined cadres committed to a utopian ideal; both employed ruthless violence against adversaries and traitors; and both used Robin Hood tactics to appeal to the poor and disenfranchised, filling in the void of state neglect or discrimination. Both preyed on the illiterate and abused, but offered them dignity and hope. Both had no chance of military victory; their strategy was to violently disrupt normal life until their demands for popular justice and reform were met.

My search for the neo-Maoists of Nepal led along a steep, rocky trail up and down the forest floor, past gnarled roots and mossy waterfalls and birch groves. I was traveling with a reporter from Katmandu, Gunaraj Luitel. Neither of us was prepared for the arduous trek, but after four hours we emerged, knees trembling with exhaustion, into a magnificent valley carpeted in wheat. Simple wooden farmhouses dotted the landscape; girls were carrying baskets of firewood on their heads; men were bent in the fields, plying curved scythes. There was no road, no power line, no official presence—no sign that any visitor had ever been there before.

But we knew that "they" had been there. We had heard stories of "them" slipping into villages at night, calling people together for meetings, listening to their problems. In towns along the way, people had pointed out landmarks: a police post they had ambushed at night, a bank they had robbed, a footbridge they had built. Here was where they had held a mass meeting to explain their ideology and call for recruits. Here was where they had rounded up the local drunks and paraded them through the square.

"We were afraid of them at first, but now they are welcome at every house," a farmer named Karna Kharki told us. He was forty-three, thin, dressed in mismatched, frayed shirt and pants. We had reached the village of Zungu, a cluster of wooden houses perched on the valley slope. Night was falling fast; cows were ambling toward their sheds. An old man with a wispy beard sat cross-legged before a tiny shrine, praying in a soft singsong chant. A gaunt woman with no teeth, wrapped in a traditional crimson cloth, held up a baby and laughed. Someone lit an oil lamp. There was the dull chunking sound of butter being pounded in a churn.

It was too late to leave now; we would never make it back through the forest to the main road where we had left our car. We would remain in the village until dawn. I was nervous but too exhausted to stand. At least I was wearing sneakers and jeans; Gunaraj had hastily set off from his office in Katmandu that morning in loafers and slacks. But the villagers surrounded us, clucking with reassurance. Nothing would happen, they said. The village was safe, no one would hurt us. We could sleep in a loft, there was yogurt and rice to eat. Even if "they" made a nocturnal appearance, we would be welcomed as guests.

"They drove out all the evil people who lend money and force us to work for nothing," Kharki explained. The cluster of villagers nodded; one man put his hands together, as if bound by a rope, and showed how the landlords had been shamed. "They are helping us to repair latrines and build roads. They punish people for drinking and they settle our disputes. The police insult us, but they treat us with respect. Now we have peace here, and we are very satisfied."

That evening, as I sat on a farmhouse porch in the darkness, drinking fresh yogurt from a wooden bowl and staring into the forest gloom, I wondered if the lives of these villagers had truly been improved, or whether they were simply being used as fodder for an ideological struggle they could not possibly understand, and against which they had no defense.

I also thought about what it was that drew me to places like Zungu in Nepal, and Batticaloa in Sri Lanka. It was not just the natural beauty or simplicity of the surroundings, though that added to the jarring poignancy of the experience. It was not just the news, though the sensational notoriety of Sri Lanka's child suicide bombers and the anachronistic cachet of Nepal's Maoist insurgency were what kept them in the headlines. And it was not just the violence, though I had always cared far more deeply about stories where life and death were at stake.

There was something else in me, a fascination with times and places where ordinary life was turned upside down, where crusades were launched and ideas dawned and the tyranny of mediocrity and neglect and injustice were challenged, where societies were forced by crises to come to grips with themselves and change. This was what had always attracted me to South Africa; this was why I had become so deeply attached to Chile and Haiti during their struggles against dictatorship; this was why I always looked forward to visiting Afghanistan under the Taliban, despite the constant tension and discomfort that made every day seem like a week.

I was not mesmerized by revolutionary leaders, attracted to martyrdom or inspired by utopian visions; I had never thrown down my professional journalist's mantle and picked up a polemical pen, much less a grenade. I had seen greed and pride and delusion sabotage noble theories and expose flawed heroes. I had seen youthful liberators become aging tyrants, moral discipline degenerate into gratuitous cruelty, cults replace institutions, and revolutions tear families apart. I did not believe in a struggle between good and evil, because I had seen them switch places too often.

But still, but still. There was a part of me that identified with the passionate conviction of those who sought to right all the wrongs, to throttle the status quo, to wake up the world, to change human nature. There was a part of me that wanted Tamil Eelam to exist, that wanted the villagers in Zungu to rise up against the landlords, that wanted the Taliban to stop the tide of appetite and debt and vulgarity that inevitably accompanies liberal modernization. There was a part of me that responded to every evangelical call, no matter what god it invoked, perhaps hoping that this time, somehow, I would not be disappointed.

In Nepal, though, I was soon to be quickly and horrifically disappointed — by the spectacle of gratuitous cruelty and slaughter carried out in the name of justice, by the debauched self-destruction of dynastic leadership, by the petty paralysis of democratic politics, and by the grinding despair of daily life in a country so wreathed in natural splendor, so steeped in gentle faith. When I finally found something redeeming, it was such a slender, ephemeral fragment of grace that I almost missed it in all the mayhem.

∞

Nepal is a strange little country of 23 million people, tucked along the Himalayan range between Asia's rival behemoths, India and China. It is a belt of isolated rural poverty surrounding the crown jewel of Mount Everest; a haven for international flower children and adventurers and a domestic cauldron of political tension; an hereditary kingdom that is trying to evolve into a parliamentary democracy; a pacifistic, traditional society of devout Hindus and Buddhists that has suddenly exploded into revolutionary violence.

There had been little news from Nepal in years when I arrived in the spring of 2001. Like most correspondents who covered South Asia, I spent most of my time in larger countries, worrying about such weighty issues as nuclear war, religious tensions, military coups, and Islamic extremism. Like many of my colleagues, I had never been to Nepal and had no idea how to spell the king's name, who the latest prime minister was, or what had possessed a legal leftist party to embark on a Maoist revolution.

It was the Maoists who first grabbed our attention, by launching a gruesome killing spree that left hundreds of people dead in a few months' time. Mostly, they attacked rural police posts, shooting everyone on duty and melting back into the hills. Suddenly the simmering, almost invisible "people's war" seemed to have become a real threat. The Maoists were now said to control five of Nepal's seventy-five districts, where they established parallel governments that brought desperately needed services to remote areas, but also applied brutal punishments to those who betrayed them, cutting off heads and smashing kneecaps with hammers.

Their leadership was underground, but it was not difficult to find their unofficial spokesmen. In Katmandu, the capital, a shabby little office above a sari shop was a meeting place for journalists and intellectuals affiliated with the Maoist party. Krishna Sen, a soft-spoken, bespectacled man of forty-five, edited a clandestine party newspaper. When I met him, he had just been released from two years in prison for communist activities, but his conviction seemed unwavering.

"We believe in the revolution, in total change," he told me, proffering copies of magazines in Nepali script that were illustrated with stylized drawings of Mao and Stalin. When I asked him about the death of communist ideology in Europe and across the world, he shook his head vigorously. It was not dead, he insisted, "only politically defeated. This is a long process, a long war."

In reality, Nepal's Maoist leaders seemed more pragmatic than doctrinaire, making repeated offers to negotiate with the government. Some officials were eager to launch a full-scale military crackdown, but others feared this would unleash a civil war. Most political

parties were already left of center, and most Nepalese seemed comfortable with communist ideas. In one magazine poll, 81 percent of
respondents said the greater threat to democracy was from mainstream parties, who were so splintered that Parliament had become
virtually dysfunctional.

The political crisis was worsening day by day when I left to
spend several weeks in Pakistan, so I was not terribly surprised
when my editor in Washington called my Peshawar hotel room early
one morning and asked how quickly I could get back to Katmandu.
My first groggy thought was that the Maoists had attacked the capital, but the editor said no, it was something much more bizarre. It
appeared that Nepal's royal family had just been massacred, inside
their palace, by the heir to the throne.

I bolted from my bed and rushed down to the lobby, rousing the
night manager and scanning the newswires. Details were sketchy,
but I cobbled together a quick story for the final edition of that day's
paper. I had no idea how I would reach Nepal, until I spotted a Pakistani International Airlines crew checking out of the lobby and asked
the captain for a flight schedule. By some miracle, there was one
weekly flight from Islamabad to Katmandu, and it left in five hours.

Twenty minutes later I was in a taxi, speeding along the pre-
dawn highway. I reached the airport with an hour to spare and collapsed in the lounge. Several other correspondents were already
there, shuffling through hastily assembled news clippings. We pooled
our limited knowledge, copied down the spellings of royal names,
and speculated wildly about palace intrigue. I was panic-stricken;
within hours I would land in a country I barely knew, where a spectacular and mysterious crime had just occurred. I would have to produce a dramatic on-the-scene story that night, and I had no idea
where to start.

Fortunately, the gods of journalism produced a second miracle
that day. As soon as I emerged from the Katmandu airport, my taxi
driver said the royal family funeral was about to begin, and did I
want to attend? I stashed my computer and suitcase in his trunk,
asked him to wait until I returned, and spent the next five hours witnessing one of the strangest, most haunting spectacles of my life.

The setting was a hillside cemetery, sloping down to a stream.
On the other side was an ancient Hindu pagoda with monkeys scampering across the gables. By nightfall the graveyard was filled with

silent spectators, including dozens of reporters and TV crews. In the distance, we could hear the slow beat of drums, growing closer. An immense funeral procession was making its way to the temple on the outskirts of the capital, bearing the bodies of King Birendra and most of his immediate family on litters heaped with flame-colored marigolds.

Meanwhile, we listened to transistor radios and scribbled furiously. The news trickled out, growing more bizarre with each official statement or swirling rumor. The thirty-year-old crown prince, Dipendra, was said to have stormed out of a palace dinner, angry because his mother did not approve of his fiancée. He had returned in a drunken rage, wearing combat fatigues, and sprayed automatic weapons fire across the room, killing his parents and at least eight other people, then turned the gun on himself.

Dipendra was now hospitalized in a coma, reportedly near death. But because he was still alive, monarchic protocol demanded that he be named king upon the death of Birendra. So the unconscious apparent regicide became Nepal's constitutional monarch that night, while state radio described him serenely as a sports enthusiast who had succeeded his father. The grim details were omitted, but a government official announced tersely that since "His Majesty" was physically unable to assume his duties, his Uncle Gyanendra would act as regent.

By the time the funeral procession reached the temple, it was well after dark, but candles flickered from stone pyres anchored in the stream. Occasional cries of "Long Live the King!" rose from the crowd. One by one, the royal bodies were lowered onto the pyres, hidden beneath hillocks of flowers and sandalwood, while barefoot Hindu priests, robed in white cloths from the waist down, lit torches and chanted. The flames rose and burned brightly, casting odd shadows and dancing in the water like some awful Halloween ritual. Cannons boomed, swords were raised, an honor guard saluted. There was not a sound from the crowd.

That night I wrote until dawn, and for the next week I embarked on a glorious sleuthing expedition, working as a team with Steve Farrell from the *Times of London*. We tracked down royal relatives and monarchy experts. We peeled away layers of rumor and intrigue. The palace was sealed, and most witnesses were dead or hospitalized. Officials were tight-lipped and evasive, and public clamor for an expla-

nation exploded into the streets. Dipendra died and was quietly cre-
mated; Gyanendra was hastily crowned under heavy security as riots
raged across the capital. But still the details of the massacre remained
secret.

Finally we located a man whose wife had witnessed the killings.
It took hours, but he eventually gave into Steve's relentless pleading
and agreed to talk. The next morning, we scooped the world with
exclusive details: Dipendra tending bar at a family soiree, slipping
away and returning in full battle dress, calmly blasting his father
with a submachine gun, then heading for the garden to shoot his
mother and sister. Two days later another witness, an army captain,
gave a press conference spelling out more details. He stood in front
of an easel showing a floor plan of the palace, and drew little Xes at
spots in the billiard room, dining room and patio where the prince
had felled various victims. Every American journalist in the room
was thinking the same thought: *This is just like a game of Clue.*

As I write this, I realize how flippant it sounds, but the truth is
that the royal massacre was far more like a murder mystery than a
human tragedy. None of us had ever met the victims, nor had most
Nepalis. They lived and died in a cocoon of royal privilege, ritual and
intrigue that could only be imagined. The murder scene was so
tightly sealed that not a drop of blood leaked out. There were no
tabloid photos that might have aroused horror and pity. Nepalis wept
for the mystique and stature of the monarch, not for the man or his
quarrelsome retinue of relatives, and we foreigners were free to play
detective.

Still, the whole episode left me with a hollow feeling, an unful-
filled need to mourn. I thought a lot about the prince, about what
must have driven him to such despair and rage. I interviewed people
who knew him, and fashioned a profile about a spoiled but frustrated
young man confined to an elegant prison, a fast-living skydiver
bound by the rules of a medieval monarchy, a self-indulgent playboy
barred from marrying the girl he loved, an honorary army officer
with both a taste for weaponry and a self-sacrificing streak. But I had
never met Dipendra, and I still had no feel for the man; no ending for
my story.

Just as I was finishing the profile, I ran into a French colleague
who said he had found an extraordinary book about the royal family

in a tourist shop. I thanked him, jumped up, and rushed off to find the book, a promotional volume about Nepal. On one page was a portrait of the prince, posing in his dress army uniform. On the following pages were half a dozen poems he had written, dominated by themes of patriotism, nobility, and death. One poem, entitled "Soldier," suggested that the author was ready to kill, and die, for the sake of honor. "Spray with blood I will," he vowed. The words sent a chill down my spine. "Shake this earth I will."

There were more stories to be done, more tensions and plots unfolding in the post-massacre political void. Protests and press conferences were being held, journalists were being arrested, the parliament was still paralyzed and the Maoists were stirring up more trouble. But I was exhausted, and I had an ending to my story. The mad crown prince had written it himself.

Before I left Nepal, there was one more stop I needed to make. It was a plain little building in a poor neighborhood, with no sign on the gate. Inside were rows of neatly made metal cots, boxes of newly knitted mittens and caps. On the walls were snapshots of young women working in teashops or posing with herds of goats. There were also drawings, mostly crude self-portraits of girls' faces, some weeping and others red with anger.

The building was a shelter and training center for girls called ABC Nepal. Most were teenagers rescued from prostitution or abuse. Some had been forced into marriage with much older men; many had been brought back from brothels in Bombay or other Indian cities, where they were prized by customers for their fair skin, piquant eyes, and slender figures. Two had been sold by their penniless parents to a traveling circus in India for $50 each.

I had spoken by phone with the shelter director, Durga Ghimire, and I had promised to stop by a dozen times, but the frenzy of news had always intervened. When I finally stepped inside the shelter, I was seared by the sight that greeted me. About twenty girls were huddled on a mat, engrossed in discussion. Their chatter died into silence when they saw me. Their eyes had that hard, faraway look I had seen in the street urchins of Kabul, a look that always broke my heart.

With a little coaxing, several girls began to tell their stories. One round-faced twenty-year-old recounted shyly how she and her little sister had been contracted as circus workers by their parents when they were ten and fifteen. For five years, she said, "we worked hard, and they only fed us rice and lentils. I cried every day." Her face was scarred from falling off a tightrope. When I asked if she was going home to her parents now, her smile vanished. "I didn't see them for five years," she said bitterly. "Why should I see them now?"

Ghimire said many of the girls at ABC faced shame and rejection if they tried to return to their families or villages. She estimated that more than 5,000 underage Nepali girls were smuggled into India each year to work as prostitutes. Indian authorities cooperated in returning them to ABC and other programs, where they were offered training in crafts and animal raising, as well as small amounts of seed money to start a business.

One girl on the mat stared sadly into space, saying nothing at all, so I asked if I could speak with her alone in another room. Her eyes were like huge black petals, shining briefly when she spoke but then dropping back to a dull stare. When she began to speak, her hands fluttered like tiny white birds. I could see why a man would want to possess her, but I could hardly believe that someone so young could have been abused so cruelly, by so many.

As an illiterate village girl of nine, she had been forced by her family to marry a sixty-year-old man, who drank and beat her. At fifteen, she had been raped by another adult relative. Her family was so ashamed that they sent her to India as a contracted laborer, but she quickly ended up forced to work in a Bombay brothel. Seven months later, she was discovered during a police raid and returned to Nepal in the care of ABC.

"I never saw the sun rise or set, because the windows were always locked," she said of her time in Bombay. "Every night they sent me ten or fifteen customers. Sometimes they raped me or burned me with cigarettes. Afterwards they gave us tips. We all hid them in our clothes to buy food." She said she considered herself lucky, "because some girls die in the brothels. I hope I get a good husband, but I want to tell every young girl I meet not to trust anyone."

As I was getting ready to leave, I went around the room, saying good-bye and promising to come back. Suddenly one slender girl stood up and held out her arms. I started to give her a quick hug, but

suddenly we were embracing fiercely, without a word, without letting go. She barely came up to my shoulder, and I did not know her
name. She began to sob, and I just stood there with my arms around
her, imagining the horrors she had endured, wondering if she had a
mother, wondering if anyone had ever held her like this, wishing one
hug could make up for everything, wishing I had a daughter to love.

It was only a few moments, but it was the first real human encounter I had experienced in Nepal. I had spent nearly two weeks in
professional overdrive, covering massacres and riots as if I were a
word-spewing robot, caught up in the heady race to beat my competitors, feeling little pity for a slaughtered family of eccentric monarchs
I had never met. Suddenly, as I felt this child shaking with sobs
against my chest, I began to weep too. It was the fragment of grace
I had forgotten to look for, and it was the ending I truly needed.

∽

Interlude

Baltimore——It is Christmas again, and I have landed, exhausted,
with no gifts again. I fantasized about ordering an embroidered velvet dress in Afghanistan for my goddaughter Alejandra, who is two,
but in the end I had to settle for an airport-purchased, illustrated
volume of "The Night Before Christmas," which, if I am really lucky,
I will have time to read to her once or twice before she moves on to
Barbie dolls. I also fantasized about sending her periodic letters and
pictures from my travels as my grandfather had once done for me,
mementoes she was still too young to enjoy but would treasure one
day. That idea, too, fizzled after the first packet vanished in the mail
somewhere between New Delhi and Washington.

Meanwhile, as I wrestle with the exotic problems of leading a
high-profile life among South Asian hot spots—balky satellite phones
and cancelled flights, suspicious military police and nitpicky censors,
sweaty jungle treks and teargas-filled streets—Alejandra's mother
Connie, my best friend back home, is saddled with the far more mundane, anonymous demands of parenthood.

My exhausted dawns are spent waiting at airports, hers comforting a colicky baby. My rewards are instant and public: headlines with

my name under them, history being made before my eyes. Hers are gradual and private: the delight of a child meeting her first cat or learning to pronounce a new word. I both envy and pity Connie, as I'm sure she does me. I can barely predict what my life will look like six months from now; she can predict all too well what hers will look like for the next twenty years.

On bad days, she stares out her office window in Washington and wishes she were winging her way to some foreign mission, free of diapers and tantrums and house payments. On bad days, I stare at the framed picture of her and Alejandra in my bedroom in New Delhi and think: I am producing an attic full of forgotten newspaper clippings; she is molding a whole new person.

Tomorrow I'll be meeting Connie and Alejandra in Washington, and I'll make sure to schedule at least one reading of "The Night Before Christmas." I know it by heart, and I want my goddaughter to grow up with the same magical wonder, the same love of words that have never left me: *"The moon on the breast of the new-fallen snow gave a luster of midday to objects below. . . ."*

The truth is that she barely knows me. I am an intermittent and unreliable visitor in her life, someone associated with holidays, ceremonies, photographs—with surprise rather than reassurance, with moments rather than hours. But I like to think that if I can make the moments special, maybe they will add up to something after all. Maybe she will absorb a little of my inspiration, and maybe I will earn a little of her love.

First, though, I am rushing from the airport to keep another appointment, a much sadder holiday reunion with a man I have known and cherished all my life, a meeting that will probably be our last. My uncle George is dying. He lies here in a hospital bed, gaunt and withered and trembling, like a leaf about to fall. Outside the window are the brown winter woods of the Maryland countryside he loves; lying on the bedside table is an album of poems and photographs assembled by the children he adores. But I can see he is in great pain, bewildered and angry and humiliated. For the first time in a life of unshakeable faith, my uncle is beginning to doubt God. *If he loves me, why is he letting me suffer so?*

It is a question so many people must have asked in their final hours, staring into the blackness and desperately searching for a glimmer of grace. Now a wise man of ninety, a devout Roman Catholic who gently prodded me for years to believe in the quenching fountain and the ardent flame that nourished his soul, is putting the same question to me, a wayward child who always shrank politely from his sermons. How can I answer him? Is this why I have rushed from the airport? Is it my turn to be strong and reassuring, to banish the doubt and fear I myself have harbored for so long?

I take my uncle's parched hand in mine, begging him not to give up. I find myself telling him how his faith has inspired me to look for signs of hope in the most godforsaken corners of the earth, where the evidence of divine indifference to man's greed and cruelty abound, but where I have always managed to find someone or something — most often a kind gesture from a poor person — that shamed my own unbelief. I tell him how I have always carried a verse from Brahms's German Requiem tucked in my wallet. *All flesh is grass, even the flowers of spring wither away, but the word of the Lord endures forever.* If the most beautiful music ever composed was inspired by faith, if Brahms and Beethoven and the psalm-writers believed, is that not enough?

I know as I stand here, with my suitcase in the hospital corridor, that this is the last time I will ever see my uncle. He looks a lot like my father, and once he is gone, my father will be the last surviving member of his generation in the family. I'm sure I'll miss the funeral, just as I missed my aunt's the year before, during a trip to Afghanistan. It was a rare gathering of a widely scattered family, and I think everyone else managed to attend, except a cousin who was traveling in Vietnam. My father sent me an e-mail about the ceremony, typically terse and understated, but much later another cousin told me she thought she had glimpsed tears in his eyes. I wonder how he is feeling now, knowing that soon he will be the only one left.

My uncle seems calmer; the nurse has given him a pill and he is drifting off to sleep. His hand slips from my grasp, his eyes close. I take a long last look at his face, sunken into the pillow, and I try to remember him from countless summer evenings, sitting on the porch of his cottage at sunset, watching the sailboats bob in Nantucket Harbor and talking to me about God. Those evenings have all blurred together now, those childhood summers have become a single, distant memory. But these few hours by his hospital bed, this unexpected gift — the chance to comfort a dying man who once comforted me — will remain embedded in my heart, like an aching crystal sliver, for the rest of my life.

CHAPTER EIGHT

The Face in the Coffin

A mighty fortress is our God,
A bulwark never failing;
Our helper he amid the flood
Of mortal ills prevailing;
For still our ancient foe
Doth seek to work us woe;
His craft and power are great,
And, armed with cruel hate,
On earth is not his equal.

. . .

And though this world with devils filled
Should threaten to undo us,
We will not fear, for God has willed
His truth to triumph through us . . .
Let goods and kindred go,
This mortal life also;
The body they may kill;
God's truth abideth still.
His kingdom is forever.

—Martin Luther, 1529 A.D.
(trans. Frederic H. Hedge,
1853)

STORM clouds were rolling in from the South African coast; rain was pounding the windshield. I had risen before dawn to follow a park ranger through the bush, tiptoeing past giraffes nibbling on treetops, baboons grooming each other in a clearing, a white rhinoceros browsing with her baby. My visit had been a dreamy sojourn after a week-long United Nations conference in Durban, a brief illusion of limitless time and space for creatures that were rapidly running out of both. I was both awed and saddened as I drove away from the park, lost in thought as I stared out at the rain.

An hour or so down the highway, my mobile phone started beeping; I had been out of range for two days in the game reserve. It was midafternoon on September 11, seven hours ahead of the American east coast. The caller was a South African journalist I knew in Durban. I could barely hear him, but his voice was sharp and urgent. *Have you heard? There has been a terrible attack in your country, in New York, in Washington, you must turn on the news, you must get back to the city, it sounds very bad.*

I frantically twisted the radio dials, but I could hear only disjointed phrases amid the crackling storm static. Not until I reached my hotel in Durban and turned on the television did I understand the enormity of the disaster. I watched, paralyzed, as the second suicide plane crashed into the World Trade Center, over and over again. I wanted to clutch someone's hand, but I was alone, in an antiseptic hotel room in an unfamiliar city at the edge of the world. I reached out to touch the TV screen, but the scene being replayed over and over seemed unreal, like King Kong swatting at toy planes from a skyscraper. At some level, I knew this terrible day would change the world forever, but I had not yet realized how swiftly and dramatically it would change mine.

∾

By the next morning I was headed back to South Asia, already sucked into a frenzy of journalistic panic. My editors wanted me to get as close as possible to Afghanistan, where U.S. officials were already beginning to cast blame for the terrorist attacks. Over the past six months, the Taliban regime had become increasingly isolated, religiously hardline and defiant of world opinion. And they were still harboring Osama bin Laden, one of the few figures believed capable of orchestrating such a breathtaking, sophisticated scheme.

I had not been inside the country in months, because Taliban officials were denying most visa requests from the Western press. At the same time, the regime's intolerance toward all foreigners, and foreign faiths, had taken a startling turn for the worse. On August 5, Taliban police raided the Kabul office of a Christian-based charity, Shelter Now International, that built low-cost houses, ran bakeries, and installed drinking water systems in Afghanistan and northwest Pakistan. The authorities in Kabul had long suspected SNI of having a secret religious agenda, and now they claimed to have proof.

To the Taliban, proselytizing or converting to Christianity was a grave crime, punishable by death. All foreigners were explicitly warned not to preach to Afghan Muslims. Now, officials said they had caught two American volunteers at SNI, twenty-four-year-old Heather Mercer and twenty-nine-year-old Dayna Curry, visiting an Afghan home with translated Bibles, Christian CDs and audio tapes. Both young women were arrested and jailed on suspicion of trying to convert Muslims, while police detained the rest of the agency's Kabul staff for good measure: two Australians, four Germans and sixteen Afghans.

The Afghans were in the gravest danger. If found guilty of abetting conversions, they faced almost certain execution. When news of their arrests reached Afghan refugee communities in Pakistan, people were outraged and terrified. In one camp near Peshawar, I spoke to several relatives and colleagues of the detained Afghan workers, who were mostly drivers and helpers at SNI. They adamantly denied the charges. "My brother is a good Muslim. He prays five times a day. He helped the freedom fighters defend Islam against the Russian troops. Why has this terrible thing happened to him?" demanded Noor Mohammed, a longtime refugee.

But it was the plight of Mercer and Curry, both volunteers sent by a Baptist church in Texas, that captured international attention and concern. The story of their arrest was featured repeatedly on U.S. television networks, and two of their parents flew to Islamabad, pressing American diplomats to intervene. Finally they secured a brief visit with their daughters in prison, but no promises of a reprieve.

After September 11, they began to fear the girls would be used as hostages or worse if bombs started falling on Kabul, and they started avoiding the press to avoid antagonizing the regime.

I was anxious to talk to them, though, and when I found out they were attending Protestant International Church, I decided to slip into a Sunday service and introduce myself. The congregation had dwindled considerably, because many Western embassies and charities had recalled their employees home. But in the stark white, half-filled chapel, the atmosphere was radiant with faith. The service was led by Curry and Mercer's pastor from Texas, whose message seemed benevolent and inclusive. He led prayers for Afghan Muslims and their rulers. He asked God to grant wisdom to the Taliban, to instill courage in the girls and bring them out of prison to safety.

But there was a militant undercurrent in the room, a fervent call to religious battle that seemed to echo the Islamic absolutism of the Taliban and their radical brethren in Pakistan. The words to one of my favorite hymns, "A Mighty Fortress Is Our God," suddenly rang with a new, crusading tone. The verses recited from the book of psalms, calling for an evil enemy to fall into "fiery pits," could have emanated from a mosque loudspeaker in Peshawar or Karachi. Just like the madrassah students in their skullcaps and robes, the good Christian people singing these hymns around me were unshakeably convinced that God was on their side.

At one point Curry's mother stepped up to the pulpit. She spoke of her daughter's concern for the widows and children of Afghanistan, and of her yearning to help others. But she also called her a "prayer warrior," a phrase used by evangelistic groups that aggressively spread the Christian Gospel. When I spoke to her later, she said her daughter had seemed completely unafraid in prison, because "she trusts in God to take care of her."

I understood, then, that these young women were not merely charitable volunteers; they were indeed Christian missionaries. The question was, how far had they gone? Had they deliberately risked bringing the wrath of the Taliban on themselves, and worse, on their Afghan colleagues? Were they frightened young do-gooders who had made a foolish mistake, or religious zealots on a crusade no less burning and utopian than the Taliban's, calmly putting their heads in the lion's mouth?

With the suicide attack on the World Trade Center and the Pentagon, Islamic terrorism became the overwhelming focus of U.S. foreign policy, instantly eclipsing the complexities of regional politics in South-Central Asia. The Bush administration, convinced that Osama bin Laden had played a role in orchestrating the attacks, demanded that the Taliban turn over their notorious guest or face military assault. Washington also offered President Musharraf an equally blunt choice: abandon the Taliban and join the international anti-terror crusade, or risk Pakistan's being demonized as a nuclear terrorist state.

Islamabad, usually hushed and bureaucratic, became a nexus of international tension and political drama. I flew directly there from Johannesburg and landed on September 13th. For the next month I worked at a fever pitch. The pace of developments was dizzying, the stakes were high, and the swirl of rumor and debate constant. Often I wrote until well after midnight, and my room at the Chez Soi became a sea of half-read newspapers and half-empty coffee cups. My only escape was taking my dog, Rafi, for quiet walks in the neighborhood, early in the morning, before another exhausting day of news-gathering.

Musharraf, a pragmatic military strategist, realized he had no room to maneuver. One week after the attacks on New York and Washington, he announced he was halting all support for the Taliban, in the interests of global security and Pakistan's "critical concerns." By casting Pakistan's lot with the West against the Taliban, though, Musharraf took an enormous risk. He abandoned a neighbor that shared a 1,500-mile border and ancient ethnic ties with his country. He challenged the largely untested "street power" of the domestic Islamic groups that had spawned the Taliban, and he laid open the split between professional elements of his military establishment and those with a pro-Islamic agenda.

Whatever the fallout at home, Pakistan's military leader knew it would be worse abroad if he sided with the Taliban, tarring Pakistan as a terrorist state and risking Western military wrath. By doing the right thing, he made himself the instant ally of a world that had once shunned him as a dictator. He hoped its gratitude would translate into tangible, monetary rewards that could boost Pakistan's prospects for economic recovery and lessen the appeal of Islamic radicalism to its alienated poor.

Intellectual leaders in Islamabad, as well as a majority of moderate Pakistani Muslims, agreed that Musharraf had correctly opted for the lesser evil, although many felt he had done America's bidding with unseemly haste, and everyone warned he would have hell to pay in the mosques and madrassahs. The divide between Pakistan's split personality—one part secular and progressive, the other religious and traditional—seemed poised for dangerous confrontation.

Rifaat Hussain, a professor at Quaid-I-Azam University and one of the most thoughtful analysts in Pakistan, put the question rhetorically: "Do we swim with the current of world opinion against terrorism, or do we condemn ourselves to being on the wrong side of history?" Pervez Hoodbhuy, a liberal physics professor and one of the country's few anti-nuclear activists, put the choice even more starkly. "Pakistan had to choose between going along with America or becoming another Iraq," he told me. "Our foreign policy was being held hostage by the fundamentalists, and September 11 brought it all to a head."

The Islamic parties, and the excitable Urdu-language press, lost no time excoriating Musharraf as a Western patsy and leaping to Kabul's defense. Sunni Muslim groups formed a coalition called the Afghan Defense Council, which warned that the United States would provoke a holy war if it attacked Afghanistan. Qazi Hussain Ahmed accused Washington of trying to "accelerate the clash of civilizations," while Fazlur Rahman said a U.S. attack on Kabul would be a "declaration of war against the entire Muslim world."

Across the Koran belt, radical mullahs began whipping up their disciples into war frenzy. In Peshawar, I watched hundreds of young Muslim men pour out of Friday prayer services, vowing to take violent revenge on America if the bombing started. They held up straw effigies of President Bush, set them on fire and stomped gleefully on the ashes. Some carried posters of Musharraf as an American lapdog, others held up portraits of bin Laden, heroically wreathed in glowing light. An elderly man pointed into the swirl of younger marchers and declared, "Today I am Osama, he is Osama, every Muslim is Osama!"

That day, in that crowd, I first heard the astonishing assertion that the attack on the World Trade Center had been an American-Israeli plot. One excited young Islamic student swore that four hundred Jews had been warned not to go to work in the tower that day. Another said no, it was four thousand. This was a conspiracy against Islam, an excuse to attack Muslim countries. I argued that this made no sense, that Jews had been killed too, but the rumor was too powerful to quash.

Soon, I started hearing it in Islamabad, too—in politicians' drawing rooms, even from a military spokesman. So deep was the hatred of Israel among Pakistani Muslims, and their impotent bitterness over U.S. policy in the Middle East, that even those who knew better were willing to spread a ludicrous lie over the ashes of tragedy. Affluent Pakistanis might not feel the desperate rage that drove fanatical Muslims to become suicide bombers, but they harbored enough enduring grievances that even middle-class professionals, clearly moved by the loss of life in New York, said they could understand why some Muslims felt grim satisfaction at the assaults on American symbols of power.

ରୀଠ

At the same time, Musharraf was extending quiet feelers to try and forestall an Afghan Armageddon. Alarmed at the prospect of a Western military attack and the creation of a political void in Kabul, the general nurtured the hope that Pakistan could exert a friendly, moderating influence on the Taliban. He allowed Taliban diplomats to remain in the capital and sent several delegations to Kabul, including his senior intelligence chief, to try and reason with the leadership.

Musharraf also tried to walk a narrow tightrope between cooperating in the anti-terror campaign and surrendering Pakistan's sovereignty to a Western invasion. He agreed to share intelligence and allow Western warplanes to land at Pakistan bases, but he insisted that no Pakistani troops or territory could be used in any attack. "Pakistan can never join in any hostile action against Afghanistan," a foreign ministry spokesman said. "We are deeply conscious that the destinies of the two people are intertwined."

But the Taliban refused to back down from their defiant defense of bin Laden. This drama played out at their embassy in Islamabad, where Ambassador Abdul Salam Zaeef faced an unruly scrum of camera crews on his lawn day after day. No matter what the shouted questions, he stuck to his script, repeating in a forlorn monotone that bin Laden remained an honored Muslim guest, that no one had presented evidence connecting him to terrorism, and that he could never be abandoned to foreign infidels.

With a Western military assault looming, the Taliban made an apparent attempt at compromise, calling a meeting of Islamic clerics which recommended that bin Laden be asked to leave when he felt it was safe and convenient. To the Taliban, this was a major concession; to the United States, it was a meaningless ploy to buy time. Washington's patience had run out.

On October 7, allied jets began bombing Afghanistan. Musharraf moved quickly to preempt a domestic revolt on several fronts, placing Fazlur Rahman under house arrest and removing three senior military officials with conservative Islamic views. But over the next week, riots erupted in several cities, with mobs destroying banks, theaters, fast food outlets, and a UN compound.

Most urban disturbances exhausted themselves without serious violence, but holy war fever was spreading in earnest among the tribal areas of northwest Pakistan. Radical mullahs and parties exhorted followers to take up arms in defense of Islam. Thousands of men responded to the call, including peasants with old rifles. The border was officially sealed but easy to slip across, and as the bombing continued, there were reports of ragtag "armies" crossing into Afghanistan in search of a holy war.

The semiautonomous tribal agencies were off-limits to foreigners, with all access roads under military guard, but I managed to spend two days driving through Malakand, a tribal region north of Peshawar, with a Pashtun friend. Virtually every village and town was swept up in the jihadi fervor. Young men crowded excitedly around displays of bin Laden posters strung across village markets. Booths had been set up to raise funds, decorated with glossy pictures of assault weapons. A convoy of trucks was loaded with blankets and other supplies to help the Taliban. Loudspeakers broadcast taped Arabic chants that declared, "Long life to Taliban, long life to Osama, death to America."

Each time we stopped, we quickly drew a crowd and lingered only long enough to speak to one or two people before jumping back in our car and moving on. The atmosphere was angry and electric, and there were few police visible. Men scowled and pointed when they saw me, and I felt far more vulnerable than I would have before the U.S. military assault began.

In the bustling market town of Batkhela, I spied several Osama posters outside a metalwork shop up, asked the driver to back up, and ducked inside. Nineteen-year-old Shahid Hussain was seated on the floor, neatly dressed and cordial. He said he was working part-time in his father's shop, while studying to enter medical school. But in the past month, his life had taken a radical turn, and his mundane ambitions had been brushed aside for a more passionate cause.

After the military assault on Afghanistan began, Hussain had joined hundreds of other young men and signed up as members of a local movement led by a militant Islamic cleric. According to his plastic membership card, Hussain and the other boys had vowed to fol-

low the path of "virtue," taken a brief training course in target practice and physical endurance, and agreed to fight an Islamic holy war
in Afghanistan if their leaders requested it.

"I am a Muslim, so jihad is my first obligation. It is more important than my career," the young man said earnestly. He was handsome, articulate, and bright, probably the focus of his parents'
dreams. Now his only hope was that they would allow him to go for
jihad. "If the ground war starts, we will all close our shops and go.
Even if we are martyred, we know we will not die."

In another spot along the main road, a crowd of perhaps a thousand men gathered around a loudspeaker truck as dusk fell. A man
in a turban was shouting hoarsely, reciting prayers in Arabic for the
successful resistance of the Taliban against the infidels. Some of the
men noticed me and began shouting angrily. There were no other
women or foreigners anywhere to be seen.

A nervous tribal policeman rushed up, waving at us with his rifle
to get in the car and leave, but an older man in the crowd took my
arm and ushered us to a nearby guest house. He turned out to be a
local official and an activist of Jamaat-I-Islami. He apologized for
the crowd, saying people had become "very emotional" over the U.S.
attack.

"Most of the time they are peaceful and occupied with their
lands, but when something endangers their religion, it awakens
them," he said. A number of farmers and shopkeepers had already
left for Afghanistan after listening to *fatwas*, or religious orders, issued by Islamic clerics. "I argued against it, but jihad is a dream for
Muslim youth. When a *maulvi* says you should go, it makes people
ashamed if they refuse. The government can interfere, but it can't
stop them."

While the world fixated on the horrors of Islamic extremism, Pakistan's worst fear was having anti-Taliban warlords from the Northern Alliance seize power in Kabul, unleash an ethnic bloodbath and
send a new flood of Pashtun refugees across the border. Both pub-
licly and covertly, officials in Islamabad scrambled to orchestrate a
broad-based political alternative by seeking out "moderate" Taliban
leaders, organizing Pashtun tribal resistance and promoting the re-

turn of the elderly former Afghan king, Mohammed Zahir Shah, who had been exiled in Italy since 1973. All these efforts came to naught, and one ended in gruesome tragedy.

In late October, a meeting of Afghan tribal elders, clerics, and former anti-Soviet fighters in Peshawar, intended to promote unity and reconciliation, was undercut by political feuding and boycotted by the king's agents. A few days later, grim news came that Abdul Haq, a former Pashtun guerrilla leader who had slipped into Afghanistan to rally Pashtun tribes, had been captured by the Taliban. As his pursuers closed in, Haq made frantic satellite phone calls to friends in Washington, pleading for an American air strike, but the response was too little and too late. Haq was tortured, "tried," and executed the same day.

In the West, Musharraf's about-face transformed him from pariah to ally. He was feted in Paris and London, and visited by the U.S. Secretaries of Defense and State. He urgently requested his new friends to limit their bombing campaign and rein in the Tajik and Uzbek warlords who opposed the Taliban. But they politely ignored his advice, giving money and weapons to the ethnic militia leaders and continuing to bomb Kabul and other areas, ratcheting up Islamic outrage inside Pakistan and pushing Musharraf farther into a corner. Even moderate Muslims began to turn against the military campaign and Musharraf's hand in it.

For the foreign press, information from inside Afghanistan was frustratingly sketchy. The Taliban had ordered all journalists to leave the country, and others who entered through Northern Alliance territory were stranded behind the front lines. Hundreds of others, like me, remained stranded in Pakistan for weeks, clutching at wisps of news and rumor from across the sealed border. Back in Washington, Pentagon briefings stressed American efforts to avoid civilian casualties, but refugees reaching Pakistan described stray bombs wreaking havoc in residential areas.

In an Afghan refugee camp near Islamabad, I met a gray-bearded man named Mohammed Sardar, wandering disconsolately among the shacks. He said he had just arrived from Kabul on an urgent mission, after sneaking across the border. In his pocket was a sheaf of letters, in painstaking Pashto script, which the elders of his community had written after staying up night after night, huddled in panic and listening to bombs fall. The letters were addressed to President Bush, the other leaders of the allied coalition, and the secretary-general of the United Nations.

"The world must know what is happening in Afghanistan," Mr. Sardar told me, his voice trembling with emotion. "The terrorists and leaders are still free, but the people are dying and there is no one to listen to us. I must get to President Bush and the others and tell them they are making a terrible mistake." One night, he said, a bomb aimed at a radio station in his community had fallen on a house, killing all five members of the family who lived there. "There was no sign of a home left," he said. "We just collected the pieces of bodies and buried them."

There was no way I could confirm Mr. Sardar's story, but I was sure he was telling the truth. I detested the Taliban as much as anyone, but I also knew how easy it was for U.S. officials to gloss over the human cost of a military assault no one could see on the evening news. I wanted them to read this story, and I wanted to reassure this anxious little man that I would deliver his message. When I told him that President Bush's office was near mine in Washington, and that he might see my report, Mr. Sardar seemed satisfied and handed me his bundle of letters with a sigh of relief. His mission was accomplished.

Authorities in Washington may not have worried too much about one errant bomb, but they were definitely alarmed and angered by the reports of civilian casualties streaming out of the Taliban embassy in Islamabad. Day after day, Ambassador Zaeef appeared on the lawn, and a hush would fall as he read out the latest cables from Kabul. His voice was nearly inaudible, but his claims were explosive and impossible to confirm or refute: American bombs had struck urban neighborhoods, schools, even hospitals.

The black-turbaned envoy was not without a sense of humor. When someone asked whether the Taliban possessed anthrax, he said they had no idea what it was. When another journalist asked whether they had control of nuclear weapons, he gave a rueful grin. "We can't even produce glass," he retorted to titters from the lawn. American officials in Pakistan were not amused. They were winning the ground war and losing the psychological one. Under U.S. pressure, the Musharraf government warned Zaeef not to use his diplomatic privileges to foment propaganda. The next day the lawn was

empty, and the day after that. Then the embassy was shut down altogether.

The last time I saw Zaeef was at his guest house in Islamabad,
looking tired and depressed, fingering his prayer beads. I had always
found him a complex figure, devout but not fanatical, shy but reason-
able. In one interview months before, he had hinted strongly to me
that he opposed destroying the Buddhas. This time, he clung to the
party line, weary but dutiful. Osama was a guest, the Americans
were criminals, innocents were being slaughtered.

But by now his world was closing in, his government was on the
run, and he had no place to hide. Soon he would be arrested, turned
over to the U.S. military, permanently silenced and erased from public view. I still try to picture him sometimes, a skinny prisoner in an
orange jumpsuit, languishing in a wire cage on a big American base.
I wonder whether he remains a true believer, whether he prays five
times a day, and whether that is enough.

∽

By early November, the Taliban regime was disintegrating and journalists were pressing against the Afghan border. One intrepid *Washington Post* correspondent, Keith Richburg, crossed a snow-covered
mountain pass from Central Asia on horseback, joining a group of
colleagues stranded with the Northern Alliance troops in a bleak,
muddy town fifty miles north of Kabul. The rest of us remained
trapped in Pakistan, working feverishly but marking time.

There was no lack of colorful stories in Peshawar, where I spent
several weeks interviewing refugees and rioters and tribal chiefs. But
the real news was happening across the Khyber Pass, and I was desperate to be there. Bombs were dropping on villages, militias were
clashing in the dark, American special forces were hunting for terrorists. Most sane people would be dying to get out, but I was dying to
get in. It was the biggest story in the world: one of those moments
when power changes hands, one ideology defeats another, and history is written. It is for such moments that journalists exist, and live.
Everything else, no matter how compelling the subject or how artful
the prose, is filler.

For me, Afghanistan also held a powerful mystique. Every one
of my visits under the Taliban had been a nerve-wracking foray into

hostile territory, yet every one had produced extraordinary stories of survival and cruelty, hunger and perverted zeal. Now this same country was about to be liberated from Taliban control. Fear of chaos had replaced fear of oppression, but there would be a chance to tell a different kind of story, to witness the rebirth of a society whose soul had been snuffed out.

Kabul fell on November 14, with Taliban troops abandoning the capital after five weeks of relentless bombing. I imagined scenes reminiscent of other historic liberations I had witnessed — the night Argentina's first civilian president was elected in 1983 after years of military rule and millions of people poured into the streets of Buenos Aires, the night Ferdinand Marcos fled Manila in 1986 and a jubilant wave of people swept toward his empty palace. In Kabul, I pictured men shaving off their beards, women ripping off their veils, music in the streets. Oh, how I wanted to be there.

The border was still shut and no exit visas were being issued, but certain Afghan exile groups with political connections offered to help us get across in return for covering their triumphant return home. The first foray collapsed when a mysterious guide, whom we had agreed to meet at 4 A.M. at a house in Peshawar, never appeared. Then we refocused our hopes, camping for several days on the lawn of a tribal militia leader from Jalalabad who had promised to lead a press convoy across the border. The yard filled with journalists and tribal fighters, equally disheveled and impatient.

Out of frustration, I pleaded with Pakistani authorities for help and secured a permit to visit the border. As I was driving toward the Khyber Pass with my tribal police escort, we passed a row of trucks and jeeps. I spotted several familiar faces and realized it was a convoy of journalists. I leaped out of the car, flagged down one vehicle and tossed my bags in the back. But the policeman dragged me out, insisting that he had to escort me back to Peshawar. I stomped and shouted, drawing more police to the scene. Finally I had to watch in helpless rage as my colleagues apologized and went on their way to Afghanistan.

That night, back in my hotel in Peshawar, I was miserable. I felt like a complete failure. I thought I might be fired, and I could hardly bear to call my office. I pulled myself together enough to write a quick story about the convoy, but my stomach was in a knot of panic. I stayed up all night, and at 8 A.M. I was waiting outside the office of the senior Pakistani official who could authorize exit visas. Several other journalists arrived, then a dozen. The official promised to see what he could do.

All day we waited on the lawn, while the crowd of supplicants swelled to more than two hundred. It was November 17, and the Taliban forces had now reportedly fled from Jalalabad. Some of the camera crews became aggressive and insistent, shoving their way into tiny offices, getting into fistfights, jamming their visa applications on top of everyone else's. Periodically a clerk emerged and shouted a name. The lucky soul would grab his visa and sprint for the car.

By midafternoon, the crowd was thinning and my name had still not been called. The border closed at 5:00, and it was an hour away. Two friends who had driven that morning from Islamabad retrieved their permits and departed. A few minutes later, my name was finally called. I started punching my cellphone, imploring my friends to wait, but they were already on the highway and their driver said it was too late to turn back. I had no car, no police escort, and no time. I stood in the road with my computer and duffel bag, feeling as if the entire world had abandoned me, and burst into tears.

Then my luck changed. Another group of journalists had rented an old schoolbus, and they decided to make a last-minute dash for the border. When we reached the immigration post, we discovered it had shut down for the evening Ramadan meal, but would reopen later that night. There were perhaps one hundred of us waiting there, listening to radio reports of more bombing and armed clashes with Taliban troops across the border. Finally the visa officer strolled back to his desk, picked up the first of a mountain of passports, and started typing with two fingers. It was pitch black outside. We sat on crowded benches, watching the pile diminish with agonizing slowness and wondering anxiously what lay ahead in the dark.

Across the room, someone began whistling a familiar song. On impulse, I jumped up and followed the sound. The whistler, a middle-aged European man, held out his arms and we danced in a little circle, singing the lines together. *"Fly me to the moon, and let me play among the stars, let me see what spring is like on Jupiter and Mars . . ."* There was a smattering of applause, and we collapsed in astonished laughter, the tension broken for one blissful moment.

It was well after 10 P.M. when our bus chugged through the metal gates and across the border. The name of a girls' school was stenciled on it, and the dashboard was decorated with paper flowers and tiny pictures of Mecca. There were a dozen of us on board, strangers at the time, and a jeepful of militiamen ahead, escorting us into the unknown. Eerie shapes loomed in the desert darkness, silhouetted against the headlights. Boulders, bushes, then a man's turbaned head with the bulbous steel snout of a rocket launcher poking up from his backpack.

Suddenly the bus stopped, and several dozen armed men swarmed around it, staring at us and chattering in excited Pashto. Three of them clambered aboard, their assault rifles clanking against the door, their faces fierce and weather-beaten. I held my breath. The oldest man surveyed us for a moment, then spoke a few words. I turned anxiously to my translator, a friend from Peshawar named Najibullah. He was grinning with relief. The chieftain had said, "Welcome to Afghanistan."

We waited there a long time, listening to walkie-talkie crackle as our militia escorts tried to determine if the highway was safe. Taliban forces had abandoned the area, but three tribal militia factions were skirmishing over who would take control, and their leaders had been locked in tense negotiations in Jalalabad. Finally we continued on at a crawl, and reached the city long after midnight.

There was no gunfire, but every few blocks an armed sentry appeared, shouting at us to halt, until our militia escorts explained who we were. We wound through the deserted streets and turned into the Spinghar Hotel, an old estate with a palm-lined drive and a dilapidated rose garden. Until two days before, the establishment had been run by the Taliban. The grumpy desk clerk said all the rooms were full, but the worn lobby sofas looked more inviting than the bus. I was still full of adrenaline, though, and my day was not yet done. I threw my gear in a corner, plugged my computer into a wall socket and began to write.

∽

The void left by the Taliban's hasty departure was chaotic and tense. Jalalabad was filled with rough rural gunmen from various militias, hundreds of whom were camped on the lawn of the Governor's Mansion, surrounded by an astonishing array of heavy weaponry, while their leaders negotiated inside. By night, they looted the city at will, ransacking UN charity offices and roaring through the streets in stolen utility trucks.

Najibullah, who had worked at a UN drug-control project in Jalalabad but fled to Peshawar from the bombing, prayed that his office had been spared. But when we entered the compound one morning, disaster greeted us. The windows had been smashed, the kitchen and bathroom fixtures ripped out, the office equipment stolen. In the yard, an enormous generator had been set afire and a four-wheel-drive vehicle battered to scrap. Najibullah, a shy and formal man, slumped on the porch, with his head in his hands, hiding his eyes.

The regional Taliban forces and their Arab allies had fled south toward the White Mountains, a rugged border area where bin Laden had once lived in a fortified mud compound. But they had left numerous traces of their presence and their chilling agenda. In one abandoned house, we found a jumble of uniforms, bandoliers, landmines, and military manuals in Arabic, with illustrations showing how to aim a rocket launcher at a moving human target and how to set a landmine to explode at the slightest touch. Neighbors told us the Arabs had stayed indoors, traveled in trucks with darkened windows, and not even allowed their children to play outside.

On the outskirts of the city were a hydro-electric dam and a scenic riverside bluff where Arab fighters had set up a camp. The grounds had once been landscaped, as if for a summer estate, but now they featured a new plaster mosque, a shed stuffed with rockets, and a camouflaged bunker that looked like a ship's cabin, decorated with posters of Mecca. Below, in a cluster of huts, we were shown a room full of chemicals in bottles and sacks, many with skull-and-crossbone labels, where the Arabs were said to have concocted explosives and conducted experiments with the help of chemists from the regional university.

But this was already old news, and we were eager to move on to Kabul. On the morning of November 19, a convoy of about eight taxis, jeeps, and trucks left the Spinghar and headed out on the highway to Kabul. I was in the fourth vehicle, riding with a Dutch television reporter. The road was slow, dusty, and full of spine-jolting craters, but we were too engrossed in conversation to mind. We were comparing our experiences in other war-and-riot zones, and musing on the motives that kept drawing us back to the next high-risk assignment, to the next life-and-death struggle in places with unpronounceable names.

Part of it, we agreed, was the addictive thrill of danger that sharpened our senses and emotions. Part of it was the competitive drive to beat other newspapers and networks. We also shared a horror of surrendering to the complacency of desk jobs and comfortable suburban lives, where the worst one had to face was an appointment with the dentist or the IRS and, perhaps, the occasional, vaguely disturbing reminder of paths untaken, novels unwritten, dreams deferred. To chronicle others' hardships and conflicts was a way to stay alive, on edge, engaged, even if our Western passports and credit cards usually allowed us a quick exit from looming conflagration.

Finally, we both admitted that morning, there was that heady assumption that we could survive anything, peer over the brink of an abyss without falling in, fly close to the flame of revolution or riot or religious wars without being seared. We had both come close to death before; his translator had been killed in Sarajevo, I had been nearly shot by drunken paramilitary snipers in Haiti, we had both been trapped in riots and crossfire. And here we were once more, heading into chaos and hoping to witness history.

As we chatted on, the terrain grew more barren and isolated; stony hills rose on our left and a river rushed below on our right. There was not a soul in sight. We pulled over for a bathroom break, and when we resumed driving, the next taxi ahead of us was almost out of view. Suddenly, it spun around in a cloud of dust and raced back in our direction. As the driver passed, he motioned frantically for us to follow. His back seat was empty.

As we sped back toward Jalalabad, my stomach knotted in dread. After twenty minutes the cabbie swerved into a gas station. Hands shaking, he poured out his story in breathless Pashto, and an Afghan journalist translated: six men wearing turbans and robes, and carrying Kalashnikov rifles, had emerged from the hills, pulled his passengers out of the car, pelted them with stones and then begun to fire. He had fled without looking back.

This, then, was the nightmare that turned all our pretensions to dust, our abstract calculus of risk to real numbers and names. Two journalists had been in that car, an Australian cameraman named Harry Burton and an Afghan photographer based in Islamabad named Aziz Haidari. Both worked for the Reuters news agency, and Aziz was a friend of mine, a jovial man with steel-blue Pashtun eyes. The night before, we had sat together in the freezing balcony of the Spinghar, laughing in exasperation over our recalcitrant laptops. Now both men were probably dead. If we had been 500 yards closer to the spot, perhaps we would be dead too.

Back in Jalalabad, all the foreign journalists gathered in the Spinghar ballroom, milling tensely, trying not to panic but fearing the worst. A second taxi driver arrived, and we learned that another car in the convoy had been halted by the same gunmen. Its three passengers — Julio Fuentes, a Spanish newspaper reporter; Maria Grazia Cutuli, from Italy's *Corriere della Serra*; and an Afghan guide — had been hauled out and forced down to the riverbank at gunpoint. The driver said he too had fled in terror.

We were all angry and frightened, anxious to act but uncertain what to do. Several people said we should form a search party; someone else said we should inform the governor. Chris Tomlinson, an Associated Press reporter from Nairobi who had once been a U.S. army medic, kept a cool head and began issuing quiet orders. All of us took furious notes and peppered the two nervous drivers with questions, partly out of anxiety and partly because we knew that, whatever else this was, it was a big story.

Through the crowd I spotted Najibullah. There was a stricken look on his face, but it instantly softened to relief. He rushed up and grabbed my shoulders — an emotional gesture for such a reserved Muslim man — and murmured, "good, good." A few minutes later, I saw Rone Tempest from the *Los Angeles Times* talking on his satellite phone to someone back in the States. That morning on the highway, he had been in the truck right behind mine. Now he was nodding to a question I couldn't hear. "No, that's not correct. She's okay," he said. "She's right here."

Yes, I was still alive, and I too needed to make a call. My father, half-asleep in Connecticut, answered hello. It was just after 5 A.M. there. Over the years he had become accustomed to receiving my calls at odd hours from distant trouble spots, but I was always cheery and casual, editing out any hint of illness or danger. This time, though, I couldn't bear to imagine him turning on the radio and hearing a sketchy report about Western journalists being killed in Afghanistan. I told him there had been an incident on the road but that

I was okay. Still groggy and puzzled, he thanked me for the call, and we hung up.

That night, when I sat down at the computer, my fingers felt numb. I couldn't find the right words; I could barely find the right keys. This was a front-page story, but I did not want to write it, because that would make it true. In a way, it helped that I had to use standard, third-person newspaper language; I could not inject my emotions into the news. It wasn't until the eleventh paragraph that I obliquely referred to my own involvement. The terse, seventeen-word sentence read like a silent, clenched scream: *"About a dozen other journalists in the convoy, including a reporter from the Washington Post, escaped unharmed."*

It wasn't until the next afternoon, when I was confronted with four wooden coffins in a blood-spattered hospital morgue, that I felt the full horror of what had happened, and of what had almost happened. The bodies had been retrieved by a militia squad, heaved into an ambulance, and delivered to the Red Cross hospital. A large crowd of journalists gathered, and camera crews tried to shove past the armed militiamen guarding the morgue entrance. Chris Tomlinson jumped up on the balcony and announced that anyone who tried to enter the building would be shot.

Finally a doctor emerged and asked for help identifying the bodies. Several foreign reporters had been friends with Harry, Julio, or Maria, but I was the only person there who had known Aziz. Two riflemen opened a crack in the door and let us slip inside. Four thin boxes lay on the concrete floor. A barefoot orderly was swabbing away blood. He stooped to open four small hinged lids, each exposing a rigid face swathed in a nest of blood-flecked cotton. I steeled myself to look into each box. The third face was Aziz, but it was mottled and dark, like a bruised stone. I hardly recognized the blue-eyed, joking cameraman I knew.

In those few horrible seconds, I realized I was staring at a death that could easily have been my own. I imagined my face in the coffin, my life extinguished without warning, my memories and dreams erased, my good-byes never said. I imagined strangers sorting through my belongings, calling my parents, reading my will. *One upright piano, to Arlington County Schools . . . One topaz pendant, to my goddaughter Alejandra . . . Five hundred shares of stock, to Doctors Without Borders . . . One sealed letter, to be given to my parents . . . Three cartons of notebooks, a thirty-year record of my private pilgrimage through life, to be destroyed by my attorney.*

Someone tapped me on the shoulder; it was time to leave. The coffin lid was being closed; I had to do something. I didn't know any proper Muslim prayer for the dead, so I raised my palms and murmured the only one I knew. *Bismillah al-rahman i-rahim, Allah, ilaha, il-allah, mohamedoon, rasool-ullah. Praise be to God, the most merciful and gracious, God is great, there is no God but God, and Mohammed is his prophet.* Then the lid shut, and Aziz was gone.

∾

With the highway far too dangerous to travel, we remained stranded in eastern Afghanistan, cut off from Kabul and the scenes of joyous liberation being replayed endlessly on CNN and BBC television. But there was more than enough news here to keep our minds off the tragedy: more political struggles among local militias, more Arab hideaways discovered. One day we chased reports of a "bomb" landing in a backyard, which turned out to be a projectile full of anti-bin Laden leaflets. Another day we followed rumors that a secret laboratory had been found containing vials of nerve gas. (Much to my relief, Afghan militiamen vehemently refused to let us into the compound.)

Once we were resigned to making the best of it, Jalalabad turned out to be a much more revealing window than Kabul into Afghan society and its response to the fall of the Taliban. In ways both subtle and shocking to outsiders, very little seemed to have changed at all. Women shopping in the bazaars still shrouded their heads and bodies beneath veils. Men still wore beards, though many crammed into barber shops to have them trimmed back from the long, scraggly style that was de rigeur under the Taliban.

The city's radio station returned to the air after five years of enforced silence, but the only programs it aired were cautious news reports and austere Koranic chants that even the Taliban would have approved. While I was at the station interviewing the director, the dusty dial-phone on his empty desk suddenly gave a wheezy jangle, and both of us jumped. It was the first time I had ever heard a telephone ring in Afghanistan.

Although Jalalabad was a large, bustling city of 250,000 people, sitting squarely on the major route from Pakistan, its daily life was governed by cultural and tribal traditions as conservative as any Pashtun village. The militiamen roaming the streets in pickup trucks were not Taliban troops, but they were illiterate rural fighters raised on religion and war, and the public feared them too. One young guard who sat all day outside the Spinghar, cradling his Kalashnikov, confided to me that he had never held a pencil. The gun, he said, was "my only qualification for a job. It is all I know."

Still, there was one enormous difference: Now that the Taliban and Arab troops had melted into the hills, no longer were citizens being forced to make an exaggerated show of devotion to the religion they already worshipped. In a spinach field outside the city, a farmer told me he had always worn a beard and had no plans to change. "Afghan Muslims were never against wearing beards. What they hated was that the Taliban forced them to," he said. "I am a good Muslim. I wouldn't shave off my beard even if you made me king of America, but I would defend to the death my right not to wear one."

For women and girls, tradition weighed even more heavily, Taliban or no. In the privacy of their homes, I met women teachers and doctors who dressed in gaudy splendor, with bright gowns and glittering costume jewelry. As soon as they stepped outside, however, they were transformed into dull-hued blobs again. The veil was an entrenched part of their culture, not easily removed. But at least now, they said, they were no longer beaten by the police if they didn't wear one.

Within days of the Taliban's departure, regional officials announced that girls were welcome to return to school. On opening day, 500 girls thronged the dirt courtyard of one elementary school. Many were teenagers who had stayed home for five years and were now nervously enrolling in fifth or sixth grade, fearful that they had forgotten all their lessons. There were no books or chalk or desks, and most teachers were older, bearded men who scowled and barked as they waded through the shrieking playground crush, raising their sticks in menace.

Nearby, several dozen mothers sat on benches, veils rolled back over their hair as they filled out enrollment forms. I was visiting the school with Scott Baldauf of the *Christian Science Monitor*; we strolled over to the women and sat down to chat. They were shy but adamant about wanting their daughters to be educated. Scott and I were both scribbling notes, but suddenly he looked up at me with an astonished grin and said, "You know, this is the first time I've talked with a woman in Afghanistan face to face." I thought for a moment, and realized what a pleasant surprise it was to be conversing naturally with these mothers, to look into their eyes and see hope and pride instead of fear—or blank blue mesh.

The new authorities were eager to accommodate us, though their handling of the press was ham-handed. The security chief, militia leader Hazrat Ali, often visited the Spinghar with an armed retinue. One morning as several of us were rushing out the hotel door, a guard leaped up and blocked our way with his rifle, saying, "Press conference. Everyone stays here."

Another day Ali's aides informed us we would be taken to see some Pakistani prisoners. We ended up following them for miles, passing village after village and finally halting outside a large shed surrounded by armed men. The door was thrust open and someone said, "You have ten minutes." We were momentarily blinded by shafts of sunlight, pouring through cracks in the dark shed. Gradually we made out rows of shapes huddled under blankets in the gloom. The shapes stirred and murmured when they saw us, and a few men sat up, blinking.

It was virtually impossible to interview them, and there was no way to confirm anything they said. But I dropped to my knees and tried to scribble a few names, snatch a few sentences. They were farmers from the tribal areas, and they had answered the call of their imams to come fight jihad against the Americans. But when they reached Afghanistan they had found no Americans, no holy war, and no one who wanted their help. Most had been arrested wandering on the roads. Now, all they wanted was to go home.

∽

There were about forty of us at the Spinghar, mostly veteran correspondents, used to taking risks. We were all potential competitors, based in a dozen countries, and most of us had never met before. But after the highway killings, we instinctively began to behave protectively toward each other—traveling in groups, making head counts, sharing information we once would have kept to ourselves.

None of us wanted to leave, but none of us wanted to die either, and we knew our Western passports and sophisticated gadgetry were no guarantees of safe passage home. At dinner, we found ourselves recalling other colleagues who had died in the Balkans or the Middle East, and passing around snapshots of our children and pets. The hotel was so full that we were sleeping four to a room, and so cold that we slept in our clothes under numerous heavy blankets, which made the thin metal cots sag nearly to the floor.

Sometimes, as we shivered in the dark, the window glass would rattle as if a mild earthquake had struck. That meant another B-52 was dropping bombs in the mountains to the south, where several thousand Arab and Taliban fighters were believed to be hiding in a fortified complex of caves known as Tora Bora. Within two weeks, Tora Bora would be under full-fledged military siege and international media focus; hundreds of fighters would die in the bombing, and tantalizing rumors would linger that bin Laden had been one of them.

Back home, meanwhile, it was Thanksgiving season. This was my favorite holiday, but one that often found me in circumstances with neither cause nor occasion to give thanks. This time, though, it seemed the perfect excuse to lift our spirits. I sounded out a few colleagues, and Jake Sutton, an eccentric Welsh cameraman and artist, volunteered to help. Together we scoured the city bazaars, coming up with eight scrawny turkeys, a sack of pomegranates to substitute for cranberries, and mountains of vegetables. All afternoon, huge pots simmered over campfires behind the hotel. The dining room manager, catching the spirit, transformed the barren hall into a magical setting of flowers and candlelight. Rone Tempest, who had survived the caravan tragedy with me, offered the single bottle of Bordeaux he had saved in his pack, and we poured a thimbleful into each glass.

At dinnertime, forty of us gathered around a long, glowing table. Some were scruffy strangers who spoke no English and had never celebrated Thanksgiving before. Others, in the course of a few days, had become my friends for life: Rone and Jake, Chris and Scott, Tim Wiener from the *New York Times*, Mike Taibbi of ABC. For once, even in jeans and a gravy-spattered shirt, I felt like a real hostess. I stood and offered a toast to our distant families, gathered friends and missing colleagues. We sipped in silence, a moment of communion and grace that none of us would ever forget. Then we all tucked hungrily into the feast.

ᔆᔆ

Interlude

Kabul——I wake up suddenly in the dark, my heart beating heavily. It has been four months since the ambush, but sometimes in my dreams I still see spattered blood, shards of glass, sprawled bodies. Now I remember. I've had a new nightmare, triggered by a new tragedy. In it, a man is beckoning to me, holding a radio and shouting, *"Did you hear? They just bombed a church in Islamabad!"*

I have been living in the Muslim world for several years now. I have been polite, objective, open, gracious. I have dressed modestly in deference to Muslim feelings, sat for hours hunched on the floor with my feet falling asleep, restrained my impulse to defend the West when some illiterate mullah railed about prostitution and pornography. I have fasted all day with Muslim friends, and broken fast with them at dusk. I have explained my faith to Muslims who expressed curiosity, but my mission has been to understand theirs, not to challenge it.

I was relieved when I heard that Heather Mercer and Dayna Curry had been freed unharmed after Kabul fell. It was a cinematic rescue: Taliban troops spiriting them out of prison, then abandoning them in a truck container in the desert, Afghan troops setting them free and American military helicopters swooping down to grab them, guided to the spot by a bonfire of burqas.

And yet the more I learned about their case, the more I became convinced they had deliberately sought to confront Islam in the worst possible place, that they had been molded and encouraged to become Christian crusaders by evangelical mentors back home. They were the perfect foil for their Afghan captors: equally certain of their righteousness, and equally willing to sacrifice themselves for it. Their zeal had been honed not in the madrassahs of Pakistan, but in the churches and classrooms of the American Bible belt.

Back in Texas, their pastor said they believed in "laying down their lives" for God, and that traveling to a country at war, showing Christian books and films in a Muslim home, were risks they had taken gladly. For them to deny Jesus, he said, would be like "putting a fish in water and asking her not to swim." Taliban officials used a slightly different metaphor. "The Shelter Now people have been preaching for a long time," Foreign Minister Muttawakil had said. "Their tentacles are everywhere."

It wasn't that I didn't admire the courage and tenacity of these young women; in some ways they reminded me of myself. And yet my own training and experience had led me to very different views: a mistrust of all absolutes, a distaste for all proselytizing, a horror of all religious conflict. I never hid my Christianity, but I confined it to that plain brick church in Islamabad, where I would retreat to take a deep breath on Sundays after listening politely all week to angry Muslim students chanting against the infidel West.

From the beginning of 2002, when I took up full-time residence in Afghanistan, I made a point of visiting Islamabad once a month, ostensibly to stock up on supplies and cash, but also to replenish my spirit. I was looking forward to Easter, when the congregation gathered in the Margalla Hills for an early-morning ceremony.

Then, one Sunday morning in March, the terse bulletin blared from my friend's radio in Kabul: *Five dead in Islamabad church bombing.* I knew immediately it was Protestant International. In subsequent reports, officials described the details: Two unidentified men had burst into the morning service, hurling grenades at the congregation. Windows had shattered, people screamed and dove for cover, blood and bodies lay strewn across the floor. Five killed, at least fifty wounded. That meant almost everyone in the church.

My first panicked thought was to find out if Cindy and my other friends had survived. Using my satellite phone, I dialed every church member's phone number I knew, but I could never get through. I scrolled through the newswires, looking for clues, and finally spotted a story that quoted Cindy as a witness. Only then was I certain she had survived. Another friend had saved herself by diving under the piano, but an American woman and her daughter were among the dead.

The attack fit a terrible pattern emerging across Pakistan. Radical Islamic groups had threatened to retaliate against Christians for the bombing of Afghanistan, and terrorist gunmen had opened fire in another Pakistani church in October 2001, killing fifteen worshippers. In January, President Musharraf vowed to crack down on reli-

gious extremists, but they responded with a series of attacks on foreigners, including the kidnapping and beheading of Daniel Pearl, a
reporter for the *Wall Street Journal*. Many Westerners had fled Islamabad, and now the only religious sanctuary for those who remained
had been violently assaulted.

Once I was sure my friends were safe, I sat down to write. I
knew the history of the church, what it looked like, what it meant to
the members. I felt frustrated not to be there, and I wanted to con-
tribute. But once again, my professional distancing mechanism
kicked in. The story I wrote that night made no mention of my affili-
ation; it simply described the church as an unpretentious place where
Christians found comfort and community. The story was sober and
bland. It did not scream what was pounding in my head: *Those bastards. I hope they fry those sick bastards*.

When I jolted awake the next morning, I was full of pent-up
rage. Evil had struck at precisely the place I had felt the safest in a
country 10,000 miles from home. I suddenly realized that this was
the definition of terrorism: a deadly assault at a time and place where
it was least expected, where people were most unguarded and absorbed in ordinary life. I imagined the attackers, angry young Muslims brainwashed to hate foreigners and Christians, discussing when
and where to carry out their plot. What better target than a Sunday
morning church service?

The truth is that the grenade blasts at Protestant International
shocked and angered me in a way that the assault on the World
Trade Center never could. I knew there was no comparison in the
magnitude of the crime; the suicide planes in New York killed close
to 3,000 people; the grenades in Islamabad killed five. I knew one
attack was an orchestrated challenge to an entire country and its way
of life; the other an impulsive gesture against a small, easy target.

But to me, the World Trade Center attack would always be a
horror movie on my TV screen in Durban. What happened at Protestant International was very, very real. This was not a distant symbol of financial imperialism, a towering structure that seemed to defy
God, a lightning rod for the grievances and twisted rage of Islamic
extremists. This was my church — my church! — a modest building
with rows of folding chairs where I had meditated on many Sunday
mornings. These were not strangers, stumbling bloodied and dazed
from the blast; they were my friends. Now the chapel was locked,

the congregation scattered. There would be no sunrise Easter service. There might never be another service at all.

In the months after the September 11th attacks, I was distressed by their polarizing impact on American society and its relations with the Muslim world. I do not believe in the clash of civilizations. I am as uncomfortable with militant Christianity as I am with militant Islam, with the idea of "prayer warriors" as well as "jihadis," with the image of crusaders "marching as to war." I believe life is more complicated than a struggle between good and evil, and that the solution lies not in pitting one religion against another, but in searching for common ground and compassion among people of all faiths.

Most of the time, this search is a large part of what motivates me, what keeps me balanced and open and "objective" in my work, what keeps me poking in the ruins of human predation and intolerance for fragments of grace. But sometimes, when I think about what happened on that spring Sunday morning in Islamabad, I feel like throwing down my pen and strapping on my armor instead.

CHAPTER NINE

Rebirth

Laila, Laila, it's New Year.
My heart is pounding.
Laila, Laila, it's New Year.
God's world will end in two days.
I have sorrow in my heart today.
The spring has arrived, but mine has not.

I will sit on your path until you come.
I will make any sacrifice you want.
I have no gift more valuable than my life,
but I fear you will not want that.
Laila, Laila, it's New Year.
God's world will end in two days.

—Sung by Farhad Darya

 THE first time I saw the Shomali Plain, it looked like an atomic wasteland. Frozen, dust-colored fields were strewn with tortured shapes: charred grapevine stumps, headless military tanks, hacked-off tree trunks. Ruined villages floated past the car window, their mud walls sagging like sad, melted sandcastles. There was no sprig of green, no hint of hope.

That was in December 2001, shortly after Northern Alliance troops swept south into Kabul, opening up Shomali for the first time in years of warfare. The once-verdant valley had been a major battle-ground in the anti-Taliban fight; its people were mostly ethnic Tajiks who supported the resistance, and Taliban troops had dynamited their wells and torched their vineyards in revenge. Lurking under the soil were deadly relics of earlier combat: thousands of landmines planted by the Soviet army.

213

Yet within weeks of the Taliban's departure, an extraordinary change began creeping into this frozen, desolate landscape. All winter and spring I traveled the Shomali road, driving between Kabul and the new U.S. military base at Bagram air field. With each trip, I glimpsed more signs of life: A solitary farmer with a shovel, digging up his old grapevines. A pile of fresh white stones and a green Islamic flag placed on an abandoned grave. A family trudging toward a village with bundles of bedding on their heads.

By April, Shomali was bursting with activity. Colonies of plastic tents sprang up beside abandoned villages. Brigades of farmers worked in the vineyards, uprooting scorched stumps and tossing them into trucks to sell as firewood, preparing the earth for planting. Squads of de-miners slowly cleared roadsides and paths with trowels and sticks, marking their progress with rows of red-and-white painted rocks. Teams of men worked the treadles of flanged wooden devices, cranking up buckets of mud from choked irrigation wells. Silhouetted against the barren brown hills, the contraptions reminded me of the windmills in *Don Quixote*.

Whenever I stopped and talked with families trickling back to their homes, I was struck by how much they had lost—and by how determined they were to rebuild their lives. In the village of Karabagh, where farmhouses lay in ruins and birch groves had been burned black, I found Mashad Mohammed, a father of eight wearing a patched tweed jacket over ragged pajamas, perched on the half-collapsed roof of the house he had built twenty-nine years before. Once, it had featured wood-framed windows and a rose garden. Now it was a heap of charred beams, and Mohammed was trying to salvage the least damaged ones to sell in the city.

"The Taliban drove us out with sticks and whips. Then they set the houses on fire. I could see the smoke and flames rising in the distance," Mohammed recalled. Squatting in the yard, he pointed to a porch where his children had once played, and started to weep. "Now I am finally home, but I am so confused. I am too old to build my house again, and I don't know what to do."

But some of his neighbors were already hard at work with shovels and axes, rebuilding the school, chopping down damaged trees and weeding overgrown fields. They had all returned from Kabul and were living in UN tents near their old homes. A tank truck pulled off the highway, and dirt-streaked children scampered into line with plastic buckets to collect water for washing and cooking.

On another day, I spotted Ghulam Sayeed and his family clambering out of a bus from Kabul and piling several huge bundles beside the highway. I offered them a lift, and we set off down a dirt lane toward their village. Rusted, half-sunken pieces of Soviet tanks littered the land like old hurricane debris. Far ahead, snow glinted from the peaks of the Paghman Mountains.

"I used to grow grapes. It was a hard living, but I was proud of my vines," Sayeed told me as we jolted along. He had spent the last several years selling fruit from a pushcart in Kabul, but now he was eager to get home and start working the soil again, even if his family had to camp in the ruins of their former house. As we entered the deserted village, the farmer apologized for not being able to offer me tea. Then he issued an invitation so unexpectedly gracious, and so full of hope, that it brought tears to my eyes. "Come back at harvest time, and we'll have lots of grapes," he said.

When I think about the rebirth of Afghanistan after the collapse of the Taliban regime, I like to picture the transformation of the Shomali Plain. It is a simpler, happier scenario than the squalid free-for-all that unfolded in Kabul during 2002—the poisonous power struggles, the rapacious landlords and aid siphoning schemes, the caravans of homeless returning refugees, the hopelessly overloaded water and power systems of a city catapulted from repressed ruin to explosive uncertainty.

First, though, came the honeymoon. Day by day, I could feel the capital evolving from a silent, cowed city to a bustling, gridlocked metropolis filled with the din of honking horns, blaring radios, and pounding hammers. Sidewalks became workshops full of half-built school desks and satellite dishes; shops overflowed with stacks of truck tires from Iran and crates of bottled water from Dubai.

Those early months of post-Taliban rule were as extraordinary and intense as any I have ever experienced as a journalist. This was one of those rare times and places where history had been turned upside down, where virtually everyone had a story to tell, every building harbored ghosts, every mundane transaction seemed an astonishing achievement, every raised flag or rehung portrait was symbolically significant.

Literally any chance to meet Afghan women was newsworthy, and their stories of survival and subterfuge were fascinating. One teacher had operated a clandestine school for girls, shifting classes between apartments to thwart the nosy Taliban police. Another women's organization held all its meetings in moving taxis. Some women were still shy with foreigners, but for the first time I could knock on doors and try my luck without fear of being denounced or detained. After years of furtive snapshots, it was a luxury just to stand outdoors and photograph children swinging in a park or shoppers haggling in a bazaar. I also took many portraits of families, who posed with pride and invariably asked for copies.

Most people in Kabul were grateful for the U.S. attack, and they warmly welcomed Americans like me who followed in its wake. There had been some bombing damage in the capital but few civilian casualties, and even grieving families seemed to accept their loss as a cost of liberation. In one apartment where an errant U.S. bomb had killed a three-year-old girl, I interviewed her parents, a policeman and a teacher who had both lost their jobs under the Taliban. They stared glumly at snapshots of their daughter in frilly dresses, but then the father roused himself and said he had a message for the American authorities.

"Please tell them we don't blame them for what happened," he said. "We lost our little girl, but we know those pilots did not do this deliberately. I appreciate the American attacks, because they saved our country from barbarism."

At first, most foreign journalists stayed at the InterContinental Hotel. The winter was freezing and conditions were abysmal, but none of us cared. Many rooms had inadequate heat, poor light, and no hot water, but the decrepit building came alive with the Taliban's departure—transformed from a haunted, empty palace to a raucous, jam-packed dormitory. I spent twelve-hour days on the street, soaking up as much as I could. Then I came back to my chilled room, ordered a pot of green tea, and sat down in my parka and boots to write.

At midnight, I would file my stories by holding a satellite phone antenna out the window of a frozen, pitch-black corridor, balancing a computer on my lap and wearing a miniature miner's lamp on my forehead so I could see the keys. My only treats were taking an occasional hot shower (courtesy of Annie Garrels from National Public Radio, who had a better room), and bringing a daily plate of leftovers to a family of stray dogs that lived behind the guardhouse.

At first, nothing in the capital worked. Traffic lights, phones and typewriters were long dead. Office files and furniture had to be thrown out after being left to rot for years. And yet every day brought new signs and scenes of liberation. Girls' schools reopened without chairs or chalk, but with great fanfare. Beauty parlors had no water or electricity, but customers were happy to make a gossipy manicure last all morning after years of living under house arrest.

The first Eid, a holiday following Ramadan that exudes the same joyous, salvational atmosphere as Easter, took on extra significance. Suddenly, the instinct to scrimp gave way to an impulse to spend, and depressed cave-dwellers became expansive hosts. For three days, the drab midwinter city burst into color and action. Children flew once-banned kites; adults bought festive new clothes. At Massoumi's Bakery, the flushed and flour-coated staff worked sixteen-hour shifts to meet the demand for holiday pastries. Customers pulled up in taxis and filled the trunks with cakes to offer visiting friends and relatives; the patio out back was carpeted with cooling metal cookie sheets.

"When the Taliban were here, they enjoyed Eid for themselves, but no one else could," said Sayed Muzaffaruddin, the kitchen supervisor, as I watched him one early morning, rolling out dough by lantern-light. "Now, people can walk freely, wear what they want, listen to music, and watch movies. They are buying more for this Eid than they have in years."

Kabul's central movie theater reopened, and I went to see my first film ever in Afghanistan—a B-grade Bollywood action flick. The seats were hard, the film was scratched and the actors spoke Hindi, but the show sold out, and the audience of young men cheered the slapstick heroism with unabashed delight. Posters of Sylvester Stallone and Jean-Claude Van Damme, as well as coquettish Bollywood starlets, added a sheen of garish gaiety to the city's muddy markets.

The American embassy began functioning for the first time in a decade, although it was transformed into a bunkerized compound with a perimeter of razor wire, guard towers and floodlights. Russia and India, Germany and France, Iran and China followed suit, refurbishing their shuttered buildings and Kabul's pariah image. The United Nations gobbled up building after building as its network of agencies and cottage industry of Afghan subcontractors expanded. By mid-year, there were more than 1,000 nonprofit agencies in the capital.

After years as a ghost city, Kabul rapidly refilled with returning refugees, who flowed across the border from Pakistan at a far faster rate than the dilapidated city could absorb. By summer the capital's population had doubled to 2 million. Every day, dozens of cargo trucks rumbled along the highway from Peshawar, filled with families and belongings. They arrived with excited dreams but few realistic prospects; most had neither jobs, homes, nor support networks awaiting them. Thousands ended up occupying abandoned ruins.

On two days in March, I climbed onto buses full of returning families and followed two of them to their destinations. The Shahs landed unannounced on a cousin's doorstep in a poor section of Kabul, dumping carpets, bicycles and a washing machine in the yard. The Sawans were dropped off outside the mud-walled hillside home they had fled years before, now empty and half in ruins. The men unloaded trunks, boxes of family photos, even a caged parrot. Then, as the bus lumbered off, everyone posed for a group portrait in the barren dirt yard. Kobra Sawan, the matriarch, smiled gamely. "We're finally home," she said. "We're going to love it here."

There was promise and possibility in Kabul's chaos, energy and freedom in its cacophony. As the capital groaned uncertainly to life, make-do entrepreneurship quickly filled the gaps. Acres of used car lots appeared overnight; storefronts became computer training programs, crammed with young adults desperate to catch up with the world. A gust of globalism blew through the streets, displacing the ruin of war and skipping an entire technological generation. By summer, the city's decrepit dial-phone system was still unusable, but everybody who was anybody had a mobile unit on his belt.

When I opened my window at dusk, the din of television and traffic drowned out the muezzins' call to prayer, and I had to remind myself not to be annoyed. That love song blaring from a radio would have earned someone a beating just a few months ago. That gunshot and scream on the Hindi film soundtrack would have been real. The Taliban had outlawed the noise of ordinary life; now it was back with a vengeance, and who was I to object?

And yet there was something too frantic in the burst of commerce and diversion, as if everyone knew the window of opportunity might slam down at any moment. Business was booming, but mostly thanks to the influx of international humanitarian and development agencies, which paid Afghan workers five times the local wage and created an instant demand for luxury housing, goods, and services. Crime was low, ethnic hostility under control and Taliban fighters nowhere to be seen—but only because 4,000 UN peacekeeping troops patrolled the capital in camouflaged tanks.

One merchant, whose shop overflowed with stacks of newly imported truck tires, told me in April that his business had gone up 30 percent. "If the country becomes stable and secure, I expect it will go up 100 percent," he said, "but we are still waiting for real change to come, for warlordism to end. If these things do not happen soon, we could lose everything again."

Afghanistan was recovering not only from five years of Islamic rule, but from the civil war mayhem of the early 1990s and the polarizing communist era of the 1980s. The country had veered between violent extremes for a quarter-century, destroying institutions and poisoning personal relations. Millions of people had been killed or wounded, displaced or driven into exile. No one trusted anyone; blood bonds and social rites no longer insured against a stab in the back.

Kabul was still an atavistic city of survivors and refugees, toughened by hardship and violence. People had spent years crouching in caves and waiting for the next bomb to shatter the windows. It was a place where each new group of liberators had turned into oppressors, where children had learned to shove and kick and cheat and steal to eat, and where everyone had committed or endured shameful acts to survive. Removing the Taliban did not erase the habits or memories burned into a generation.

One day I watched in horror while a food giveaway program in a schoolyard degenerated into a primitive, nightmarish scene: Thousands of women and children clawing their way toward trucks piled with wheat, and police beating them back with branches and belts, just like the Taliban. There was more than enough for all, but no one believed it. Another day I tried to interview families at a food handout in a park, but I was soon surrounded by a mob of jeering, rock-throwing boys and had to flee.

Everything had been stripped away except instinct. Respect for law, merit and civility had vanished, leaving only fear of power and scheming sycophancy. Virtually no one obeyed the hapless traffic policemen waving quaint "stop" paddles. Instead, intersections became jousting arenas where powerful utility vehicles—often carrying military VIPs—barged through inching swarms of dented taxis, buses, and trucks. I saw drivers punch each other, SUVs almost run over pedestrians, and militiamen point loaded rifles at cabbies blocking their way.

Dogfighting, banned by the Taliban because it encouraged gambling, quickly resumed in the capital, where high-stakes matches were often held after Friday prayers. I could never bring myself to watch, but I did attend several games of buzkashi—violent, exhilarating free-for-alls on horseback, in which the rider who grabbed the goat's headless carcass became fair game for everyone else. There were rules but they had nothing to do with fairness or safety; only strength and aggression mattered. As virtually every player grappled for the carcass, riders had their teeth knocked out and horses were gashed by flailing hooves. By the end, the field was often a churned-up mass of mud and blood.

Greed and corruption flourished in the new frontier. Landlords evicted poor Afghan families, renovated houses, and rented them to foreign tenants at ten times the price. Foreign charities became goldmines for theft and nepotism; government jobs went to insiders' relatives. Refugees lined up at the municipal building to claim old government land deeds, but officials sold the valuable plots to their friends. Cell-phone and video shops opened on every block, but looted and shell-pocked factories remained empty and idle for lack of serious investment.

Despite the new spirit of freedom in the air, the gratuitous cruelty of the Taliban—especially the notorious Vice and Virtue Ministry goons—left a sullen, angry mark on the urban populace. I don't think I met a single man in Kabul between the ages of seventeen and thirty who had not been harassed, beaten, or jailed. Older professional people who became my close friends had been victimized as well. The indignities were still fresh, and some would leave scars for life.

My translator in Kabul, a polite medical student named Najeeb, took me to see an abandoned jail where he had been briefly confined for the crime of playing chess, forced to sleep in an open dirt patio and subjected to daily Islamic lectures. My driver, Fawad, showed me another prison where he had spent several weeks for possessing a music cassette. Usually nonchalant, Fawad grew agitated as he peered inside a row of open, empty cells.

"This is where they beat me with six lashes for making tea," he said, pointing to a filthy corner in one barred cement room. "This is where I wrote, 'Death to the Taliban.'" As he left, he gave the wooden cell door a sudden, vicious kick. "These men were not Muslims, they were barbarians," he muttered.

And yet there was a palpable public urge to shake off the Taliban pall. One of the most moving experiences I had during those first months was at the national stadium, which the Taliban had converted from a sports arena to a punishment gallery. The regime disapproved of boisterous athletic competition, requiring soccer players to wear long pants and fans to refrain from cheering. Instead, officials urged the public to gather after Friday prayers and watch adulterers being lashed or thieves having their hands cut off. I never witnessed one of these grim spectacles, and most Kabulis wanted to forget they had. The stadium acquired the stigma of an old gallows, haunted by unhappy ghosts.

Not long after the Taliban fell, however, officials announced that a free soccer competition would be held there, and hundreds of men and boys clambered up the cement bleachers. The two teams were wearing shorts, and the loudspeaker played folk ballads. I sat in the stands, smiling at the whoops and groans that accompanied each near-goal. A shopkeeper, watching the game with his young son, told me he had seen Taliban stab condemned men to death on the same field. "Everyone hated it and tried to leave," he said.

At halftime I headed down to talk to the players, and a ripple of murmurs spread through the stands. I was the only woman there, and I knew the buzz was about me. My first instinct was to shrink inside my scarf and ignore it. But on impulse, as I started onto the field, I turned back and waved. To my astonishment, the crowd burst into applause. They were thanking me just for being there. It was at that moment, I think, that I realized Afghanistan was truly free.

Just over a month after the Taliban fell, a new interim government was installed in Kabul. It had been cobbled together at a conference in Bonn, hastily convoked by the UN even as Taliban forces clung to their last strongholds in November. Afghan leaders from four major ethno-political factions negotiated under intense foreign pressure, and after ten days they reached an uneasy power-sharing agreement.

On December 21, Hamid Karzai was sworn in as the country's interim chairman. He seemed tailor-made for the job: a Pashtun tribal leader and educated ex-diplomat, he had fought the Taliban but was not saddled with the violent past of other Afghan militia bosses. As Karzai took the oath of office, clad in a majestic striped silk tribal robe, he called on all Afghans to "come together as brothers and sisters. Let us be good to each other. . . . Let us forget the sad past."

But the veneer of political unity was paper-thin. Karzai enjoyed international support but commanded no personal army, the true measure of influence in Afghanistan. Real power lay with the warlords of the Northern Alliance, especially Tajiks from the Panjshir Valley, who felt entitled to rule after helping the West defeat the Taliban. Karzai headed the government, but Panjshiri leaders controlled key cabinet posts, and Defense Minister Mohammed Qasim Fahim, a semiliterate but shrewd Panjshiri, was the most powerful man in Afghanistan.

The Foreign Ministry, to my pleasant surprise, became a professional bureaucracy once more. On my first visit, I was astonished to recognize the same press officers I had known only as bearded, turbaned Taliban employees. Now shaved and dressed in ill-fitting Western suits, they sheepishly welcomed me back. The walls were mildewed and the typewriters broken, but the forbidding atmosphere had vanished. Abdullah, the new minister and chief government spokesman, was another Panjshiri and no friend of Karzai, but he played his part with dignity and aplomb.

Despite his weak position, Karzai also rose to the occasion, exuding serene, self-confident authority. He joked with journalists, received endless delegations of tribal elders for tea, and made uplifting speeches that vowed to steer the country toward democracy, reconciliation, and prosperity, though always with a prudent nod to Islam. He surrounded himself with educated Afghan professionals who returned from Western exile to take up cabinet posts.

I especially liked Amin Farhang, a thoughtful man who gave up a university post in Germany to become minister for reconstruction. When I followed the directions to his new office, I was shocked to recognize it as the old Vice and Virtue Ministry. His modern corner suite, featuring plush beige carpeting and new computers, was the same bare room where I had once interviewed a stern mullah, whose battered metal desk held an array of leather whips.

"This used to be the ministry of destruction. Now it's the ministry of reconstruction," Farhang told me, only half-joking. The executive décor was an important signal to international donors and investors. "After twenty-three years of war, the image of Afghanistan is one of Kalashnikov culture and corruption. We want to create a new mentality," he said. "We want to show we are accountable and in control. Otherwise, we will never regain international confidence."

The Northern Alliance leaders, however, viewed Karzai's exile coterie as untrustworthy, Westernized interlopers ("dog washers" was the favored epithet) on their rightful turf. Their formal relations were civil, but in key agencies, including the army and intelligence police, power was controlled by the Panjshiris. Militia commanders installed themselves in comfortable houses and roamed the city in SUVs. Their troops, ostensibly banned from Kabul, were omnipresent on the streets and often acted as self-appointed morality watchdogs.

Despite their armed rivalry with the Taliban, the Panjshiri forces were also Islamic militias with conservative values, especially regarding women. At one house rented by several male American reporters, soldiers burst in and demanded to know why they had allowed an Afghan woman inside (she had asked to make a phone call). At a hotel wedding, where the salon was curtained between male and female sections, a soldier on guard overheard me interviewing the musicians, who were waxing nostalgic for more liberal times when mixed-gender dancing had been allowed. The guard angrily cut them off, saying it was "un-Islamic" for them to suggest such a thing.

Even though women were now free to work and shop, it remained rare to see female faces in public. Inside schools and offices, they mingled comfortably with their male colleagues, but most donned a burqa as soon as they stepped out the door. When city residents began venturing out to suburban parks for picnics, most women stayed home. Their prudence was not a residual habit from Taliban time, but a live apprehension of the mujaheddin. The last time they had controlled the capital, no woman was safe. Now they were back. Everyone knew what they were capable of, and no one knew what the rules were in the confused and evolving ethos of post-Taliban society.

One day, I was interviewing a Panjshiri refugee family in a hill-side slum above Kabul, and I asked two bright teenaged sisters why they were not in school. They said their older brother, a former mili-tiaman, would not allow it. When I asked him why, the young man became flushed and agitated. "I would never let my sisters go to school; it would bring shame on the family," he said. "We mujahed-din freed Kabul. It is our city now, and we will bring our values to it."

The power struggle unfolding in Kabul was a war of both ethnic-ity and values; a clash between the forces of modernity and tradition. Nowhere was it played out more visibly than on state television. The minister of information and culture, a close aide to Karzai, locked horns constantly with midlevel Panjshiri officials over whether popu-lar romantic Hindi movies could be broadcast, and how much hair women newscasters should be allowed to show beneath their head-scarves. Both were highly emotional flashpoints in a contest to deter-mine the role and definition of Islam in Afghanistan's future.

There was also intense competition between icons, myths, and versions of history. Islamic militia leaders wanted to glorify the anti-Soviet "jihad," suppress the unsavory mujaheddin period that fol-lowed, and take credit for the country's liberation from the Taliban. Being a "jihadi" meant having the pick of government jobs, even for illiterate veterans. Any criticism of former militia leaders—many of whom were responsible for terrible human rights abuses—was recast as disrespect for the sacred jihadi legacy.

With little respect for Karzai, the Panjshiris built an official per-sonality cult around their own hero: Ahmed Shah Massoud, the aus-tere and brilliant guerrilla commander who first led his Tajik forces against the Soviets and then waged a relentless campaign against the Taliban. Massoud never lived to see Kabul freed, though; he was as-sassinated two days before the World Trade Center attacks by two suicide bombers who visited his compound in northern Afghanistan, posing as journalists.

But Massoud's heirs shamelessly marketed his legacy as a way to ennoble their cruder grasp for power. Billboards, posters, and car-pets of the craggy commander, with his fox-like eyes and pie-shaped "pakul" cap, appeared throughout the capital. On the first anniversary of his death, Kabul was transformed into Massoud City, with a towering portrait unveiled over the national stadium as children chanted paeans and officials paid homage. A newcomer might logically assume that Massoud, not Karzai, was running the country.

Some Panjshiris were genuinely attached to Massoud, though, and sought to preserve his moral legacy. Massood Khalili, a longtime aide whom I had known as the Northern Alliance envoy in New Delhi, was gravely wounded by the same suicide bomb. When I visited him six months later—wheelchair-bound and pitted with shrapnel wounds—he wept as he described his last hours with Massoud, reading poems about moments of friendship that will never come again. "I loved my commander, did I tell you that?" the crippled man blurted out.

The only figure who could compete with Massoud's powerful image was the former king, Mohammed Zahir Shah. He was eighty-seven and ailing, and he had remained aloof from his homeland's turmoil during his long exile in Rome. In power he had been self-indulgent but benign, and many Afghans remembered his reign as a time of peace and gradual modernization. Pashtuns in particular believed only Zahir Shah had the stature to lead postwar Afghanistan and heal the divisions created by successive wars and revolutions.

"I was only seven when he left, but my father always sang his praises. Our shop was always open late, there was always enough to eat, and people walked the streets without fear." That was Delagha Khwaja, a Pashtun tailor whose shop I often visited for tea while he sat cross-legged in the gloom, stitching embroidered velvet dresses. "Every Afghan yearns for those times to come again," Delagha said. "We don't want a monarchy now, but we need the king to put things right."

Under the UN accord, the king was slated to return home by June and preside over a mass tribal assembly, known as a *loya jirga*, that would select a new government. But supporters hoped Zahir Shah would take the reins of power himself. Expectations for his triumphant homecoming spread; his half-ruined family tomb was repaired and a luxurious house prepared. Even the ancient royal gardener was brought in to tend the roses. But the king's detractors were determined to make sure he remained a ceremonial figure, and rumors of assassination plots spread, repeatedly postponing his return.

Meanwhile, plans for the loya jirga generated hope and excitement across the country. An independent commission set aside quotas for women and minority delegates, while banning anyone linked to human rights abuses. Commission members traveled to every province, explaining the process in mosques and schools. Some 1,500 local delegates would be elected by open ballot; they in turn would choose a new parliament and transitional government until a new constitution could be written and nationwide elections held. It sounded and felt remarkably like democracy in action.

In practice, though, political reality often intervened. People everywhere begged the commission members to send U.S. soldiers to protect the vote, but the peacekeepers were confined to Kabul. Militia leaders muscled their way into dozens of rural delegates' seats and even won elections in the capital. I watched in astonishment as Abdul Rasool Sayyaf, an Islamic cleric who headed an especially notorious militia, rose in a school auditorium, adjusted his bifocals and read out the required oath, swearing "before almighty God" that he had no links to terrorism, crime, human rights abuses, or "the murder of innocent people."

Moments later, Sayyaf was elected to represent his home district, and loya jirga officials endorsed the vote. Journalists crowded in, asking the white-bearded cleric about reports that his fighters had robbed, extorted, and destroyed large sections of Kabul during the civil war. But Sayyaf airily waved us off, saying there was "no legal proof" of such crimes, and withdrew to bask in his victory. I left the room deeply disillusioned. I had seen for myself how much power Afghanistan's hated warlords still wielded.

When Zahir Shah finally flew home on April 18, he kept a low profile, remaining at home under guard and receiving well-wishers on the terrace. But pernicious rumors about his family's ambitions threatened to derail the loya jirga. Finally, U.S. officials pressured him into a humiliating spectacle. Reporters were called to the king's home, but he slumped silently between Karzai and the U.S. ambassador. An aide read a short statement saying Zahir Shah had "no intent to restore the monarchy," and "fully supported" Karzai's candidacy to head the new transitional regime. That was all.

On June 11, in a huge, air-conditioned tent donated by a German foundation, the loya jirga opened. What transpired during the next ten days was both a miracle and a travesty. Afghans of every description took the microphones, speaking their minds freely—often in passionate, long-winded harangues—for the first time in years. Offstage, the chemistry was often therapeutic, with women scolding warlords and ethnic rivals chatting over tea. Journalists, banned from the tent, were limited to watching the proceedings on a giant screen at the InterContinental.

In other ways, though, the assembly made a mockery of its democratic mandate. Governors and militia leaders strong-armed local delegates, quashing a pro-king mutiny. Karzai was easily elected to continue as government head, and the hastily announced new cabinet included all the original Panjshiri members, reflecting a backroom deal to keep Fahim and his cohorts on board. Finally, the assembly became so mired in factional bickering that it never got around to establishing a new parliament.

"This was not a real loya jirga; it was not able to make decisions or exercise power. But it was an opportunity for Afghans from all backgrounds to meet and talk, to sit and realize they face a common problem," said Omar Zakhilwol, an Afghan economist who returned from Canada to participate. "Maybe we were naïve to expect democracy to be born at this loya jirga, but it opened up people's eyes, and that was an important first step."

Settling into Kabul as a foreign correspondent was a daily test of endurance and adaptability, even for those of us who had been perfectly happy in dense, dirty capitals like Mexico City or New Delhi. There were no newspapers, no cafes, no telephones. Most of us moved to houses in once-affluent neighborhoods, but even exorbitant rents did not guarantee being able to take a shower, fry an egg, or transmit a story. Sometimes the light, heat, and water would all fail, usually on deadline and after curfew, at which point we invariably discovered there was no fuel left in the generators. At such moments, I tried to remind myself that unfiled features or unwashed hair were petty annoyances compared to the resigned dread I had felt every day I woke up under Taliban rule.

I still drove to the InterContinental every morning to feed my family of stray dogs, secretly looking forward to their yelps of greeting, finding a few moments of quiet communion before the day began. The security guard, a grizzled militiaman, always shook his head in amusement, but sometimes I caught him throwing leftover rice their way. Then one morning when I arrived, I knew something was terribly wrong: the mother was lying still; the puppies were hysterical. There were strange men everywhere — municipal workers spreading poisoned meat in a crude but effective anti-rabies campaign.

It was too late to save the mother. She died as she had lived, at the fringe of an indifferent society. No one had loved her but me, no one else had been allowed to play with her pups. Now our bond of trust had been erased as if it never existed, and her body was being heaved into a garbage truck. I wanted to say good-bye, to somehow honor her short struggling life, but I had to think of the puppies instead. I rounded them up and put them in my car. One was cold and trembling, and I realized she must have eaten some of the poison. I stayed up with her for two nights, wrapping her in wet towels and pouring water down her throat, and she survived.

I named her Pak because it rhymed with *sack*, which is Pashto for dog. She grew into a stout, amiable creature who spent her days digging up rosebushes in my back yard and jumping on me with joyful, muddy paws. But even after a year, every time I drove up to the InterContinental for a meeting or a news conference, I could not bear to look at the empty spot behind the guard booth where, for a few moments each morning of my frantic, armored existence in that first, post-Taliban winter, I had felt needed and loved and at peace.

At first, Kabul after dark was little different from what it had been under the Taliban. Streets were deserted and curfew was crudely enforced. Returning from a trip to the countryside, we would frantically call colleagues on the satphone to learn the military password for that night. As we entered the city limits, soldiers screamed at us from the dark, guns leveled at the windshield. As we held our breaths, there would be a tense exchange of code-words. "Sixty-three," the driver would say. "Kalashnikov," the militiaman would answer, relaxing and waving us past.

As the foreign community grew, journalists and nonprofit groups began organizing evening parties, usually featuring Pringles (the only snack initially available in Kabul shops) and a smuggled bottle of Russian vodka. At 9 P.M., there would be a sudden scramble for the door, and those who lived nearby would stroll home tipsily under the stars, which glowed magnificently from the high altitude and lack of pollution.

After months of intense reporting, with little access to the world except BBC news and eight-dollar-a-minute satellite calls, those evenings recreated a microcosm of home I desperately missed. At the house shared by National Public Radio and Voice of America, I spent happy evenings playing Scrabble and singing harmony with Gary Thomas, a VOA correspondent who always traveled with his game board and guitar, and who knew all the lyrics to my favorite songs, including "Helplessly Hoping" and "The City of New Orleans."

Initially, we tended to invite few Afghans, because the cultural barriers were high and the social rules unclear in the evolving, post-Taliban atmosphere. Should we offer drinks? Should we include wives? Gradually, a handful of ministry officials and professionals began stopping by, though all arrived stag and almost all refused liquor—except for a few who surreptitiously poured their wine or whiskey into soda cans.

At the same time, we began to receive invitations to Afghan homes. The culture was famous for its hospitality, and people were eager to compensate for the hostility of the Taliban years. Often an interview would lead to an insistent invitation to lunch, and it was such bad manners to refuse, no matter how poor the host or meager the fare, that I often forced myself to push pieces of bread around a common pot of greasy soup, and was always rewarded with a franker conversation afterwards.

Over time, I grew close to several middle-class families and began to visit them for lunch after Friday prayers. It was from them that I came to understand both the endearing and asphyxiating aspects of Afghan culture—its social taboos, family demands, and ethnic prejudices as well as its supportive kinship ties and generosity. I was shocked to discover that many English-speaking young men I knew had two mothers and numerous half-siblings. Many men went to government jobs in suits and ties while their wives rarely left home, never wore Western clothes, and spent their days squatting over primitive woodstoves and washbasins exactly as they would have in a rural village.

Afghan family life was ruled by pride, shame, obligation, and fear of gossip; individual feelings were irrelevant, especially for women. I observed arranged marriages in which engaged couples saw each other rarely, always with relatives present and often without speaking together. I attended hotel weddings where guests danced to fast, thumping music but men and women were kept rigidly segregated, while the newlyweds—often both blood relatives and virtual strangers—sat stiffly on a stage, frowning as if presiding over a funeral. I saw how families were expected to feed and shelter endless streams of distant relatives who appeared on their doorsteps, and how wives had to endure years of beatings because it would bring intolerable shame on their families to seek a divorce.

I also came to understand the hollowness and despair experienced by educated, open-minded people who had stayed in Kabul during the Taliban era, while their active lifestyles shrank to four walls and their brains atrophied from idleness. I made friends with doctors and lawyers who had spent years driving taxis or clearing land mines, with bright young men and women who had lost so many years of school they no longer felt capable of learning. For anyone who knew English and WordPerfect, Kabul was now a goldmine; for everyone else, it was an illusory Oz. And yet I also saw how families who had stayed behind gave each other moral and material support, clinging together in a world gone mad.

One family I visited often were the Sarbozes, who lived in a vast, crumbling apartment complex. The family of nine had spent the Taliban years crammed together in three rooms, singing and playing detective games at night to keep from going crazy with boredom. Now they were determined to find a meaningful niche in their reborn country. Aziz, aged thirty-one, a lawyer purged from the Taliban justice ministry, went to work as a city prosecutor, citing butchers and bakers for health violations. He took great pride in helping restore law and order to a chaotic, half-ruined city. "You have to start somewhere," he told me, setting off to the meat bazaar one day with a spring in his step and a clipboard clutched under his arm.

His older sister Shiqiba, a medical doctor, had been able to keep her hospital job under the Taliban, but she hated wearing a burqa and being segregated from male patients and colleagues. Once the regime was gone, her spirits soared and she organized a party for International Women's Day at her clinic. Later, she showed me a video of the event, beaming as she watched herself, wearing a stylish black dress, deliver a short welcome speech in careful English.

Aziz's parents, Noor Ahmed and Noorzia, endured their own indignities under the Taliban. Noor Ahmed's career as a public health engineer had been truncated in the religious purge. Now, at sixty-four, he was still brimming with ideas but had lost much of his drive. "I know about many useful things, like drainage and industrial pollution, but the world thinks there are no professional people left in Afghanistan, just religious illiterates," he said bitterly. "There are many of us who have been here the whole time, hidden under our burqas and turbans."

Noorzia, a stout, dignified woman, confided to me that once she had been washing dishes at an outdoor tap of the apartment complex, with her scarf pulled back over her hair, when a Vice and Virtue enforcer sneaked up and whipped her hard across the back. Her voice still shook with rage as she told the story, and her husband's jaw still clenched with remembered humiliation.

One thing missing from the Sarboz apartment was photographs. Aziz and his brothers kept their tiny Taliban ID photos as perverse souvenirs, though I barely recognized them scowling in scraggly beards and turbans. There was also a blurry snapshot from Aziz's wedding day—just three weeks after the Taliban seized Kabul in 1996. After that the family album was blank, as if five years had passed with no memories worth preserving at all.

After a few months, though, I began to notice photos in the apartment: Aziz giving a legal lecture; Shiqiba at the hospital party; relatives gathered for a picnic. Slowly, the Sarbozes' life was returning to normal. For me, writing the saga of this family's rebirth felt like affirming the worth of Kabul's forgotten middle class. For them, the real thrill was seeing their pictures in the *Washington Post*. There was Noor Ahmed playing with his grandchildren; Aziz in his business suit; the entire family posing on the apartment stairs. Everyone stared at the paper, beaming and pointing. Then Aziz cleared his throat. "Do you think you could bring some more copies?" he asked.

That Kabul spring also brought a rite of passage I had dreaded: my fiftieth birthday. I had always seen myself as Peter Pan; eternally adventuresome and refusing to age. Determined to defeat this depressing milestone, I decided to throw myself a party. Even a few months earlier, it would have been impossible. Now, curfew had

been lifted, wine and beer were plentiful, and Afghans and Westerners mixed more often. I invited everyone I knew and delivered invitations all over the city, half in English and half in Dari.

By mid-evening the yard was crammed with guests and food.
The Massoumi brothers brought a cake; Aziz and his father arrived
in their best suits. Foreign ministry officials and loya jirga commis-
sioners chatted with journalists from a dozen countries. A trio of Afghan musicians played in a corner, and a dozen young Afghan men,
mostly diffident translators and drivers, began clapping and circling
and shimmying with sexual energy none of us had imagined they
possessed. Later, a UN refugee worker from Colombia put on a me-
rengue tape and twirled me around the parlor. When the candles
were lit for me to blow out, I wished for nothing but that moment: a
date I had feared, in a place I had hated, turning into a triumphant
night I would never forget.

∞

The other Americans in Afghanistan, a fighting force of 8,000 to
12,000 troops, existed in another world. They were stationed out of
sight, at fortified bases from which they conducted raids on areas
believed to harbor pockets of Taliban and Arab forces. Only civil affairs teams and Special Forces officers, distinguished by their short
beards, wraparound shades and thigh pistols, had any dealings with
ordinary Afghans. There were no salutes or off-duty leaves. Officially, the entire country was a war zone.

My first encounters with U.S. troops were at the Kandahar airport, which had been turned into an ultra-secure military base. There
were triple-razor-wire rolls, bomb-sniffing dogs, and sentries whose
thermal rifle sights could sense a mouse in the grass at 500 yards.
Inside, a canteen sold Big Red, Crest, and M&Ms; messages from
American schoolchildren were taped on the walls. Most troops never
left the base, except in patrol convoys. None had been in Afghanistan
before, and in a sense they were not here now. Every time I entered
the compound, sand-blown and grumpy from multiple security
searches, a young serviceman from Georgia or New Jersey would
say, "You actually live out there? What's it like?"

The main base, at Bagram airfield, was a larger, more permanent
operation that gradually evolved into an American mini-city, with a

post office, phone-home tent, weight-lifting area, and giant PX. The canteen had an unlimited supply of plastic-pouched, self-heating meals, from chow mein to lasagne. The state-of-the-art command center had a bank of laptop computers and a giant screen tracking every military move in the country.

American journalists visited Bagram constantly, and some lived there for months, waiting for the chance to accompany a raiding party or at least film troops returning from the mountains. I made dozens of trips there for briefings, but we were barred from wandering around the base. Somewhere at Bagram was a hangar where Afghan and Arab detainees were kept in barbed-wire cages, but no one in authority would reveal the number or names of prisoners, even when their families had given us precise information. For all we knew, they might as well have been on Mars.

The troops at Bagram had a single mission: to hunt down and wipe out any remaining enemy forces. Most of their operations were in the high, barren hills of eastern Afghanistan, where hundreds of fighters were believed to be hiding in caves and ridges. In March, the allies launched Operation Anaconda, an ambitious sweep involving 3,000 Western and Afghan troops. Dropped from helicopters onto 8,000-foot slopes in the Shahikot Mountains, they endured searing-hot days and frozen, starry nights.

When the men returned, we were allowed to meet them as they staggered out of big black Chinooks under huge backpacks of grenade launchers or machine gun parts. Exhausted, filthy, and sunburned, they collapsed on the ground and described their experiences: grueling high-altitude treks, sniper attacks from distant ridges. After a handful of interviews, I realized how young and green—if highly trained and motivated—these young servicemen really were.

"It was nothing like training at all," a sergeant told me. He was blond, blue-eyed, and not half my age. "There were real bullets, and they were intended to hit you. It was scary at all times." After one mortar attack from the hills, he said, "you learned fast. As soon as you heard the hissing, you got down. As soon as you heard the boom, you got up and ran again."

The men never actually got close to an enemy fighter, though. If a few snipers' heads popped up along a ridge line, the officers called in air strikes and the site was pounded with bombs. They found surprisingly few bodies, but abundant evidence of human activity in abandoned caves and camps: half-eaten meals, clippings of just-cut hair, and boxes of alarm clocks waiting to be attached to explosive detonators.

Far trickier and more hazardous were the raids on occupied villages, mostly in Pashtun areas where there was suspicion of Taliban presence or support. Combat squads would descend on a mud-walled hamlet, kicking in doors and shouting while attack helicopters hovered overhead. Sometimes Afghan men would be handcuffed and led away as their wives and children ran out, weeping and shrieking. This was murky political terrain; such raids were often based on tips from other Afghans with unclear motives. Sometimes confusion and panic, coupled with modern military might, led to tragedy.

In July, I was visiting Islamabad when heard the first sketchy but sensational reports: the Americans had bombed an Afghan village wedding; Afghan officials said there were forty dead, mostly women and children. It had happened in Oruzgun Province, a rugged Pashtun region that had been home to both Taliban leaders and an anti-Taliban force organized by Karzai. The story was explosive, and I knew I had to reach the village as fast as possible.

The next morning I landed in Kabul, grabbed a taxi and headed south toward Kandahar, steeling myself for the dust-choked, spine-killing, fourteen-hour trip. By the time darkness fell, we were still in the desert and the driver was growing nervous. At 10 P.M., three soldiers at a checkpost blocked our way; there were gunmen ahead and all traffic must halt until dawn. In the darkness I could see a dozen cargo trucks, their drivers huddled under blankets in the sand.

I knew I was stuck, but I refused to give up on my story. There was a rundown café behind the checkpost, with a buzzing generator. I lugged my computer to the porch, plugged it into a dangling socket, connected it to my satphone, and voila! I had instant access to every wire report. American officials said their planes had attacked after coming under anti-aircraft fire; villagers insisted the only shots were from guests firing celebratory rifle rounds as part of Pashtun wedding tradition.

I couldn't reach the scene, but I could still write what I knew. For two hours I typed in the steamy darkness, batting away bugs and trying to ignore the circle of silent turbaned men that gathered to watch me and my exotic paraphernalia. At 1 A.M. I punched the "send" command, packed up my gear and fell fitfully asleep in the back of the taxi, with my arms looped through half a dozen equipment straps. My story, filed from a desert truck stop, made the front page.

By the next morning, I was at the Red Cross hospital in Kandahar. A tiny boy with a chest wound was curled on his side, stuck with tubes and moaning in pain; an uncle said both his parents had been killed in the assault. "Fifteen people from my home are dead. I don't know why the Americans hate us," the man said, cradling the boy in his lap. A young woman lay with her leg in a cast, her party dress splattered with blood. "We were all so happy and clapping. Then the bombs came and I saw people running and shouting and falling," she said.

The next day I reached the village after a hellish, seven-hour jeep journey through the badlands of Oruzgun. I was traveling with Ivan Watson from National Public Radio, a brash young adventurer whom I hated that day for being able remove his shirt in the scorching heat. We were greeted by the local elders, who swore they were loyal to the government and showed us AK-47 rifles given to them by Karzai to help overthrow the Taliban. They spoke bitterly of being falsely denounced to the Americans by their local enemies, of U.S. troops sweeping through the village after the assault and handcuffing women to men—a sexual outrage in Islam.

Finally we came to the scene of the slaughter: A mud-walled compound with an arched doorway leading to a large dirt courtyard. In the entrance lay a jumble of plastic sandals, untouched—or possibly arranged—as if to preserve evidence. Inside sat an old woman, wailing and rocking. She told us several hundred women had gathered to dance and sing on the night of the wedding, while the men went to a separate place. Then out of the sky swooped a noisy plane or helicopter, circling and firing down. Many women and children had been killed, and many injured.

It was a gruesome story, repeated by many witnesses. And yet we saw no blood, no bodies, just some holes in the dusty walls and some fragments of shredded gray metal. Were we being duped? Was this a Taliban village in disguise? Could the Americans, with their precision bombs, have made such a terrible mistake? Back at Bagram, officials continued to insist that U.S. reconnaissance planes had faced "sustained hostile fire," and that helicopter gunships had responded. In the end, we remained skeptical of both versions. Forty-eight people had died, and both Afghan skulldug-gery and American overkill had played a role. More than that, we would probably never know.

Whenever I traveled to areas where American troops had been hunting for Taliban and al Qaeda fighters, I was struck by the dis-connect between their narrow mission and Afghanistan's complex re-ality. In many places, ethnic rivalries, tribal squabbles, corruption and warlordism loomed much larger in people's fears than attacks by al Qaeda. To many Afghans, the Western military crusade to root out Islamic terrorism seemed an abstract obsession, while the presence of local bullies was a daily threat.

For the foreign troops, distinguishing friend from foe was a tricky and dangerous business. Tribal leaders glibly denounced per-sonal enemies as "Taliban" or "al Qaeda," and one militia chief called in a U.S. airstrike against a convoy from a rival group. Villagers begged the Americans for protection from warlords but then pro-tested indignantly when the Americans arrested tribal leaders sus-pected of collaborating with the Taliban.

Equally treacherous were relations between the Western forces and their erstwhile allies, the Northern Alliance militias. To ensure the defeat of the Taliban, U.S. military and intelligence operatives plied these groups with money and weapons, regardless of their re-cords. Now, some of these same militia leaders turned against the Karzai government, refusing to accept its authority and running their regions like armed fiefdoms, even as the U.S. military continued to depend on them for help in the anti-terrorist campaign.

In Khost, an eastern provincial capital near the Pakistan border, Karzai named Hakim Taniwal, a soft-spoken sociology professor, as governor, and he received me warmly in his official guest house. But just blocks away, troops loyal to Bacha Khan Zadran, a tribal war-lord who had fought the Taliban alongside U.S. forces, physically prevented Taniwal from entering his office. Zadran, who thought he deserved to be governor instead, held the province hostage for months, blocking the highway and shelling the airport, until he fi-nally tired of the fight and retreated to his rural lair.

In Herat, a province bordering Iran, militia commander Ismael Khan ruled as self-proclaimed "emir." A stern Islamic conservative, he banned the Internet from his realm and subjected women to hos-pital chastity tests. His power was financed by customs duties, which he refused to turn over to Kabul, and he enjoyed demonstrating his vigorous grip to the foreign press. On one visit, I followed Khan in an official caravan where children lined the roads holding up his portrait. Later he took a photogenic sunset gallop on a white stallion, and at midnight the indefatigable "emir" was still at his desk, receiving Heratis' humble requests for help in land disputes and divorces.

In Kandahar, a sand-swept southern city that had been the Taliban's religious base, the bazaars offered a post-Taliban smorgasbord for every taste—opium paste and Osama bin Laden candy, kung-fu videos and fighting partridges, kites and burqas in rainbow colors. Karzai's appointed governor was Gul Agha Shirzai, a vulgar but shrewd militia leader who had helped rout the Taliban, yet many Kandaharis remained in mourning for the toppled Islamic leaders and fearful that chaos and crime would fill their wake.

Early in the year, I visited a cemetery in Kandahar where veiled women wept over the tombs of slain Taliban officials. One laboriously carved epitaph listed the achievements of a slain Taliban governor: a builder of mosques and madrassahs, a fighter against communists and enemies of Islam. As my translator read from the stone, I realized this was the Taliban's history of itself. The movement had left no monuments or memoirs; its only written legacy was in memorials to its dead. In another cemetery, emotional crowds of men and boys swarmed the fresher graves of Arab fighters, seeking a blessing from their martyred souls. When I tried to interview them, I was pelted with rocks.

The region that intrigued and repelled me most, though, was the north. In part, this was because it had been cut off from the rest of Afghanistan for so long. The Salang Tunnel, a mountain highway pass that linked the north to Kabul, had been bombed shut by Massoud in 1997, and the road became a war zone. Terrible things had happened above the Salang—revenge massacres, ethnic atrocities— but they had been largely shrouded by the fog of war, with few outside witnesses, and tens of thousands of inhabitants had fled as far as southern Pakistan.

As soon as the Taliban left, many northerners were anxious to return home. The Salang was frozen shut, but thousands of people trekked up the highway, slipped through holes cut in the ice, and walked through. One day in January, so cold my camera batteries froze, I watched a stream of families, some with only sandals on their

feet, disappear down crude ice steps into the frigid, pitch-black tunnel, carrying babies, suitcases and sacks of merchandise. I decided to
climb down too, and lasted five minutes. The tunnel felt like a meat
locker with an arctic wind blowing through it. As Afghans brushed
down and past me into the dark, I hurriedly struggled back up to the
light.

By late spring, the Salang had melted enough to admit cars, although crawling through the mile-long tunnel was a four-hour nightmare of toxic fumes, inching trucks and deep icy ruts. Two hundred
miles north lay Mazar-I-Sharif, the regional capital built around a
historic blue-tiled Islamic shrine. The city had long been in the grip
of Gen. Abdurrashid Dostom, an Uzbek warlord and Northern Alliance member, who issued his own currency and required visitors to
register at his own "foreign ministry."

Dostom had a reputation for ruthlessness and cruelty; the see-
sawing battle over Mazar between his forces and the Taliban had
been marked by mass slaughter and reports of prisoners being sealed
inside trucks to die. But by the fall of 2001 he had become a crucial
ally in the Western military assault. Soon after the installation of the
Karzai government, the shrewd general reinvented himself as a shirt-
sleeved politician, hiring a public relations team and treating journalists to lavish meals in his personal headquarters.

On a trip to Mazar in May, I watched in fascination as Dostom,
aged forty-seven, presided over a convention of his revived political
party, calling on Afghans to build a "real democracy" that would be
"free, united, peaceful, and secure." The same day he easily won election to the loya jirga after a tentful of illiterate Uzbek elders marked
Xes across the ballot printed with his symbol, a globe. He eagerly
took up Karzai's call to disarm regional militias, but his real intent
was to emasculate a rival Tajik commander, Mohammed Attah,
whose troops constantly clashed with his.

Two months later on a trip with several other journalists to Shibberghan, Dostom's hometown several hours from Mazar, I glimpsed
the cruel truth about the defeat of the Taliban's northern forces,
largely at Dostom's hands. Thousands of surrendered Taliban fighters were still detained in the local prison, and we were told that some
were about to be released. Entering the compound, we saw a sea of
emaciated, silent men squatting on the ground. There was little time
to talk, but I sensed that awful secrets lay behind their stony stares.

An official started to read off names, then decided to throw open the iron gates. The men rose in disbelief, some limping, others dropping ragged bundles and racing for the exit.

Outside, dozens of prisoners' families were waiting, and they shouted out names in the dust and din of the oncoming rush. Many had traveled long distances to be there; several villagers said their sons had been forcibly conscripted in the final months of Taliban rule. I watched one elderly man reach up to embrace his gaunt, shivering son and try to put his own cloak around the boy's shoulders. It was a gesture of unbearable tenderness; a fragment of grace in a field of broken men. I had lost my translator in the melee, but the power of that scene would have been diminished by words. I just stood and stared, knowing this was the moment I had traveled 400 miles to witness.

Most of the prisoners at Shibberghan were "ordinary" Taliban, illiterate villagers of no political consequence. The tougher, more senior captured fighters, both Afghan and Arab, had been confined at Qala-I-Jangi, a mud-walled military fort nearby. In November 2001, a group of these desperate, defiant prisoners had staged an uprising at the fort, killing one American CIA agent; shortly after that they had nearly all been wiped out by massive American bombing.

As we were driving past the fort, we stopped on a whim; to our surprise the military guards were happy to show us the site of the conflagration. Hesitantly, we climbed down into the cellar where the Islamic fighters had made their hopeless stand against the infidel invaders. It was a charred hole, strewn with filthy, blood-spattered black cloths. I realized that the rags were the trampled turbans of the dead; all that remained of the once-powerful Taliban mystique. I wondered if these men, trapped in an underground inferno, had really believed they were going to paradise.

I didn't know it then, but the ghosts of Shibberghan were far greater in number. There were rumors of hundreds, perhaps thousands of Taliban prisoners sealed into trucks after they surrendered, and arriving at Dostom's prison dead or dying. In August, *Newsweek* published a horrifying account of the death caravan; drivers described men screaming for air and sticking blackened tongues out holes in the searing-hot containers; other witnesses described seeing the trucks opened at the prison with bodies flopping out like fish.

The corpses were rumored to have been buried in mass graves in the desert, but neither the Karzai government nor UN authorities in Kabul dared investigate for fear of retaliation by Dostom. There were also reports that U.S. special forces, working with Dostom to defeat the Taliban, had known of the atrocities and done nothing to stop them. An Irish journalist, Jamie Doran, made a film suggesting U.S. forces were complicit. The Pentagon strongly denied the charges, and several Afghans who collaborated with Doran were beaten or killed, apparently by Dostom's men.

Perhaps, one day, the mass graves of northern Afghanistan will be dug up, as they were in Argentina and Rwanda, with bones and bits of cloth revealing clues that can help identify the victims and prosecute the killers. But even if that day never comes, the descriptions from witnesses are damning enough. One man, whose face was hidden in the Doran film, said he saw a truck being opened up, with half-roasted corpses tangled in a slime of blood and vomit and feces. "I will never forget that smell as long as I live," he said.

∾

On the surface, life in Kabul was relatively safe and civilized. The ubiquitous UN peacekeeper tanks, the soldiers shopping for carpets on Chicken Street and tousling urchins' hair, created a lulling sense of security. An occasional rocket landed in the city, reminding the public that unseen enemies lurked nearby, but the attacks were erratic and rarely caused damage.

Meanwhile, American and UN military trainers were working hard to forge a new, multiethnic national army, a professional fighting force that would be loyal to the central government and, one day, rid Afghanistan of warlordism forever. Every few months, another class of trainees would perform on the UN military parade ground, conducting precision drills and mock assaults for an audience of beaming foreign and Afghan officials.

But Karzai and his government were vulnerable to an array of enemies, both internal and external. Afghanistan remained awash in weapons and roiling with rivalries. The culture of democracy was new and untested; the culture of intimidation and score-settling was old and entrenched. Every few months, another violent political crime shattered the capital, reminding the public and the world how precarious the country's post-Taliban peace really was.

The first incident was a murky assassination, disguised as an attack by an excited religious mob. The victim was Abdul Rahman, the minister of tourism and civil aviation. The setting was Kabul's airport on the night of February 14, where thousands of Muslims had been waiting several days for flights that would take them to Mecca for the annual hajj pilgrimage. Rahman boarded another plane en route to India, but the angry crowd of hajjis surrounded it. In the darkness, Rahman was stabbed and beaten to death. A few hours later, Karzai appeared on state TV, shaken and angry. He denounced a high-level plot involving Panjshiri officials in three ministries, and vowed to investigate the slaying.

The next day the foreign affairs minister, one of Karzai's Panjshiri rivals, announced that there had been no such plot, and that Rahman had been killed by the mob. But conspiracy rumors continued to swirl, and numerous sources told me Rahman, another Panjshiri who had feuded with Fahim's faction, had been knifed by personal rivals inside his plane, then pushed out into the angry crowd. Several of the alleged plotters were reported to have fled to Saudi Arabia and then quietly returned home. But no formal investigation was ever completed, and Karzai—who stood in grim silence next to the top Panjshiri ministers at Rahman's funeral in a misty hillside cemetery—never referred to it directly again.

Five months later, an even bolder assassination took place: Vice President Abdul Qadir, a veteran tribal politician from Jalalabad and the highest-ranking Pashtun in Karzai's new cabinet, was gunned down at midday on July 6 as he drove out of the Public Works Ministry in his black Landcruiser. When I arrived there half an hour later, the vehicle was still crashed into a ministry wall, riddled with bullet holes and surrounded, belatedly, by UN troops. Qadir's bloody prayer beads were still on the front seat. Afghan officials at the scene said two killers had escaped in a taxi, and they vaguely attributed the slaying to "enemies of Afghanistan."

This time a high-ranking investigative commission was named, but no one expected the truth to come out. Many Pashtuns suspected the Panjshiri cabal, but conveniently for whoever the killers were, Qadir had been a controversial man with an endless supply of enemies, from rival militia leaders to opium poppy traders to his own relatives. Still, the fact that a vice president could be slain with impunity, outside his office in midday, meant that no Afghan leader was safe.

The assassination and its international fallout exacerbated tensions between Karzai and Fahim. The president complained that the defense minister was trying to stack the new army and the security ministries with ethnic loyalists. Fahim was infuriated when Karzai's Afghan military guards were replaced by American commandos. When the *Post* printed a story by Susan Glasser and me about these tensions, Fahim called a press conference just to deny it. Susan had left Kabul by then, and I had to sit through the event, dutifully taking notes with a frozen smile, as Fahim fulminated about Western media bias and lies in the *Post*.

Despite the tightened ring of security around Karzai and the capital, minor rocketings and other attacks continued to occur periodically. Officials blamed them on a shadowy array of enemy forces including Taliban loyalists, al Qaeda remnants, Pakistani spies, and followers of Gulbuddin Hekmatyar, a fugitive militia leader and one-time American favorite in the anti-Soviet conflict.

On September 5, real terror struck. It was a busy afternoon, on a street crammed with shoppers. A small explosion was heard, drawing curious onlookers. Minutes later, an enormous blast shattered windows and strewed the street with bloody bits of flesh. The bomb, planted in a parked taxi, killed twenty-six. This was not a furtive potshot; it was the kind of calculated attack I had seen in Kashmir and many of my colleagues had seen in the Middle East. We had no idea who was responsible, but their aim was clear: to terrify and kill as many people as possible.

My colleagues and I grimly roamed the streets, interviewing shopkeepers and police, photographing bloody footprints and glass shards. Kabul's main bazaar, one block away, was always jammed with trinket salesmen and money changers and pickpockets; now there was only dead silence. At one point I felt a tap on my shoulder, and turned to see a long-lost friend—an Afghan lawyer who had once been my taxi driver in Islamabad, and who had just brought his family home to Kabul. We hugged in the swirling crowd, caught between happiness at the chance reunion and horror at its circumstances.

As dusk fell, most journalists headed to the Foreign Ministry for a briefing that yielded little but official expressions of horror. I left the building, and a few minutes later my mobile phone rang; it was a colleague saying I should rush back. Traffic was completely jammed, so I ran the last five blocks. Abdullah, the minister, was back in the briefing room, his face ashen. Karzai had just been attacked by a gunman while visiting Kandahar; the uniformed man had fired into his car from a few feet away, then been shot dead by Karzai's American bodyguards.

The president survived unharmed—indeed, the astonishingly resilient Karzai appeared on TV hours later, chuckling and remarking that such attacks were "to be expected" in his line of work. But as we absorbed this new shock, the same thought gripped us all: It was too much of a coincidence; it had to be a coordinated plot. And then this: If the gunman had succeeded, or if another succeeded next time, the country would literally fall apart.

∾

A year after the rout of the Taliban, Karzai was still in office, but he rarely ventured out of his security bubble now, and the country seemed to be drifting from one disappointment to another. In the capital, the postwar bustle continued; more exiles returned, more weddings were held. But roads remained cratered and factories closed. Regional warlords still resisted central authority, and political promise was replaced by deepening cynicism. International attention waned, the stream of aid slowed, and some journalists left for the Middle East, where a new American military campaign was brewing.

For those of us who stayed, life grew easier by the day. Power failures were less frequent, ministries acquired e-mail, Internet cafes sprouted across the city, and a new international supermarket sold imported dog food, French cheese, and Scotch whiskey to anyone with a Western passport.

But I too was growing disillusioned. I admired Karzai for trying to set an example, but virtually no one followed it. I saw few acts of altruism and far too many incidents of bullying, cheating, and malice. I was surrounded by people who smiled and fingered prayer beads as they stole. No deal was final, no answer was straight, and every circumstance, from a job application to a riverside picnic, was an opportunity to take advantage. Meat donated to feed the emaciated Kabul Zoo animals vanished; so did cement donated to build schools.

I even caught myself shouting in exasperation at the wheedling widows who surrounded my car. I felt as if Afghanistan, after three decades of utopian but extremist causes with violent endings, was becoming just another nasty Third World bazaar.

Whenever I felt especially demoralized after a day of petty hostilities and lewd stares and garbage-piled sidewalks, I sat for a while in my garden and tried to cling to the few fragments of grace that had filtered through the squalid haze. Almost always they were unexpected, generous gestures from people who could not afford to make them.

One day, when I was shopping for blankets in a bazaar, I bumped straight into Mohammed Sardar, the little gray-bearded man who had traveled to Islamabad with his packet of letters asking President Bush to stop the bombing of Kabul. He was overjoyed to see me, and he insisted repeatedly that I let his wife cook me dinner in thanks. Three times I agreed to visit his home, in a poor district on the outskirts of the capital, and three times I backed out, ostensibly because something more urgent came up.

I thought guiltily of the classic fable about Afghan hospitality I had once read in an extraordinary photo-journalist's book called *The Victor Weeps*. It was about a Pashtun man who thrice refused a friend's dinner invitation, then accepted another's. The spurned host, chancing upon the two diners, was so insulted that he fetched his gun and shot them both dead. Mr. Sardar, however, bore me no ill will. I was a busy foreign journalist, he was a nobody. He sent his son to my house one day, on foot, carrying a heavy bundle. It was a set of chipped enamel pots wrapped in a shawl. Inside was an entirely cooked dinner for six.

Conclusion

ALL perception is relative. I am back in New Delhi, a city I once dismissed as a sweltering, mildewy, bureaucratic labyrinth full of wheedling beggars and haughty clerks and gloppy food and infuriating traffic. Five years later, as I return to pack up my long-abandoned office after months of living in Kabul, coping with frozen showers and spine-jolting roads and violent power politics, Delhi suddenly seems like an oasis of civilization and freedom.

The boulevards feel strangely smooth and wide, the traffic seems orderly and polite. The foliage is green, the breeze is fresh, the parks are neatly tended, the marble lobbies are air-conditioned. There are newspaper stands and public phones on every corner, bookshops and bank machines and health clubs tucked into brightly lit plazas. There are slender girls in jeans chatting on cell phones and chubby kids lining up for Big Macs. And, for the first time in months, nobody is gawking at me in the streets.

Of course, I am only back for a few days, to say good-bye at the end of my regional tour of duty. I have spent too little time in India to miss it, but for a brief moment, the idiosyncrasies and excesses that once drove me to distraction seem endearing. Once I regarded the thick stack of morning newspapers as a chore to be tackled: now they have become a smorgasbord to be savored. Once I dreaded the endless triplicate forms awaiting me at various ministries; now they seem like miraculous evidence of a functioning state. Once I fumed at the studied disinterest of clerks and commuters and secretaries; now I am grateful to be anonymous.

As I crisscross the city on a final round of errands and farewells, I glimpse common sights that suddenly seem uniquely special. The hand-painted movie posters of buxom heroines and snarling gangsters. The bony cows pulling lawn mowers across public parks. The mischievous monkeys grabbing bananas from the fruit carts outside

245

the Ministry of Defense. An elephant patiently waiting at a traffic light. The barefoot boy who races up to my car window at the Moti Bagh Flyover, tossing a penny-tabloid inside and hoping I will buy it.

Despite these reassuringly timeless details, though, some things are not the same. India has become a nastier place since I left, less tolerant and more suspicious, less gracious and more raw. Incidents of terrorism and mob violence, the worst in years, have jangled the country's nerves and hardened its heart. Tensions between Hindus and Muslims, kept in check for a decade, are now seething again.

Although the Vajpayee government took credit for the long lull in religious violence, I knew it was only a matter of time. Rama and I had spent months interviewing Muslims across India, discovering a vast yet scattered and powerless minority of 140 million people, still scarred by Partition, ostracized by the Hindu establishment and held back by its own traditions. Discrimination was outlawed but ubiquitous: police bias, job denials, dirty looks. The Hindu nationalist movement, encouraged by some official sectors, was becoming bolder and more aggressive, promoting causes that had led to violence in the past. There were no incidents of mass hatred, but only the right spark was missing.

In February 2002, the spark ignited in Gujarat State. A trainload of Hindu activists, participating in a revived campaign to build a temple on the site of a historic mosque, was attacked and burned, leaving fifty-nine dead. Hindu riots erupted in retaliation. For a solid week, rampaging mobs torched and looted Muslim homes, slashed and beat Muslim strangers and neighbors alike. "Mothers were skewered on swords as their children watched," Celia Dugger wrote in the *New York Times*. "Young women were stripped and raped . . . doused with kerosene and set on fire."

The region's Hindu-led police and political establishment did little to intervene. When the religious rage was spent, after two months of sporadic violence, nearly a thousand people were dead and the depth of communal hatred lingering a half-century after Partition was exposed anew. The Vajpayee government, while officially espousing religious tolerance, had allowed Hindu nationalism to reach new emotional extremes and political ambitions, with tragic results.

At the same time, the heightened threat of Islamic terrorism was exacerbating tensions between India and Pakistan. Just three weeks after the September 11 attacks in the United States, Muslim guerrillas assaulted the legislative assembly in the Kashmir city of Srinagar, killing thirty-eight. On December 14, another suicide squad attempted to storm New Delhi's parliament house—the most prominent symbol of Indian democracy—setting off a gunbattle that left thirteen dead.

Indian officials blamed two Pakistan-based Islamic guerrilla groups, Lashkar-e-Taiba and Jaish-e-Mohammed, and demanded that Musharraf shut them down. India warned it would "liquidate the terrorists and their sponsors," and might even attack militant training camps inside Pakistan. The Indian ambassador was recalled from Islamabad, extra troops were deployed to the border, and the two nuclear powers veered extremely close to war.

The Bush administration, dependent on Musharraf's new cooperation in the anti-terror campaign, could do little more than urge restraint on both sides and politely prod Musharraf to rein in the Islamic groups. But the harsh anti-Pakistan rhetoric emanating from New Delhi, both more aggressive and more frightened than any I had heard in five years, seemed to echo America's own transformation from self-confident, magnanimous superpower to wounded, snarling behemoth. India, an elephant stung by ants, was bellowing in rage against its democratic restraints.

Returning to India during a period of such hostility was a disconcerting experience for me. I wanted to do a bit of sentimental sightseeing, but had I learned too much about the region's cruel history—especially the bloodthirsty, six-century reign of the Mughal emperors—to be dazzled by its monuments. Shah Jehan, who commissioned the delicate floral mosaics of the Taj Mahal to memorialize his wife, also overthrew his father and murdered half his family to reach the throne. Tughluk, whose crumbling fort I had often visited to watch scampering monkeys, was a brutal tyrant with an army of slaves and spies who invented novel tortures and expelled the entire population of the capital in a fit of pique.

I was still awestruck by the Jama Masjid, the majestic central mosque of Old Delhi, with its wide empty plazas and barefoot pilgrims napping in the shadows. But since my first visit there, I had experienced Taliban rule in Afghanistan and terrorism in Pakistan, and I had seen how Muslims were reviled and persecuted in purportedly secular India. Somehow, the knowledge of these things made the splendid old mosque seem shabbier; a false beacon surrounded by alleys full of flies and disappointment and seedy corruption.

Rekindling personal ties also proved difficult after such a long absence. I was warmly welcomed back by Michael Sullivan from NPR and Jim Teeple from VOA, with whom I had shared some true adventures, especially the uplifting Hindu festival on the Ganges and the nightmarish earthquake in Gujarat. But many of my colleagues had already moved on to new assignments in Beijing or Jerusalem or Mexico; couples I knew had split up; phones had been disconnected. There were new officials in the ministries; new clerks in the shops; even new beggars on some of the corners.

My old house was empty now, the patio strewn with fallen branches, a chain padlocked across the gate. My books and clothes were in boxes, Ravi's drawings were gone from my office walls, and the staff had already moved into a new house, chosen by the incoming correspondent from Washington. Asha and Ashok were happy to see me, we laughed and hugged, but I could also see sadness, and a bit of distance, in their eyes. They were anxious to please the next foreigner on whom their survival would now depend, and their loyalties had already shifted.

The worst moment came when we had to decide what to do with my dog, Mundan. I couldn't take her back to Afghanistan, and no one I knew in Delhi wanted to keep her, so I reluctantly decided to leave her at a shelter run by a Hindu charity. As I drove away from the house with Mundie in the back seat, Asha began to weep into her sari cloth. She didn't say a word, but I knew she was reliving our odyssey to the Ganges, the shivering dawn with the screaming baby boy, the train trip back to Delhi with the smuggled puppy, so very long ago.

I suddenly felt overwhelmed by frustration, guilt, and a vicarious sense of powerlessness; by the immutable stratification of Indian society, by the whims of wealthy employers that dictated the lives of the poor. After three years of feeding and brushing and walking Mundie, Asha could do nothing to stop her from being given away. After all the midnight news crises and monsoon housefloods and shared confidences and cups of tea, I too was leaving forever. I would keep sending the Pandeys cards for Christmas and Ravi's birthdays, but I could never make up for abandoning them. By the time I saw their little boy again, he would probably be a grown man.

∾

Closing shop in Islamabad was traumatic in a different way. It had always been a businesslike capital for me, with fewer personal memories and friendships, but it had also been a comforting base in a volatile region, a quiet and secure oasis where I felt at home. But when I returned to pack up, just before Christmas 2002, the atmosphere had chilled and security was tighter. A surge of Islamic terrorism and angry demonstrations in the months after September 11 had driven many Westerners away, and the small community of foreign journalists had been badly shaken by the kidnapping and murder of Daniel Pearl, a *Wall Street Journal* correspondent.

I did not know Danny very well, but we had crossed paths at the Chez Soi in happier times. In January 2002, while I was immersed in the ebullient novelty of post-Taliban Kabul, he was on the trail of underground Islamic fanatics in Karachi, hoping they would lead him to information about a British man who had been arrested on an American Airlines flight with a bomb in his shoe. Instead, Danny was lured to a secret rendezvous by e-mail, held prisoner for days while his captors sent out a series of Internet demands, and then beheaded in a videotaped execution.

At the time, many journalists in Afghanistan commented on the irony of being safer there, in a country we had once feared and loathed, than in Pakistan, which was far more modern and well-policed. We also debated whether we would have taken the same steps that led Danny unwittingly to his death. I had always been cautious in riots and quick to duck crossfire, but even more wary of dealing with secret groups or strangers I didn't trust. Still, all of us had been in rapidly shifting circumstances, unfamiliar with local languages, dependent on strangers, forced to make instant choices with little but instinct to guide us. All of us could have been Daniel Pearl.

The gruesome crime and international scandal deeply embarrassed Musharraf, who had recently vowed to crack down on Islamic terrorist groups and declared that the true "jihad" should be against poverty and illiteracy. After Danny's death, Musharraf ordered a massive manhunt that led to a number of arrests and convictions, but many militants were quietly released. Even a military president who had allied himself with the West against al Qaeda did not have sufficient political muscle to rein in Islamic violence in his own country.

There were other ominous signs that Pakistan, caught between the push toward worldly modernization and the drag of religious traditionalism, was slipping backward. A coalition of Islamic parties, long pooh-poohed as a radical fringe, emerged from national elections in October 2002 as the country's strongest political bloc. In Peshawar, where the Islamic groups won control of provincial power, the mullahs toned down their fanatical anti-Western rhetoric and adopted a new vocabulary of constituent service, but then introduced full-fledged Shariah law and proposed a Taliban-like religious police to enforce it.

Still, Islamabad remained a cocoon of modernism, and I was happy to be back at the Chez Soi for several days. There were few guests now, and almost no journalists at all, but the staff had dutifully fed Rafi and the white cat and kept my room ready in case I suddenly appeared. I spent several days packing up my belongings, reliving many intense months as I waded through waist-high stacks of newspapers. There was a photo of Musharraf, solemnly addressing the nation on TV after the coup. There were anti-Taliban troops celebrating in liberated Kabul, and mobs in Peshawar burning effigies of President Bush, and Kashmiri villages in flames.

I could hardly believe I had seen and lived through and produced so much, in such a short time. But when I was finished culling and purging and boxing, the room where I had spent so many late nights at my laptop, surrounded by papers and phone lists and coffee cups, looked like a stranger's quarters, an impersonal cubicle that bore no trace of me or my frenetic existence there. I had arranged to ship Rafi and the white cat home to the United States. Next time I returned, there would be no more quiet morning walks in the neighborhood, no one waiting for me to put a bowl of milk on the porch.

Other places once special to me were no longer the same, either. Protestant International Church had been repaired and reopened, but my friends from church were long gone, and the building now conjured up images of terror instead of sanctuary. I had worked hard in Pakistan to understand Islam and fit into a more conservative religious culture. I still loved the muezzin's call, and I was sure the Muslim prayer recited on all Pakistani International Airline flights had helped guide my plane safely to Lahore one summer night, after we pitched wildly through the most terrifying thunderstorm I have ever experienced. But when my church was bombed that Sunday, I found myself railing against a faith that inspired young men to slaughter innocents—and angrily standing up to defend my own.

Most of all, I would miss the little attic in the women's shelter where I had spent so many quiet hours with Fawzia and her children. There were probably other families living there now, with their own tales of abuse and hardship, but I did not know them, and they had not loved me. There would never be another weekend afternoon reading books and drawing Bible scenes in that secret, sun-filled room up those narrow stairs, where no bad news could find us.

∾

I had deeply conflicting feelings about leaving Afghanistan, a country where I had experienced such extremes of heat and cold, such buoyant hopes for deliverance and such disillusionment at the power of habit and greed, ignorance, and fear. I had known moments of real happiness there—tending to my assortment of stray dogs, playing Scrabble and singing old Dylan songs, walking home before curfew under a clear starry sky, scooping out pomegranates for a Thanksgiving feast, picnicking beside the Salang River, celebrating my birthday. For a while, I had actually made a home there too, with canaries singing in the back yard and Farhad Darya on the tape player and green tea for breakfast. But I never felt really clean or rested, and never went a day without having to grapple with power failures, punctured tires, dust in my teeth, grasping beggars, hostile glances.

My friendships with other foreign journalists were especially ephemeral. One evening we would be sipping wine by the fireplace; the next morning they would be gone on a plane to Hong Kong or London or Istanbul, perhaps forever, scribbling e-mail addresses as they dashed out the door. My friendships with Afghans were limited in a different way; some seemed open and modern at first, but I gradually discovered that their family lives were a dense thicket of obligation and rank and ritual from which no one could escape. Even without the Taliban, Afghan society remained closed and conservative, a place even the most adaptable foreigner could never really feel comfortable or at home.

There had been a time when merely crossing the Khyber Pass had filled me with a sense of adventure and privilege and awe, when a thousand hopeless faces had pressed against barbed wire to watch me walk unhindered through the gates. Now my trips to Kabul were brief, uneventful plane rides, surrounded by bored international consultants. The airport immigration agents barely looked up as they stamped our entry visas. There had been a time when every face under every turban and burqa held the promise of a story; every bazaar seemed crammed with exotic goods and history. Now I had been disappointed and importuned and lied to so often that I no longer believed anyone.

I still wanted Afghanistan's democratic experiment to succeed, wanted its rebirth to be real and meaningful and bring out the best attributes of a people finally freed from the perversity of war and ideological extremism. But this was a country with few heroes, only survivors, weighed down by boulders of vengeance and greed and tradition. Change would come very slowly, if ever; trust would take a generation to rebuild. The prospect was depressing and wearying. After more than a year in Kabul, my senses were sated, my notebooks overflowing, my conscience dulled. To salvage what remained of my inspiration and outrage and hope, I had to get away for a while. It was time to go home.

Epilogue

All flesh is as grass,
And all the glory of man
As the flower of grass.
The grass withereth
And the flower thereof falleth away,
But the word of the Lord
Endureth forever.

—Johannes Brahms,
"A German Requiem"

In the end, only three things matter:
How fully you have lived,
how deeply you have loved,
and how well you have learned
to let go of things not meant for you.

—Old Buddhist saying

IT is a cool summer evening, and I am sitting on the front steps of my cottage in Arlington, Virginia, sipping lemonade and listening to the insect-whir in the trees. Rafi is snoozing beside me, and the white cat is chasing fireflies in the crabgrass. It is a perfect moment at the end of a season of rare solitude and serenity. I have spent the last six months in cloistered luxury, sometimes taking all morning to pursue an elusive thought. Now my book is done. I have no idea whether it will resonate with others, but at least it has grappled with some of the questions whirling in my head.

Meanwhile, I slowed down and peered closely and took time for things and people I had neglected for years. I spent hours weeding my overgrown yard and read entire books under my grape arbor. I learned my neighbors' names for the first time, deepened relationships

253

I had put on hold, and spent a wonderful final week with my closest friends at Chincoteague, breathing the salt air and watching the herons fishing in the reeds. I could get used to this leisurely pace and private peace, to musing instead of reacting, browsing instead of skimming. It has the ring of a different kind of truth.

And yet I also know it is another form of escape, a temporary retreat from a public mood and political direction that have saddened, bewildered, frightened, and infuriated me. Six months ago, I came home from South Asia to an America I barely recognized. This time, it wasn't the excesses of consumption and libertinage, the super-sized portions and cleavage-obsessed TV shows that sent me into culture shock. It was something new — the fear and suspicion in the air, the aggressive security measures and the casual erosion of legal rights, the replacement of debate with flag-waving, the swagger of people in authority and the meekness of everyone else.

The nation, still shocked and vengeful after the attacks of September 11, seemed to have forfeited all reason. A zealous chief executive was on the warpath, the Congress was cowed and the networks were gung-ho. It seemed as if America's worst tendencies had been legitimized by a single day of horror, and its proudest values were being jettisoned in the name of preserving them.

There were color-coded terrorist alert levels, retina scans at the gym, secret trials and prisons, and new laws allowing the police to see who was checking out spy novels from the library. There were newspaper editorials calling France our enemy, authoritative voices suggesting that torture was acceptable and dissent treasonous. There were caravans of fortified SUVs on the highways and recordings in subway stations telling me to watch out for "suspicious individuals" and not to be alarmed by the sight of heavily armed men.

Muslim immigrants and visitors had their dignity and rights yanked away. An exiled Kurdish doctor, once gassed by Saddam Hussein, was deported. A dignified Pakistani cabbie confided to me that after thirteen years of picking up passengers from the same D.C. hotel, he was suddenly barred from using its restroom. Another friend from Pakistan, a newspaper editor visiting Washington on a fellowship, was seized outside his office by armed federal agents and hustled off to jail, merely because he had misunderstood the confusing new registration process for foreign Muslims.

I had just spent the better part of five years in the Muslim world, and I had begun to understand the deep ambivalence, the admiration tinged with resentment and mistrust, that many people there felt about the West, and the United States in particular. I had lost friends and colleagues to Islamic terrorism, but I had become close to moderate, enlightened Muslims as well. I cringed at the religious demonization taking place in both worlds, and I felt an urgent need to act as some sort of a bridge between them.

Instead, working alone all spring and cut off from my garrulous public profession, I felt isolated and depressed, appalled at what was happening around me but impotent to have any impact on it—or even the illusion of impact that seeing my name in print usually brought. I seethed in airport security lines and scribbled angry screeds in my journal. On the subway I read of bombs falling on Baghdad neighborhoods and burst into tears. After work I retreated to my yard, tearing out weeds and lopping off branches. I felt as if I was hanging on by a thread to everything I thought I knew and believed about my country.

I was also jealous. Many of my colleagues had rushed to Iraq in the wake of the American invasion and were filing dramatic daily stories, while I toiled in a vacuum, engaged in what was starting to seem like an irrelevant literary exercise. I slipped into habits I detested, eating too many canapés and drinking too much sauvignon blanc at think-tank receptions. I paced in my office, staring out the window, no longer sure I had anything meaningful to say. I belonged back in the foreign trenches, getting hot and dirty, interviewing real people and making their struggles come alive to the next day's readers.

My brooding abruptly changed direction on May 9, when an old and close friend was killed in Iraq while on assignment for the *Boston Globe*. Elizabeth Neuffer was a journalist who had followed a life path nearly identical to mine: raised in the same privileged corner of New England, driven by the same ideals, and drawn to the same kind of hellish hot spots that took her far from her roots. In Kabul, she had missed my fiftieth birthday but we celebrated her forty-sixth, and we posed for a snapshot in front of the InterContinental Hotel. With our fair hair and blue eyes, our dowdy headscarves and pudgy winter parkas, my father later observed, "you look like twins."

Elizabeth was killed in a car accident while crossing the Iraqi desert. It seemed a perversely mundane and senseless death, but it

occurred in the context of a tense and chaotic post-war society. She
was very much in her element that day. I could picture her racing
back to Baghdad, eager to tell the stories of ordinary people she had
met. I had made similar dashes across risky, unfamiliar terrain, anxious to start writing, already forming the first descriptive phrases in
my mind. This time, it really could have been me.

She had just published her own book, a labor of outrage and
courage that had sent her knocking on doors across Bosnia in search
of ethnic murderers and following investigators to exhume mass
graves in Rwanda. She wrote with eloquent rage about peering into
trenches that contained "not only the bones of dead men and boys,
but also civilization's hope that evils such as genocide were a thing
of the past."

Over the years, Elizabeth and I often talked about our mutual,
intense desire to travel the world and chronicle its struggles and right
its wrongs. We talked about the guilt of being brought up in such a
rarefied environment, the contradictory pulls to settle down and take
flight, the emotional distancing that accompanied our peripatetic
quests. Once, she gave me some heartfelt advice. Her father had recently died, but she had taken a break from her far-flung crusading
to spend time with him first. "You need to do the same thing, before
it's too late," she told me. "If you don't, you'll always regret it."

On a beautiful morning in late May, I drove through rural Connecticut to her hometown, about twenty miles from mine. It had been
many years, but I recognized the winding roads lined with stately
oaks and beeches. I recognized the white Protestant church where
her friends and family gathered, and I knew the hymns by heart. As
I listened to the eulogies, I was amazed at how much inspiration she
had given others despite a frenetic existence, and at how rooted she
had managed to remain while skimming across the earth.

I also remembered her advice, and I slipped away from the service early to spend a few hours with my parents. I visited them several times during my spring sojourn in the States, watched them
adapt to shrinking horizons in their new retirement complex, sensed
them growing frailer and more forgetful in just a few months. I knew
they missed their old gray clapboard house overlooking the Connecticut River, but I was stunned when they told me that the new owners, whose tastes were grander and more modern, had decided to tear
it down.

My mother gamely suggested we drive over to look at the spot, but I couldn't bear the thought. Without realizing it, I had secretly clung for years to the image of that silent house by the silver water at dawn, those swans bobbing in the cove, as I crossed desert highways and stared at hotel ceilings thousands of miles away. Somehow, I always imagined the house would remain, with my mother's sewing table in the cellar and my father's desk in the den and our old dog Peter's grave under the pine tree.

As I roamed South Asia during the last five years, those memories of home became especially important. I lost friends and colleagues to assassinations and accidents, I covered earthquakes and cyclones, I witnessed royal murders and senseless martyrdoms. People I knew and cared about paid the ultimate price for risks I continued to take, mourning briefly and moving on again. I took pride in traveling fast and light, fitting into new cultures, absorbing new realities and putting them into prose. I became expert at making entrances and escapes.

But as long as that house was there by the river, somehow I felt protected, like Ravi being immersed in the Ganges at dawn. I could survive anything, I would always be welcomed back, and I did not have to confront the evidence of my own family's encroaching mortality. There would always be another Christmas party, another summer evening on the terrace; the breeze from the water would always rustle the reeds and rattle the screen door.

Now, suddenly, it was gone. I felt a kind of panic, as if nothing in my life were permanent, as if time had finally caught me acting half my age and had punched through my frantic defenses against growing old and losing those I loved. I was still not sure, despite what I had told my uncle on his deathbed, whether I was ready to face the few deaths that really mattered to me. I was still not sure where I belonged, happily weeding my garden or swept up in the next intoxicating gust of wind that came along. My life was a work in progress, a leap of faith without an epiphany, a book without an ending. But at least I had finally begun, in these months of introspection, to confront its contradictions.

Just as I was finishing my final chapter, the foreign editor of the *Post* called and asked if I could go to Iraq. Conditions there were risky and unpredictable; American soldiers were being attacked every day. It was extremely hot and increasingly nasty. I didn't hesitate for a moment to say yes, though my heart stuck in my throat. This time, I had thought a great deal about the costs of my addiction. I had just lost a twin in the same desert I was about to cross. It was still where I wanted to be, but this time I needed some extra insurance.

I called a friend, a creative master carpenter, and told her I wanted to build an addition onto my cottage in Arlington, with a reading nook and a music den and a room for the cats and dogs. We met a dozen times before I left, we pored over paint chips and blueprints, we discussed sliding doors and recessed lights. Just imagining the project felt reassuring, like throwing out an anchor at sea. I had no idea what lay ahead, but now I had a new image to cling to, of a sturdy nest with Rafi and the white cat waiting for me on the front steps. This time I was sure that no matter how far I drifted, I'd be back.

—Arlington, Virginia
July 2003

Recommended reading

This book is largely drawn from my own recollections, private journals, and published writings from South Asia, including numerous articles from the *Washington Post*. I also drew on articles in American newspapers and magazines, including the *New York Times*, the *New Yorker*, the *Los Angeles Times*, and the *New York Review of Books*; Pakistani newspapers and magazines including *Dawn*, the *Friday Times*, the *Herald*, and *Newsline*; and Indian newspapers and magazines including the *Hindu*, the *Indian Express*, *Asian Age*, and *India Today*.

For a deeper or more detailed reading of the events, issues, and societies covered in this book, I recommend the following:

On India

Ali, Agha Shahid. *The Country Without a Post Office*. New York: Norton, 1998.

Bumiller, Elisabeth. *May You Be the Mother of a Hundred Sons*. Kolkata, India: Penguin, 1991.

Dalrymple, William. *City of Djinns*. London: Flamingo/HarperCollins, 1994.

Joshi, Manoj. *The Lost Rebellion*. New Delhi: Penguin, 1999.

Mishra, Pankaj. "Death in Kashmir." *New York Review of Books*, Sep. 21, 2000.

— — —. "Kashmir: Unending War."*New York Review of Books*, Oct. 19, 2000.

— — —. "The Other Face of Fanaticism." *New York Times Magazine*, Feb. 2, 2003.

Naipaul, V. S. *India: A Million Mutinies Now*. Viborg, Denmark: Vintage, 1998.

— — —. *India: A Wounded Civilization*. London: Picador, 1977.

Roy, Arundhati. *The God of Small Things*. Noida, India: Penguin, 2002.

Thakur, Sankarshan. *Guns and Yellow Roses: Essays on the Kargil War*. New Delhi: HarperCollins, 1999.

Tully, Mark. *No Full Stops in India.* New Delhi: Penguin, 1992.
Vijayan, O. V. *Collected Short Stories.* New Delhi: Penguin, 1998.

Selected articles on India by the author, from the **Washington Post**:

"A Good Voice Is Silenced: Kashmir's Loss Is Also Mine." Outlook, June 9, 2002.
"At the Confluence of Heaven and Hell." January 29 and 30, 2001.
"Ten Years of Ruin in Kashmir." June 21, 1999.
"The Young Boy and the River: On the Banks of the Ganges, a Family Flows with Tradition." March 14, 2000.

On Pakistan

Bennett, Jones Owen. *Pakistan: Eye of the Storm.* New Haven, Conn.: Yale University Press, 2001.
Constable, Pamela. "Pakistan's Predicament." *Journal of Democracy*, Jan. 2001.
Durrani, Tehmina. *Blasphemy.* Ferozsons, Pakistan: South Asia Books, 1998.
— — —. *My Feudal Lord.* London: Corgi, 1994.
Goldberg, Jeffrey. "Inside Jihad U: The Education of a Holy Warrior." *New York Times Magazine*, June 25, 2001.
On the Abyss: Pakistan After the Coup. New Delhi: HarperCollins, 2000.
Rashid, Ahmed. "Pakistan on the Edge." *New York Review of Books*, Oct. 10, 2002.
Stern, Jessica. "Pakistan's Jihad Culture." *Foreign Affairs*, Nov./Dec. 2000.
Weaver, Mary Anne. *Pakistan in the Shadow of Jihad and Afghanistan.* New York: Viking, 2002.

Selected articles on Pakistan by the author, from the **Washington Post**:

"In Pakistan, a Gentler Side of Islam." Oct. 20, 2001.
"In Pakistan, Women Pay the Price of 'Honor': Maiming, Killing Accepted Response to Percieved Sin." May 8, 2000.
"Pakistan's Moral Majority: Islamic Fundamentalist Fervor Poses Challenge to Military Regime." June 22, 2000.

On Afghanistan

Anderson, Jon Lee. "After the Revolution: The City of Kandahar, Post-Taliban, Is Full of Reminders That the Taliban Were Not Always What They Seemed To Be." *New Yorker*, Jan. 28, 2002.

— — —. "Letter from Afghanistan; City of Dreams; A Peace of Sorts Comes to Kabul." *New Yorker*, Dec. 24–31, 2001.

Dehganpisheh, Babak, John Barry, and Roy Gutman. "The Death Convoy of Afghanistan." *Newsweek*, Aug. 26, 2002.

Elliot, Jason. *An Unexpected Light: Travels in Afghanistan*. London: Picador, 1999.

Griffin, Michael. *Reaping the Whirlwind: The Taliban Movement in Afghanistan*. London: Pluto Press, 2003.

Kaplan, Robert. *Soldiers of God: With Islamic Warriors in Afghanistan and Pakistan*. New York: Vintage, 2001.

Maley, William, ed. *Fundamentalism Reborn? Afghanistan and the Taliban*. New York: New York University Press, 1998.

Rashid, Ahmed. *Taliban: Militant Islam, Oil, and Fundamentalism in Central Asia*. New Haven, Conn: Yale University Press, 2001.

Sheikh, Fazal Ilahi. *The Victor Weeps: Afghanistan*. Zürich: Scalo Verlag, 1998

Selected articles on Afghanistan by the author, from the **Washington** Post:

"The Conflict in Covering the War." Dec. 2, 2001.

"Into the Land of the Taliban." Sep. 27, 1998

"Buddhas' Rubble Marks a Turn for Taliban." March 20, 2001

"Some in Kandahar Mourn the End of Taliban Rule." Jan. 16, 2002.

"Middle Class, Again, in Afghanistan: The Family That Stayed Despite War and Repression Finds a New Sense of Purpose." July 26, 2002.

Other Recommended Books

Agee, James, and Walker Evans. *Let Us Now Praise Famous Men*. Boston: Houghton Mifflin, 1941.

Hedges, Chris. *War Is a Force That Gives Us Meaning*. New York: Public Affairs, 2002.

Neuffer, Elizabeth. *The Key to My Neighbor's House*. New York: Picador, 2002.

About the Author

Pamela Constable is a foreign correspondent for the *Washington Post*. During a twenty-eight-year career in journalism, she has also been a reporter for the *Baltimore Sun* and the *Boston Globe*. She has traveled on assignment in more than thirty countries; lived for extended periods in Chile, India, and Afghanistan; and collected stray animals on three continents. Her first book, coauthored in 1991, was *A Nation of Enemies: Chile Under Pinochet*. She is currently based in Kabul, Afghanistan, but between assignments she makes her home in Arlington, Virginia.